THE
BUSINESS-SAVVY
PROJECT
MANAGER

THE BUSINESS-SAVVY PROJECT MANAGER

Indispensable Knowledge and Skills for Success

GARY HEERKENS

McGraw-Hill

New York   Chicago   San Francisco   Lisbon
London   Madrid   Mexico City   Milan   New Delhi
San Juan   Seoul   Singapore   Sydney   Toronto

The McGraw·Hill Companies

Library of Congress Cataloging-in-Publication Data is on file.

Copyright © 2006 by The McGraw-Hill Companies, Inc. All rights reserved. Printed in the United States of America. Except as permitted under the United States Copyright Act of 1976, no part of this publication may be reproduced or distributed in any form or by any means, or stored in a data base or retrieval system, without the prior written permission of the publisher.

4 5 6 7 8 9 10   IBT/IBT   1 9 8 7 6 5 4 3 2 1

ISBN 0-07-144307-X

The sponsoring editor for this book was Roger Stewart and the production supervisor was David Zelonka. It was set in Caslon 224 by Patricia Wallenburg.

Printed and bound by IBT Global.

 This book is printed on acid-free paper containing a minimum of 10 percent recycled, de-inked fiber.

McGraw-Hill books are available at special quantity discounts to use as premiums and sales promotions, or for use in corporate training programs. For more information, please write to the Director of Special Sales, McGraw-Hill Professional, Two Penn Plaza, New York, NY 10121-2298. Or contact your local bookstore.

CONTENTS

PART TWO

APPLYING SOUND BUSINESS PRACTICES
AT THE ENTERPRISE LEVEL   97

PART FIVE

APPENDIXES 303

INTRODUCTION

Less than 150 words into this book, you will encounter a series of statements that I will refer to as *revelations*. These revelations seek to expose one of the most critical issues facing the practice of project management today. Simply stated, it is the failure of many companies—companies of all sizes and shapes—to recognize projects for what they actually are: financial investments.

Some of the revelations provide a shocking view of exactly what can happen when projects are treated more like science projects or idea playgrounds than business ventures. An alarming number of companies I have encountered, for example, systematically promote just about any "good idea" to project status, with little or no meaningful business-based analysis. Almost invariably, this practice eventually translates into wasted money and resources, as time (and a vast expenditure of cash) reveals that some weren't such good ideas after all.

Other revelations I provide reveal how an inflexible adherence to the triple constraints (cost, schedule, and scope) typically wins out over the maximization of cash flow. And, in nearly every case, the company remains blissfully unaware of the lost opportunity, because they just simply don't look at projects as investments.

After listening to countless tales from practicing project managers, engaging in a multitude of discussions with corporate managers, and encountering a wide range of experiences as a consultant, I wrestled with the decision of whether to refer to these revelations as "atrocities." At first, I thought that the use of that word might be overly dramatic. Now, I'm not so sure.

However, all is not lost! In fact, I see many signs that some change is beginning to occur within and around the project management discipline—change that is destined to result in a strong marriage between the world of project management and the world of business. There is little doubt that many people want it, and it is happening. My frustration comes from observing the *rate* at which this union of business and project management is materializing. Personally, I'd like to see it happen much faster.

A key factor in understanding how to speed up this process comes in acknowledging that only part of the change required to address the aforementioned atrocities—or, revelations—can be driven from the top down. The rest (in fact, the lion's share) will have to be driven by practitioners.

By becoming a business-savvy project manager, you can make a huge contribution to the cause. You can display a level of comprehension about your company's business that transcends the current norm. You can propose, manage, and report on projects using the language that your management truly understands—language such as *cash flows*, *financial risk*, *strategic alignment*, and *business impact*. You can help your management begin to view projects in a different way. Armed with a working knowledge of how the discipline of project management can make a meaningful, positive *economic contribution* to the "bottom line," I believe that the business-savvy project manager can elevate project management—as a discipline as well as a profession—to higher ground.

This is the underlying philosophy and purpose behind this book.

One of the greatest challenges I faced in writing this book is knowing when to stop—where to draw the line and send the book off to be published. The study of business is almost incomprehensibly huge. But I don't think it's necessary for practicing project managers to know *everything* about business. Project managers should, however, understand *the connection between the world of business and the world of project management*. This is where I chose to draw the line.

Even with that limitation, there remains a considerable amount of information to be dispensed in this book. As you read on, recognize that all the information presented to you will assume either of these two basic forms: (1) knowledge and skills that you could apply immediately (i.e., *how to prepare a business case for a project*); and (2) information directed toward building a solid knowledge base that will prepare you to excel in the future of business-based project management (i.e., *a study of organizational management*).

Structurally, the book is organized into four main areas of focus. Chapters 1 through 4 concentrate on *building foundational knowledge*, including useful information on organizational management, cost management, and even a brief visit into the worlds of finance and accounting. Chapters 5 through 7 concentrate on *applying sound business practices at the enterprise-wide level*, namely, the study of project portfolio management. Chapters 8 through 11 include the most "hands-on" area of focus from the perspective of the practicing project manager. These chapters concentrate on *applying sound business practices at the individual project level*, with primary emphasis on learning how to conduct a project financial analysis.

The final chapter, Chapter 12, stands alone, concentrating on *preparing the project business case*. The project business case rep-

resents the convergence of everything covered in all previous chapters—and more. Although it is the cornerstone of business-based
project management, many companies do not do a very good job of
preparing project business cases. Even more do none at all. With that,
we've come full circle—back to the revelations mentioned previously.

Who was this book written for? I envision this book having two
target audiences. First and foremost, practicing project managers. By
incorporating the lessons offered in the book, business-savvy project
managers simply will manage projects better. But there's more at
stake than just better projects. Business-savvy project managers can
enable important advances in how project management is perceived
by companies. Regrettably, many of today's organizational managers
view project managers as little more than a pair of hands—a coordi-
nator of predetermined work products or a preordained outcome.
Thus remains the perception that just about anybody can "do project
management." Excellent project managers know this is not true. But
how can they convince others of this? Well, one way is to display and
apply the knowledge and practices presented in this book.

The second target audience—though not specifically identified
in the title—are organizational managers. The reality is that this book
is not *only* for project management practitioners. Nothing would
please me more than to have mid-managers and corporate executives
read the book and better recognize the critical linkages that exist
between the way you and I manage projects and the way they manage the company.

In fact, several of the revelations described at the outset of the
book are strongly tied to this group. My fervent hope is that organizational managers come to recognize that the discipline of project management has the potential to contribute much, much more than it
does in many companies today. As just one example, most of the project managers I speak with are not invited (or even allowed) to participate in the "front end" of the overall project life cycle—when many
of the critical decisions are made that tie projects to the business. In
my view, an excellent opportunity is lost when this happens. But once
again, how can we convince organizational managers that we could
add more value by being more involved?

By becoming *business-savvy project managers*.

Enjoy the book!

PERMISSIONS

Description of the balanced scorecard approach reprinted by permission of Harvard Business School Publishing from *The Balanced Scorecard*, by R. S. Kaplan and D. P. Norton, the Harvard Business School Publishing Corporation, 1996; all rights reserved.

Definition of core competences reprinted by permission of Harvard Business Review, from *The Core Competence of the Corporation*, by Gary Hamel and C.K. Prahalad, May–June 1990, the Harvard Business School Publishing Corporation, 1990; all rights reserved.

Formula for, and description of, Pacifico's profitability index method is used by permission of John Wiley & Sons, Inc. from *Project Management: A Managerial Approach*, by Meredith and Mantel, 1993.

Figure 6-6 (stage-gate value analysis) and description is used by permission of John Wiley & Sons, Inc. from *Project Management: A Managerial Approach*, by Meredith and Mantel, 1993.

Discussion on the financial concepts Market Value Added and Economic Value Added is used with permission of Blackwell Publishing, Ltd., and is adapted from "EVA™: Fact and Fantasy" by Stewart, G.B III, *Journal of Applied Corporate Finance* (Summer 1994).

Figure 6-8 (using poor man's hierarchy to select attributes for evaluation of new product portfolio projects) and description is used by permission of John Wiley & Sons, Inc. from *The New Project Management*, by J. Davidson Frame.

Discussion on the four business questions is used by permission of John Wiley & Sons, Inc. from *eXtreme Project: Using Leadership, Principles, and Tools to Deliver Value in the Face of Volatility*, by Doug DeCarlo, Jossey-Bass Publishers, 2004.

Table 1-2 (changing perspectives) is used with permission of John Wiley & Sons, Inc. from *The Project Manager's MBA*, by D. Cohen and R. Graham, Jossey-Bass Publishers, 2000.

Description of cash management cycle and adapted illustration (Figure 2.3) is used with permission of John Wiley & Sons, Inc. from *The Project Manager's MBA*, by D. Cohen and R. Graham, by Jossey-Bass Publishers, 2000.

Reference to term "project outcome life cycle" and subsequent discussion is used with permission of John Wiley & Sons, Inc. from *The Project Manager's MBA*, by D. Cohen and R. Graham, Jossey-Bass Publishers, 2000.

Quote that illustrates a multidomestic strategy is used with permission of The McGraw-Hill Companies from "It Was a Hit in Buenos Aires—So Why Not Boise?" *BusinessWeek* (9/7/1998) by David Leonhardt.

Description of primary competitive strategy used with permission of Perseus Books, L.L.C. from *The Discipline of Market Leaders*, by M. Treacy and F. Wiersema; 1995.

Quote that illustrates transnational strategy is used with permission of The McGraw-Hill Companies from *Management: Function and Strategy*, by T. S. Batemen and C. Zeithaml.

Table 2-2 (comparing accounting systems), Figure 3.3 (information management planning mirrors organizational planning), Table 3.2 (tactics for establishing a competitive advantage), and the Pep Boys example of using IT for strategic purposes) from the *Certified Business Manager Preparation Guide*, Part 2, Volume 3, *Theory for Functional Areas*, 1st edition by Thomson Learning, 2004. Used with permission of South-Western, a Division of Thomson Learning.

Figure 3-1 (hierarchy of plans and goals) from the *Certified Business Manager Preparation Guide*, Part 1, Volume 1, *Theory for Core Areas*, 1st edition by Thomson Learning, 2003. Used with permission of South-Western, a Division of Thomson Learning.

Figure 2-5 (some focus areas of managerial accounting systems) and description of terms therein used with permission of Pearson Education, Inc., from *Cost Accounting: A Managerial Emphasis*, by C.Horngren, G. Foster, and S. Datar, 2000.

Figure 4-1 (components of the master budget) and description of terms therein used with permission of Pearson Education, Inc., from *Cost Accounting: A Managerial Emphasis*, by C.Horngren, G. Foster, and S. Datar, 2000.

Discussion on responsibility accounting used with permission of Pearson Education, Inc., from *Cost Accounting: A Managerial Emphasis*, by C.Horngren, G. Foster, and S. Datar, 2000.

Figure 4-3 (the combinations of cost assignment and Cost Behavior) used with permission of Pearson Education, Inc., from *Cost Accounting: A Managerial Emphasis*, by C.Horngren, G. Foster, and S. Datar, 2000.

PART ONE

BUILDING FOUNDATIONAL KNOWLEDGE

CHAPTER 1

Project Management as a Business Function

If you're like most people, you probably have at least some of your money tied up in financial investments. Companies are not really all that different from you in this regard. Why? Because all companies have money tied up in projects. The reality is this: *The projects that companies pursue are really just another type of financial investment.*

So, who manages *your* personal investments? An engineer? A scientist or technician?

Or someone with a title that sounds something like "financial planner" or "investment analyst"?

Well, here's some interesting food for thought: In most companies, project management has long been viewed as a technical function. Accordingly, the role of project manager has traditionally been filled by technical specialists. In many companies today, this continues to be so.

But wait a minute ... didn't we just say projects are *financial investments*?

A FEW REVELATIONS AS WE BEGIN...

If you are someone who is steeped in the traditional rules and regulations that surround the discipline of project management, prepare to be surprised. Some of the thoughts and principles that I am about to present may strike you as being outrageous.

For example, few would argue the long-standing contention that finishing a project *on time and on budget* are crucial project objectives. And I certainly wouldn't debate their importance. But let's take another look at this from a business standpoint and ask some tough, objective questions.

First, in the grand scheme of things, *exactly how important* are the objectives of completing a project on the originally specified day at the originally specified cost?

Second, isn't there actually a "larger picture" that we should focus on? Don't more important objectives exist?

The answer to the last two questions is a resounding "Yes," and simply reflects the notion that projects are an integral element of a very large framework—the framework of *business*. And so, for just about any company today, projects are (or should be) recognized as key agents in the pursuit of business excellence.

If we begin adjusting our perspective to accept the principle that project management is primarily a business function, it follows that we may have to consider adjusting our entire perspective regarding the things that represent the most important project objectives. Confused? Perhaps some of the following revelations will help clarify this point and put you in the appropriate frame of mind for reading the remainder of the book.

Revelation #1: It really doesn't matter how well you execute a project, if you're working on the wrong project!

A recurring theme throughout this book will be the notion that one of the most basic objectives of any project is to make or save money. Generating positive cash flows is a key element of nearly every business operation. On the surface, projects are pursued for a wide variety of objectives, including increasing customer satisfaction, expanding presence in a particular segment of a market, or enabling higher efficiency in day-to-day operations. But the true impetus for doing any of these things can be traced back to the same objective: to make or save money.

This certainly seems obvious, doesn't it? Not necessarily. Consider for a moment a project that is executed flawlessly, yet ends up costing more money than it saves. It almost seems silly to ask whether that project should be considered a success. And yet, day after day, week after week, countless projects like this are pursued by companies. Why? Well, for many possible reasons. What I have found, though, is a fairly consistent pattern of insufficient, flawed, or biased upfront work. And, as we will discover a bit later in the book, the upfront work is focused on ensuring that companies have identified and selected the best possible project opportunities. Only after this has been done should companies shift their attention to issues such as the pursuit of cost and schedule excellence. Sadly, this sequence is not always followed.

Let's examine how this phenomenon plays out at the personal level. Before most people enter into any kind of personal financial investment, they often spend a considerable amount of time carefully researching that investment. I'm not sure the same can be said for all companies that enter into the pursuit of new projects. The reality is that an alarming number of projects get launched without a rigorous analysis of whether they represent a sound business investment. Many are launched with virtually no analysis whatsoever. And, in an alarming number of cases, projects are launched on little more than the notion that they "seem like a very good idea."

A famous adage in the world of project management says doing the right project and doing the project right are two different factors, both of which must be given serious consideration. This is quite true. However, the question "Are we doing the right project?" often is underplayed or largely bypassed, while the question "Are we doing the project right?" often is examined in excruciating detail.

To illustrate, I can tell you that I frequently receive telephone calls and e-mails from potential clients requesting services such as delivering a training course on how to use project scheduling software, assisting them in setting up and administering an earned value measurement process, or facilitating a session on how to construct a work breakdown schedule. I receive considerably fewer calls asking me to coach project managers on how to develop a solid business case or to advise senior managers on how to develop a strategically aligned portfolio of projects. In short, I have observed more examples than I care to admit where companies agonize over issues related to excellence on project execution, directing this attention at projects that they should not even be pursuing in the first place!

Revelation #1 is founded in the notion that the issue of *doing the right project* is a business consideration; whereas, the question of *doing the project right* is a logistical consideration. Although both considerations are important, it's crucial to recognize that the questions must be asked *in the correct order*. Finding out that a project has not achieved the desired business impact after it has been executed flawlessly is simply not good business.

Revelation #2: There are times when spending more money on a project could be smart business—even if you exceed the original budget!

To some, this statement may seem outrageous. I suspect that this revelation is most unsettling to those who firmly believe that bringing a project in "on budget" is one of the ultimate measures of project success. However, imagine that you are managing a project and come to recognize that an additional expenditure of $50,000 (over the original budget) would result in additional cost savings of $200,000 for your company. The appropriate decision here seems obvious, doesn't it? Yet day after day, week after week, countless project managers would not be given the opportunity to pursue this seemingly logical business decision. Sadder still, most would actually be discouraged from making a business decision such as this—all in the name of sticking to the original budget. Management's rationale?

Flexibility and variances from project plans equate to disorganization and chaos. The reality? A lack of flexibility can sometimes lead to missed opportunities.

This exact scenario played out (quite painfully) for one project manager with whom I had a recent conversation. She told me of a large project that she was working on for a major U.S. corporation. Her project centered on the modification of equipment in a production department that was part of one of the company's overall manufacturing operation. The project had a very strong financial justification. Its entire premise revolved around the recognition that automating equipment would allow for a significant reduction in that department's direct labor costs. Against the backdrop of this premise, I found her sad tale to be particularly ironic—and much like the scenario just described.

She told me that, as her project entered the installation phase, the engineering staff approached her with an idea. The idea was based on the implementation of a limited amount of redesign, coupled with the purchase of some additional tooling. The financial justification of this incremental change was even stronger than the original justification.

One problem, though. The incremental costs to accommodate this change had not been included as part of the original project budget. The proposal was turned down. The opportunity came and went.

Revelation #3: There are times when spending more time on a project could be smart business, even if the project is delivered after the original deadline!

This is the time-based corollary to Revelation #2. And virtually all of the issues described in that revelation hold true for this one as well. Together, this pair of revelations is directly tied to the recurring theme throughout this book—*flexibility may not always be a bad thing*. After all, anyone who is business-savvy recognizes that the business climate is ever-changing.

As mentioned, few would argue that maintaining an on-time project delivery, or trying to hold to the original schedule is an appropriate goal when managing projects. However, it is equally critical to note that fostering an organizational culture and project environment that allows sufficient latitude and process flexibility to seize businesses opportunities as they arise can significantly contribute to improving the profitability of an organization's overall project portfolio.

Doug DeCarlo, a well-respected consultant and author, eloquently and thoroughly describes this need for flexibility throughout his book, *eXtreme Project Management: Using Leadership, Principles and Tools to Deliver Value in the Face of Volatility*.

DeCarlo points out that the ultimate goal of project management is not to deliver the planned result, but rather the *desired result*. That is, the definition of success (i.e., schedule, budget, quality, scope, ROI) will likely change throughout the project, based on changing business, economic, political conditions, and a potential host of other factors. To reinforce the need for flexibility, DeCarlo urges project managers to relentlessly focus on, and update answers to, what he calls "The Four Business Questions":

1. Who needs what and why?
2. What will it take to get it?
3. Can we get what it takes?
4. Is it worth it?

When considered collectively, these Four Business Questions serve as a constant reminder to all stakeholders that the project is first and foremost a business venture.

In practice, applying the Four Business Questions should translate into practices such as continually updating the business case to reflect the latest expectations and projections.

According to DeCarlo, Business Question 1 is a statement of the customer requirements and the project deliverable at any point in time, coupled with a succinct statement of the fundamental business need and the answer to why the project is being undertaken. Importantly, the management sponsor should be viewed as "owning" the answer to Business Question 1, although the project manager may act as a facilitator who helps extract and solidify the customer need.

The business Question 2 is owned squarely by the project manager. It's her job to estimate what it will take to get the project done (e.g., schedule, budget, stakeholder participation, etc.) as the project objective is presently defined. Business Question 2 can also refer to the technical feasibility of the venture.

The answer to Business Question 3 is a result of a negotiation between the management sponsor and project manager for resources, money, and time (schedule). If the answer to question 3 is "No, we can't get what it takes," the project has to be redefined (Question 1) or a decision is made to proceed no further. If it can be done (technically, financially, or otherwise), then the fourth and final Business Question kicks in: Is the project (still) justifiable from a business perspective in light of what it will take to succeed? This is clearly the sponsor's call.

The entire key to the flexibility principle comes when DeCarlo emphasizes that the answers to the Four Business Questions can change weekly and in some cases, daily, as new information comes in.

Finally, he notes that rigid, unwavering compliance to schedule, budget, or any other project constraint can result in delivering an elegant solution that cannot be justified in terms of economic value.

Revelation #4: Forcing the project team to agree to an unrealistic deadline may not be very smart, from a business standpoint.

Unfortunately, it is not uncommon for project managers and project teams to be forced into agreeing to unrealistic project deadlines. Although completing a project as soon as possible is a virtuous objective, gearing the project's justification and approval to unrealistically aggressive deadlines can have dire consequences. Consider the project whose financial justification is based on the assumption that it will be completed in 1 year, even though the project team, through careful and intelligent planning, has determined that 15 to 16 months is required to complete the effort. In Chapter 9, Project Economics, Part II: Preparing for a Project Financial Analysis, we explore the business implication of this specific situation, because it is so common. You will undoubtedly be surprised (if not shocked) at what a simple financial analysis reveals. A lesson is to be learned from this scenario: Relying on high-quality input data (honest estimates, in this case) and pursuing rational and logical approaches (faith in the expertise of good project teams) are cornerstone behaviors in delivering consistently positive business results. Some traditional practices (like developing "stretch goals," in this case) may be popular and conceptually pleasing management behaviors, but they are not necessarily consistent with sound business practices.

Revelation #5: A portfolio of projects that all generate a positive cash flow may not represent an organization's best opportunities for investment.

So far, all the revelations we've discussed related to individual projects. But similar revelations can hold true at the organizational level as well. For example, even organizations that routinely perform financial justifications as a prerequisite to project approval can fall victim easily to Revelation #5. The culprit here is a surprisingly common phenomenon in companies today—a significant disconnect between the people who establish strategic direction and those who are charged with the job of generating new project ideas. The problem begins at budget time. One of the first things that many companies do is subdivide their overall budget, and disperse it across organizational units. As we'll discover a bit later, as soon as budgets are departmentalized, focus on what is best for the overall company has been forever lost. Each individual organizational manager now begins to focus on what is best for his organization (you can't really blame his). Unfortunately, the inevitable outcome is a suboptimized portfolio of projects.

One particular company I worked with did not realize (or believe) this kind of suboptimization was possible until they agreed to engage in an exercise in which they took all the projects listed within all their organizations and created a master project list. After some analysis, the problem came into focus. They discovered several instances in which projects in one organization were dropped because of funding constraints, while other, much less worthy projects in other organizations were authorized.

When we discuss portfolio management techniques in Chapters 5 through 7, we explore ways to ensure that this doesn't happen in your organization. And as we discover, one of the keys is maintaining portfolio balance, not across organizational units, but across strategic objectives and critical project dimensions.

THE LANDSCAPE OF PROJECT MANAGEMENT IS CHANGING

Figure 1.1 illustrates how the fundamental focus within the discipline of project management has changed over the past few decades. In the early days of project management, the focus was on the technical aspects of managing projects (the term *technical aspects* does not refer to the technology embedded within the project, but to the technology of project management, such as developing detailed task listings and carefully crafted project schedules). Normally, the primary emphasis was on perfection in scheduling and flawless execution of the project work. The principle was simple: If an excellent schedule was excellently controlled and executed, the resulting outcome was

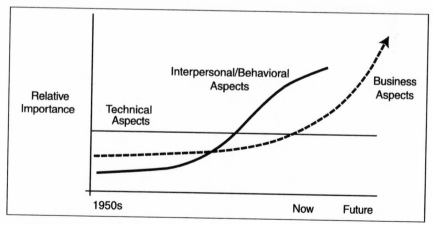

FIGURE 1.1

The growing importance of business in project management.

guaranteed to be excellent. (In Figure 1.1, the technical aspects of a project are used as a baseline of comparison.)

Throughout the 1980s and 1990s, the emphasis shifted to the interpersonal and behavioral aspects of managing projects. Although the technical aspects still were considered important, many came to realize that behaviorally based considerations, such as motivational skills, leadership skills, conflict resolution skills, and other so-called *soft skills* were a major influencer of project success and failure.

The critical importance of these soft skills remains widely acknowledged today. However, the realization is now advancing to the forefront of the project management discipline that *projects are critical agents in nearly every company's quest to achieve positive business results*. In that regard, a simple realization now is beginning to sink in for many companies. It is the realization that, to a large extent, it doesn't matter how good the schedule is, or how well the people in the project are managed interpersonally, if those values are being applied to poor business ventures. For some companies, this realization is certainly not news. But for many other companies, this realization represents a potential awakening.

Unfortunately, project managers who find themselves working for a company that doesn't appear to have recognized the existence of a strong connection between the world of project management and the world of business are now at risk. The risk comes in the form of being lured into thinking that "all this talk about business" is irrelevant. This is not good. Why? Because the connection *is* there, and it won't be long until the connection comes clearly into focus for management. As soon as this happens, attention undoubtedly will shift to them as project managers. The best thing today's project managers can do is prepare themselves accordingly.

The reality is that more and more companies today are making that connection, as evidenced by a noticeable shift in the composition of solicitations for project management professionals. Check out the Help Wanted column the next time you read the newspaper. Or try surfing any of the large Internet job posting sites. It's quite likely that you will see a growing emphasis on business knowledge and skills as a desirable project manager competency.

The connection between the world of business and the world of project management has not gone unnoticed by professional societies, such as the Project Management Institute (PMI®). To illustrate the point, consider this: In 1999, about 12% of the articles published in PMI's monthly magazine, *PM Network*, dealt with business-related topics. By 2004, that number had grown to about 42%.

Clearly, the landscape of project management is changing. And as the landscape of project management begins to change, it follows that various types of expectations will change as well.

HOW EXPECTATIONS OF PROJECTS ARE CHANGING

So, what kind of effect will this awakening of the business connection have on individual projects? The answer to this question begins with an analysis of how the expectations of projects will change. Here are a few examples of how project expectations are likely to change as we begin to embrace the project as an agent of enhanced business results:

- Technical success for any given project proposal will be assumed (except perhaps research and development projects).
- The primary emphasis in judging project attractiveness will shift toward profitability and away from those other factors used to evaluate attractiveness today.
- The business component of project proposals and project status reports will be more comprehensive and thorough.
- Post-project considerations will play a much larger role in project selection and justification processes.
- The business impact of projects will be re-examined at project completion, and in many cases, well beyond traditional completion.

These few examples illustrate how we will continue to observe a fundamental shift in the nature of project expectations—from being technically and behaviorally focused to being business-focused—over the next several years.

HOW EXPECTATIONS OF PROJECT MANAGERS ARE CHANGING

If the expectations of projects are expected to change, it follows that expectations of project managers will change as well. Generally, project managers will be expected to significantly increase their understanding of how business relates to the world of projects and vice versa. Specifically, project managers of the future will be expected to proficiently display these three attributes:

- Greater business awareness. Project managers will possess the knowledge and understanding that project management is a business-based discipline and not a technically based discipline; and possess substantial knowledge and understanding of how projects relate to their company's bottom line.
- Greater business acumen. Project managers will possess knowledge about when to apply the appropriate business principles,

concepts, or tools, why it is necessary, and the benefits to be gained by doing so.

- Greater business competency. Project managers will possess first-hand knowledge of how to use key business tools and techniques, thus reducing excessive reliance on others in performing certain business functions (i.e., deferring everything financial to "the financial group").

Some other more specific expectations of future project managers are:

- Project managers will be expected to direct projects more like a businessperson and less like a scientist, technician, or efficiency expert.
- Considerations such as impact on profitability, effect on business results, and compatibility with organizational strategy will be a significant factor in molding a project manager's leadership methods and decision-making approaches.
- Project managers will be expected to demonstrate an entrepreneurial spirit.
- Project managers will be expected to share in the responsibility for the achievement of business results.

I cannot resist throwing in an editorial comment about that last expectation. With the shared responsibility for achieving business results *should* come the practice of regularly involving project managers much earlier in the overall project life cycle, when most of the critical (and meaningful) business decisions are made. It remains to be seen whether this actually happens.

Collectively, I think it's fair to summarize the expectations listed above by simply expressing it this way: To some extent, the project manager of the future will be expected to perform and think more like an executive. This is a tall order. My personal belief is that those who are able to live up to this expectation can expect a number of new avenues of professional growth to become available.

HOW THE DEFINITION OF PROJECT SUCCESS IS CHANGING

If you ask most people today how they define project success, the answer would almost certainly revolve around whether the triple constraints of time, cost, and scope were achieved. You will get no argument from me that it is very desirable to deliver a project on time, at the agreed-upon cost, and able to perform according to specifications. It's worth repeating that these are virtuous objectives. However, it's just as important to note that satisfying the triple constraints while being a valid measure of success is certainly not the *ultimate* measure of success in a business sense.

Evaluating whether the triple constraints were satisfied is primarily a measure of how efficiently a given work effort is managed. It is not a direct metric of success in the achievement of desired business results. This is a key concept. However, many companies still seem to rely on a kind of "leap of faith" here. The inflexibility in their approach to managing project efforts seems to suggest this underlying premise: As long as the appropriate cost, schedule, and scope targets are properly set during the early stages of the project, it somehow follows that hitting these targets will automatically translate to business success. The fact is, there really is no direct connection.

There is an implied connection.

There is an indirect connection.

And there is some potential cause-and-effect, but only if no changes in the business environment occur throughout the life of the project. And as we said earlier, this is an unlikely scenario.

Satisfying the triple constraints, for example, says very little— *directly*—with regard to whether the project was a wise investment. Did the project make money or lose money? This question cannot be directly answered through the knowledge that we brought the project in on time, at cost, and according to specifications.

It also says little about whether the original business need was fulfilled, whether a given business opportunity was effectively exploited, or whether customers and users were satisfied in a way that will keep them coming back. And it says nothing about whether the results achieved from a project is likely to open new avenues of product penetration that will benefit the company in the future.

And so, what we need to do in the new, business-based project management system is to recalibrate the way we define project success. Table 1.1 illustrates some of the basic components of that recalibration process. As our perception of project management as a business function and our perception of project success become better aligned, "successful" projects will come to be defined more in terms of business impact, and less in terms of logistical excellence.

SOME OTHER SIGNIFICANT CHANGES

As we begin to characterize projects as investments and project management as a business function, other shifts in perspective—includ-

TABLE 1.1

The Measures of Project Success are Changing

Today's measures of success (focused on logistics)	Future measures of success (focused on business results)
Satisfy the triple constraints (cost, schedule, and scope)	Satisfy a strategically aligned business need
Must not exceed the original project budget … *no matter what!* *Must not* violate the original project deadline … *no matter what!*	Maximize the return on the money invested in the project
Meet the technical or functional specifications	Satisfy the "true need" or the root cause of the problem
Satisfy the needs of customers and user	Make customers and users want to keep coming back
Manage to a successful customer sign-off	Manage the overall project life cycle, including post-project

ing changes in behaviors and attitudes—are likely to occur. Project managers and members of project teams will come to view their participation, their involvement, and even the basic orientation toward projects in a very different way.

Table 1.2 lists some examples of how project personnel are likely to change their views on some basic project management issues. Generally, their focus will expand significantly. Many would agree that this is a positive move for project management, project managers, project teams, and ultimately, for organizations.

ADOPTING A TOTAL ASSET LIFE CYCLE FOCUS

Perhaps one of the most important changes in perspectives will occur in the very way we define the life of a project. Traditionally, many considered that a project's life began at the point when a solution had been determined, and ended when a predetermined result (often a specific technical outcome) had been achieved. Project planning and scheduling marked the beginning of a project, and customer sign-off marked the end. This context is quite consistent with the thought process around the triple constraints described earlier.

A much healthier perspective (from a business standpoint, at least) is achieved by recognizing that life exists before and after these "traditional" boundaries. Figure 1.2 illustrates this point. Although it shows only one simplified model of a project life cycle, an analysis of

TABLE 1.2

Changing Perspectives

Issue	Has been:	Will be changing to:
Alignment of project with company strategy	Not my concern	Key determinant of project success; valuable knowledge for me to have
Economic viability of the project	Must have been done by somebody/don't care	Something that needs to be evaluated and confirmed before proceeding too far on the project
Marketing	Done by people in the marketing department	Something that can promote higher quality decision making on projects
Cost management	Only immediate project costs are important	*All* costs and benefits incurred by project effort should be driving my decision making
Finance and accounting	Viewed as something unrelated to projects	Knowing where the project come from is useful knowledge Contribution projects make to "bottom line" is real, and should be understood

virtually any type of project life cycle is likely to portray that some sort of foundational or investigative activities occurs prior to the traditional launch of projects.

Just as important as the upfront work is what happens after the completion of what we frequently consider to be "the project." In the life of most project investments, there exists a downstream customer, or *receiver*, of a project's key deliverables. This receiver could be the consuming public, an internal or external customer, or a user group, to name a few. What happens once the project is "handed off" to these receivers is viewed by many as existing outside the boundaries of the project. This kind of short-range thinking often can lead to less-than-optimum outcomes, to long-term customer satisfaction problems, and underachieving investment results.

The process of including all these elements to define a *total asset life cycle* represents a key change in perspective and an important element in embracing project management as a business function. With the total asset life cycle perspective, we begin to move away from thinking of projects as simply exercises in managing the logistics surrounding work products and resources. We now begin to think of projects as financial investments that are inexorably tied to the company's bottom-line results.

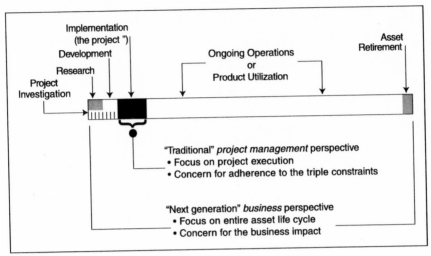

FIGURE 1.2

Adopting a total life cycle focus.

SO...HOW ARE PROJECTS CONNECTED TO THE "BOTTOM LINE," ANYWAY?

Understanding the connection between projects and the proverbial bottom line of a company is a critical piece of knowledge and understanding, especially for project personnel. It not only serves to explain why we do projects; it offers a useful framework for understanding the difference between project-related decisions that are "good for the business" and those that are not.

Describing the connection between projects and the bottom line is remarkably straightforward and can assume many forms. Sadly, however, these insights are rarely shared with project personnel.

Actually, a number of connect points exist. Perhaps one of the most straightforward ways of describing the connection of projects to the bottom line consists of defining three critical financial elements and understanding how they relate to one another.

Market Value Added (MVA)

For many companies, the underlying premise of good business is simple: Upper management's primary goal is (or should be) to maximize shareholder wealth. However, maximum shareholder wealth does not equate to a company's overall size or total market value, as Figure 1.3 seeks to explain. As you look at this graphic, consider (a) as the start-

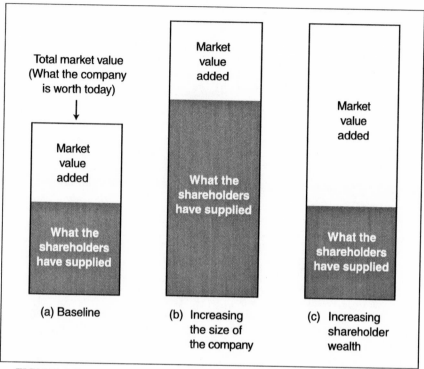

FIGURE 1.3

Focusing on the right kind of growth.

ing point for a company that wishes to "grow their business," that is, increase the company's total market value.

Total market value could be increased by raising and investing as much capital as possible, in an upward spiral of acquisition and raw asset growth (b). Unfortunately, this would merely increase the overall size of the company and do little or nothing to increase shareholder wealth.

Shareholder wealth is actually maximized by enlarging the spread between the total market value of a company's equity and the amount of equity capital supplied by shareholders (c). This difference is called the market value added or MVA, where:

$$MVA = (\text{market value of equity}) - (\text{equity capital supplied by shareholders})$$

or,

$$MVA = (\text{\# of outstanding shares})(\text{stock price}) -$$
$$(\text{total common equity})$$

Stated simply, MVA is the difference between what investors have put into the company and what they could now get out of it. Once again, in keeping with the premise of what represents good business, the goal of corporate managers is to maximize that difference.

Barring unusual and dramatic events, the growth of a company's MVA ordinarily occurs slowly and continuously over time. It is promoted and sustained when corporate management invests the shareholders' money wisely, thus leading to a series of incremental, positive financial returns from year to year. This leads us directly to the second critical financial term.

Economic Value Added (EVA)

Whereas MVA represents the cumulative effects of managerial decisions since the inception of the firm, economic value added, or EVA, focuses on managerial effectiveness in a given year. MVA may be thought of as a long-term, cumulative measure of management's historical performance, while EVA provides a relatively short-term, incremental measure of management's ability to create value using the existing assets of the firm (referring again to Figure 1.3c).

The equation that describes the EVA is:

$$EVA = \text{net operating profit after taxes (NOPAT)} -$$
$$\text{after-tax cost of capital used to support operations}$$

or,

$$EVA = (\text{Revenue-Operating Costs-Taxes}) -$$
$$(\text{Operating Capital})(\text{Weighted Average Cost of Capital})$$

EVA is calculated by taking the after-tax operating profit and then subtracting all costs associated with the capital investment required to generate that amount of profit. Stated simply, EVA measures how much money management can generate given the assets it has to work with. EVA is actually the truest estimate of a company's economic profit for the year, which is quite different from the accounting profit that we hear so much about in traditional corporate communiqués. Profit in the traditional accounting sense measures the financial return provided to shareholders, but does not reflect the costs associated with supporting the capital assets required to run the business (called the *carrying cost*).

The term of Weighted Average Cost of Capital (WACC), used in the EVA formula, reflects these two types of costs, and obviously is included in the calculation of EVA. We will examine WACC more closely in Chapter 2, The Core of Business Knowledge: Finance and Accounting.

Net Present Value (NPV)

The third and final key term is net present value (NPV). The net present value technique is a financially based method of evaluating project attractiveness. Net present value is expressed in terms of dollars, and it represents the wealth that any single project is expected to return to the company. This wealth typically comes in the form of either making or saving money. If a project has a positive NPV, it is generating more than enough cash to service the debt required to finance its execution. In other words, a positive-NPV project has the ability to accomplish three things: cover its own financing costs, provide an attractive return to shareholders, and add to the accumulated wealth of the company. The "accumulated wealth" portion is the actual net present value.

Connecting the Dots

Now that some basic terms have been defined, it's time to describe how they relate to one another. The key to recognizing the contribution of projects—beyond NPV alone—comes in recognizing that a direct cause-and-effect relationship exists between NPV, EVA, and MVA. In fact, they feed directly into one another, as Figure 1.4 graphically depicts.

The profitability realized by each completed project (measured by its NPV) contributes directly to a company's EVA. The ability to consistently identify and pursue projects that have positive NPVs dur-

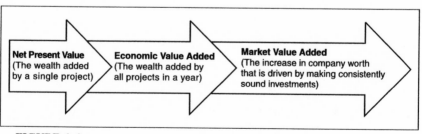

FIGURE 1.4

Generating wealth begins with high NPV projects!

ing a given year will directly result in the generation of a large, positive EVA for the company for that year. When management focuses their attention on generating large EVAs, they are behaving in a way that is consistent with maximizing shareholder wealth (their primary goal). More to the point, generating positive EVAs year after year is a strong indicator that a company's management are wise investors, and shareholder confidence will increase.

If shareholders are confident that a company's managers are wise investors, as demonstrated by the ability to generate a steady stream of high EVAs over time, they will react by bidding up the stock price. This in turn will generate an increase in the company's MVA. Although certainly not the only factor that affects its stock pricing, it is a significant one.

An important foundational premise of this book comes in recognizing that a company's ability to consistently construct a portfolio of projects with high net present values is a key contributor to its long-term economic growth. These topics will be discussed in detail in Chapters 5 through 10.

CHAPTER 2

The Core of Business Knowledge: Finance and Accounting

The key to establishing real expertise in any field of study depends to a great extent on the establishment of a solid basis of understanding of the field's underlying concepts, principles, and customary practices. In the field of business, this is a daunting task, because the field of study is almost mind-numbingly gigantic. This chapter strives to make some real headway in helping you to establish this solid basis of understanding.

As a way to reduce the sheer volume of material to a manageable size, we'll focus on some of the foundational principles of finance and accounting that have strong connections to projects and project management. As you proceed through this chapter, try to remain aware of those connections, because doing so will greatly enhance your overall understanding of how projects, project management, and the world of business interrelate.

FINANCE: THE BASICS

The study of finance consists of three interrelated areas: (1) money and capital markets, which deals with the securities markets and financial institutions; (2) investments, which focuses on the decisions made by both individual and institutional investors as they develop their investment portfolios; and (3) financial management, or "business finance," which describes the actual management of a company, and involves the various economic decisions made within companies. Although money and capital markets and investments are important areas in the study of finance, we focus on financial management, because this area of finance is most relevant to projects and project management.

WHAT IS FINANCIAL MANAGEMENT?

To conduct business, a company needs a wide variety of real assets. Some assets are *tangible* (facilities, equipment, offices) and some are *intangible* (technical expertise, trademarks, and patents). These assets are used in various ways to generate positive net cash flows (i.e., make a profit).

To obtain the money needed to pay for these assets, the company sells pieces of paper called *financial assets* (or securities), which are viewed as claims on the company's real assets. Financial assets include shares of stock, bonds, bank loans, and lease obligations.

Financial management refers to the actual management of a company. *Financial managers* are critical players in the financial management process, because their decisions influence the actual value of their company. Financial managers must make critical decisions in each of these three areas:

- Where the money will come from to pay for real assets (the financing decision)
- How the overall financing process ought to be managed (the cash management decision)
- How much the company should invest in asset acquisition, and what specific assets the company should invest in (the capital budgeting decision)

HOW ARE PROJECTS FINANCED?

One of the most important roles of a financial manager is to create value through a sound investment strategy. One way that value creation occurs is when the company acquires assets that have the capability to generate more cash for the company than they cost to acquire. Perhaps a company's most basic (and most valuable) resource is the stream of cash flows produced by its real assets.

Generally speaking, projects represent an orderly method for acquiring the assets needed to generate streams of cash flows for a company. As has often been noted, projects are one of the keys methods through which companies conduct business. Within the project context, real assets are generally acquired through a combination of direct purchase, development and building of the assets using internal company resources, or contracting with an outside firm to provide the assets. The process of spending money on projects—so as to acquire real assets and increase overall cash flow—is called the *capital investment process*.

But where exactly does the capital come from to pay for these projects?

Raising the capital needed to fund projects can come from many different sources and take a variety of different forms. However, all capital can be classified into two basic types—debt and equity. Companies may choose to use either debt or equity capital to finance the creation of their assets through projects. Most companies use a combination of both, as Figure 2.1 illustrates.

Debt financing refers to how much money the company has borrowed from financial institutions to finance its operations and invest in asset creation. In many ways, the process of debt financing is similar to the process you and I follow in taking out a loan from a bank. The cost of debt financing refers to the interest rate charged on borrowed funds. This rate is governed by the terms of the various loans the company has taken out. The overall "blended" required return, which considers all the outstanding debt, is sometimes referred to as the *current borrowing rate*.

Equity financing refers to how much money a company has received from the owners of stock (shareholders), plus the amount of money that the company has kept for the purpose of reinvesting in the company on the shareholder's behalf (*retained earnings*). The *cost of equity financing* is the rate of return that shareholders expect. Shareholders who provide capital to a company through the purchase of stock are well aware that they might have invested their money elsewhere. In essence, they continuously compare the return they receive from a given company to what they believe they could have received from other investments having an equivalent level of risk. The amount they could have received elsewhere is referred to as their *opportunity cost*. The return provided by the company they have chosen to invest in must meet or beat this opportunity cost to keep the shareholders satisfied.

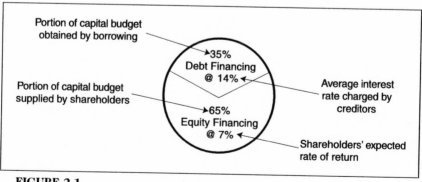

FIGURE 2.1

Capital structure for project financing.

A company's *capital structure* refers to the relative proportion, or mix, of different securities that a company uses to finance its various investment projects. It describes how the company, through decisions made by its financial managers, chooses to proportion its sources of capital. Figure 2.1 illustrates an example in which a company has determined that the optimal mix for its investment situation consists of 35% debt financing and 65% equity financing.

THE WEIGHTED AVERAGE COST OF CAPITAL

The mathematical blending of the cost of debt financing with the cost of equity financing yields the *weighted average cost of capital (WACC)*. Knowledge and understanding of what the components of the weighted average cost of capital is and what it represents is absolutely crucial to project management professionals. Once again, however, it is rarely explained to them.

As a value, WACC is applied in two important ways: first, in the process of determining whether a given project is a justifiable financial investment; second, in calculating the *carrying cost* of capital financing, thereby influencing the calculation of economic value added (EVA). As you may recall, EVA measures how much the money managers of a company are able to generate, given the assets the company has to work with. It differs from traditional accounting measures of profit, because it incorporates the cost of acquiring all company assets. The carrying cost of the entire asset base is calculated using WACC, because it represents the rate of return (or interest rate) assessed on the monies used to acquire those assets.

WACC is also the primary criteria in determining whether or not any individual project is economically attractive. Only projects that can generate a positive cash flow (i.e., positive net present value [NPV]) will contribute to EVA. Accordingly, only positive-NPV projects should be authorized. To generate this positive cash flow, a project must be able to provide a return that exceeds the WACC. Stated another way, a project manager (or anyone proposing a project) must demonstrate the ability to generate a return greater than the money being "borrowed" to finance the project. This is just good business.

Sometimes, WACC is referred to as the *after-tax* weighted average cost of capital. Because interest costs are tax deductible, the cost of debt financing ordinarily is expressed as an after-tax value when calculating the WACC. This is seen in the equations used to calculate the WACC, shown in Figure 2.2.

The example shown in Figure 2.2 assumes the same capital structure shown in Figure 2.1. This company has obtained 35% of the capital used to execute projects by taking on debt; the current bor-

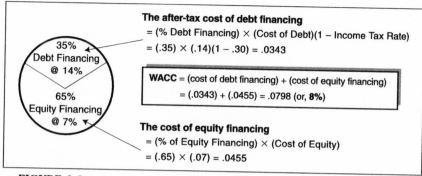

FIGURE 2.2

Calculating the weighted average cost of capital.

rowing rate, when considering all of its outstanding debt, is 14%. The remaining capital used to execute projects (65%) has been obtained using shareholders' equity.

In this example, we make some assumptions. First, we assume an income tax rate of 30% (in reality, this value would be known, not assumed). We also assume that shareholders are expecting a minimum 7% return on the money they have invested in the company.

As the equation shows, the mathematical blending of the cost of debt financing and the cost of equity financing, coupled with a provision for income tax effects, yields an overall weighted average cost of capital of 8%. By definition then, any project capable of generating a return in excess of 8% is referred to as being *financially justified*.

Companies often "adjust" the weighted average cost of capital. Typically, the WACC is raised, based upon a variety of risk factors. This concept is explored in more detail in Chapter 11, Risk Management and Decision-Making in Business.

THE CASH MANAGEMENT CYCLE

The question of how any given project is financed is just one piece of the larger process of cash management. Every successful company has a pool of cash that it uses to sustain its day-to-day operations. *Cash management* is a commonly-applied financial discipline that provides the framework for understanding how this pool of cash is applied to running a company. The acquisition, distribution, application, and conversion of cash tend to follow the same process, regardless of the type of business or the nature of the investment. Not surprisingly, this process is referred to as the *cash management cycle*. Understanding the cash management cycle is not only a useful piece of basic business knowledge, it is a helpful way of demonstrat-

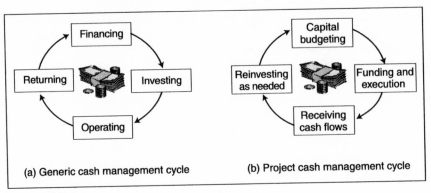

FIGURE 2.3

Cash management cycles—a strong correlation.

ing the correlation that exists between running a business and executing a project. This correlation is shown in Figure 2.3, by comparing the cash management cycle of a company's ongoing operations with the cash management cycle of a project.

Figure 2.3(a) illustrates the basic cash management cycle, which is composed of four basic steps:

- **Financing.** In this step of the cash management cycle, decisions are made on where cash can and should come from. As we discussed, the cash used to finance projects (as well as ongoing operations) comes from three basic sources: debt, stockholder purchase, and retained earnings. Retained earnings consist of those cash inflows generated through operating activities that are not returned to shareholders. Instead, these cash flows are set aside for the purpose of reinvesting in the company. Projects are one of the many ways that companies may choose to reinvest retained earnings.
- **Investing.** Once cash has been raised through financing, financial managers must determine exactly how to invest that cash. Cash can be invested in many ways, including investment in ongoing operations and investment in asset acquisition (namely projects).
- **Operating.** Here, the invested cash is applied to the ongoing operations of the company so that positive cash flows are generated. Naturally, the cash channeled into operations is expected to be exceeded by the cash derived from operations. This process is sometimes referred to as cash conversion, and is the desired, normal outcome of the ongoing operations of any successful company.

- **Returning.** The last major decision that financial managers must make is to determine how the cash received from ongoing operations should be distributed. In anticipation of the beginning of another cycle, decisions must be made about where the money should go. Some will be used to pay down the company's debts, some will be returned to the company's shareholders, and some will be retained and used to finance the initiation of the next cash management cycle.

Although the same four basic steps are involved, Figure 2.3(b) shows how these same cash management steps can be placed in a project context. Here's how the two cycles correlate:

Financing (project).   In this step of the project cash management cycle, both cycles reflect virtually identical decision-making with regard to where cash can and should come from, and where it should go. The company is viewed as having one large pool of cash, with a tendency not to discriminate between cash applied to operations and cash applied to projects. In both cases, the principle is the same: to apply cash resources for the purpose of generating even more cash.

Determining how much cash to invest in projects is at the heart of the project financing step. Once that decision is made, other decisions must be made regarding where to invest the cash. These decisions aren't straightforward, because there are many different ways of dividing up the cash. For example, a company could choose to invest in the creation of new assets, in the company's various business units, in certain product lines, in their production capability, or in their plant facilities. When considered together, the question of how much money to invest in projects and where to invest that money is commonly referred to as the *capital budgeting decision*.

Investing (project).   The decision regarding whether to invest in a specific project is ordinarily guided by a company's procedure for performing a financial analysis. Assuming that the project has an acceptable NPV, formal project approval will result. This represents the actual investment decision and triggers the release of funds to support the project effort.

Technically speaking, the actual process of investing occurs during project execution. Here, the cash invested in a project is used to purchase materials and resources for the purpose of converting the supplied cash into assets. As you might expect, those assets are expected to generate additional incremental cash flows (i.e., make money).

Operating (project).   Once a project comes to a traditional closure (customer sign-off), the assets it has produced are placed into service. Now comes the *realization* and *receipt* of the positive cash flows generated by the project. It also marks the beginning of a period that closely parallels business operations. In a sense, the company now begins to "run the project" much as it would "run the business." If the project has been determined to be financially strong (characterized by a large, positive NPV), a steady stream of positive cash flows can be expected to follow. In their book *The Project Manager's MBA: How to Translate Project Decisions into Business Success*, Dennis J. Cohen and Robert J. Graham refer to this as the *project outcome life cycle.*[1]

Returning (project).   In this step, the promised economic benefits are finally realized. It's important to note that this step of the cash management cycle (the project outcome life cycle) often can continue for several years into the future. Regrettably, this is where many companies lose touch with the cash management cycle at the individual project level, because determining exactly how much cash a given project is returning to the company may be difficult.

Typically, companies have a large volume of projects that have been completed and are (presumably) accruing financial benefits. It is not always possible—or practical—to track the contribution attributable to any single project. However, this practice should be done whenever possible, because it offers an excellent opportunity for organizational learning. For example, a verification of actual results can provide valuable insights into the methods a company uses to identify, characterize, and quantify potential benefit streams when they are generating project proposals.

Capital budgeting is the last area in which financial managers make critical decisions. The topic of capital budgeting is examined in detail in Chapter 5, Project Portfolio Management, Phase I: Identifying the "Right" Business Initiatives.

ACCOUNTING: THE BASICS

Most project managers I know willingly admit that their knowledge of the accounting discipline is quite limited. In fact, some confess that they actually try to avoid just about anything having to do with the world of accounting. Many equate the practice of accounting with a detailed analysis of debits, credits, and ledgers that most of us had to endure at some point during our academic upbringing.

However, there is much more to accounting than debits and credits. Accounting is actually a system—an information reporting system at its heart—that provides useful insights to a variety of people, including investors, company management, creditors, and a host of other key stakeholders. In fact, accounting is often dubbed "the language of business."

The fact is that accounting principles and practices have more ties to the world of projects and project management than you might think. For example, managerial accounting reports—which many of us have seen, and that managers use every day to make project-related decisions—are as much a part of the world of accounting as the more familiar annual reports.

WHAT IS GAAP?

Actually, the question should be what *are* GAAP? All financial accountants are expected to follow *generally accepted accounting principles* (GAAP) during the preparation of accounting reports. The reports prepared using GAAP allow shareholders and potential investors to compare one company with another. If companies were allowed to prepare and publish financial data using whatever format they wished, comparisons among companies would be virtually impossible. The principles embodied in GAAP are developed from history, opinions on appropriate accounting practices, and through guidelines handed down by the Financial Accounting Standards Board (FASB), an authoritative body that has been given the responsibility for the development of accounting principles.

Beyond the GAAP lies a set of basic accounting concepts. Although they may seem obvious, these concepts form the basis of accounting, are universally accepted, and are therefore worth repeating:

The *business entity concept* limits the financial data in any accounting system to that data directly related to the activities of the business. Businesses are viewed as being separate from their owners, creditors, or other stakeholders. A business owner's personal activities, property holdings and dealings, or debts are irrelevant to the accounting system of the owner's business.

The *cost concept* means that only the exchange price or cost of the transaction relating to property, merchandise, or other goods, should be entered into the accounting records. Other types of costs, such as assessed valuation, asking price, or a market appraisal, are irrelevant.

The *objectivity concept* works in concert with the cost concept. It requires that accounting records and any published reports must be based solely upon objective evidence. In dealings between buyers and sellers, only the final agreed-upon amounts related to a given transaction should be entered in the accounting records. Any intermediate or temporary values, such as revised offers, appraisals, or expert opinion, should never appear in formal accounting records.

The *unit of measure concept* requires that all financial data in accounting records should be recorded in terms of dollars (or any other legal currency). Money is considered the standard unit of measure.

The *matching concept* refers to the practice of comparing expenses and revenues in a given accounting period, thus revealing the common metric of *net income*.

All these accounting concepts are used in the preparation of various accounting reports, commonly referred to as *financial statements*. These publicly distributed financial statements offer outsiders a good view of a company, relative to its economic strength and viability, as well as the expertise of its general management. The three most common financial statements are the *balance sheet*, the *income statement*, and the *cash flow statement*. Each has a particular purpose relative to expressing the position of company.

It's important to note that, although these financial statements are aimed primarily at external entities, this does not render them irrelevant from our standpoint. Every project we execute exerts an effect (albeit it's often a small effect) on the three common financial statements we're about to examine.

MEASURING FINANCIAL HEALTH: THE BALANCE SHEET

The balance sheet is a snapshot of a company's financial condition or situation that is taken at a particular point in time. It displays three basic pieces of information:

- How the company's assets are deployed (cash vs. inventory vs. property)
- The extent of the company's *liabilities* (how much is owed to whom)
- The breakdown of *owner's equity* (shareholder contributions plus any retained earnings)

The "balance" in balance sheet is represented by this simple formula:

$$Assets = Liabilities + Owner's\ Equity$$

The balance sheet is used by external entities to answer questions such as:

- How liquid are (readily convertible to cash) the company's assets?

- How deeply is the company in debt?
- What is the size and proportion of stockholder ownership in the company?

The connections that can be seen in the balance sheet come in the form of assets (specifically, the assets that a company puts in place through project execution) and *owner's equity* (the amount of equity financing used to execute projects).

MEASURING PROFIT: THE INCOME STATEMENT

The income statement shows how profitable a company is by summarizing its sales revenue and various expenses over a specific period of time.

The type of information reported on a company's income statement may be summarized by this simple formula:

$$\text{Sales Revenue} - \text{Expenses} = \text{Net Income}$$

The operational activity within a period of time—and the resulting financial data expressed on the income statement—determines the changes that are made to the balance sheet at the end of that period. Net income is ordinarily the "headliner" on the cash flow statement.

Obviously, a strong connection exists between the income statement and projects that deal with new-product introduction or product enhancements. These kinds of projects typically focus on the generation of increased revenues.

MEASURING THE WAY MONEY MOVES: THE CASH FLOW STATEMENT

The cash flow statement describes all the changes that occur with respect to cash over a specified period of time. Figure 2.4 shows how cash flow statements are structured for most companies.

A strong and obvious connection exists between projects and all the items identified in a company's cash flow statement. As you examine Figure 2.4, you may recognize that the items identified within cash flows from financing activities are a reference (at least in part) to the funding of projects. Items listed in cash flows from investing activities represent a strong reference to the creation of assets—the literal end result of many projects. Finally, cash flows from operating activities are closely aligned with the fundamental objective of most projects. Typically, projects focus on improving business operations, allowing them to function in a more profitable way.

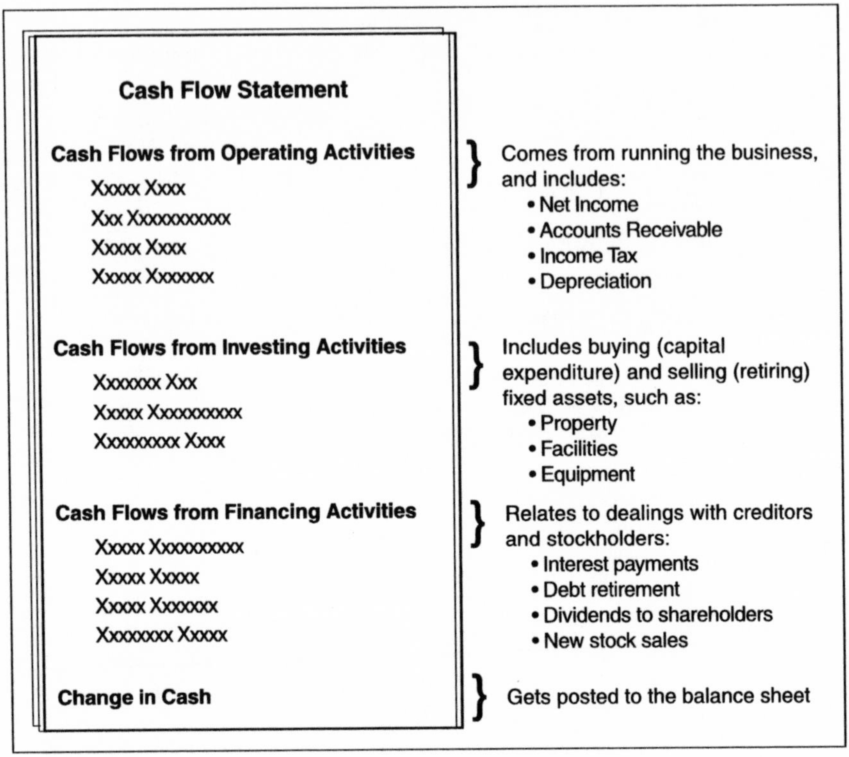

Cash Flow Statement

Cash Flows from Operating Activities
  Xxxxx Xxxx
  Xxx Xxxxxxxxxxx
  Xxxxx Xxxx
  Xxxxx Xxxxxxx
} Comes from running the business, and includes:
  • Net Income
  • Accounts Receivable
  • Income Tax
  • Depreciation

Cash Flows from Investing Activities
  Xxxxxxx Xxx
  Xxxxx Xxxxxxxxxx
  Xxxxxxxxx Xxxx
} Includes buying (capital expenditure) and selling (retiring) fixed assets, such as:
  • Property
  • Facilities
  • Equipment

Cash Flows from Financing Activities
  Xxxxx Xxxxxxxxxx
  Xxxxx Xxxxx
  Xxxxx Xxxxxxx
  Xxxxxxxx Xxxxx
} Relates to dealings with creditors and stockholders:
  • Interest payments
  • Debt retirement
  • Dividends to shareholders
  • New stock sales

Change in Cash
} Gets posted to the balance sheet

FIGURE 2.4

Cash flow statement—basic structure.

MAKING SENSE OF FINANCIAL STATEMENTS BY USING RATIO ANALYSIS

Financial statements can provide a wealth of information about a company to a variety of stakeholders. However, examining the details embedded in the three financial statements described above can be difficult. For many, a process called *ratio analysis* represents an easier way to understand a company's business position, general health, or growth prospects.

In ratio analysis, bits and pieces of information are extracted from the three basic financial statements and combined in various ways to create *financial ratios*.

Ratio analysis is frequently used by three groups: (1) company managers, who use ratios to help them analyze control and improve company operations; (2) credit analysts, such as officers of financial institutions and bond rating analysts, who use ratios to understand a company's debt position; and (3) stock analysts or investment analysts, who are interested in a company's efficiency and prospects for growth. Financial ratios provide useful information in five different areas relating to financial performance:

- **Liquidity.** Liquidity is the ability of a company to meet its short-term obligations.
- **Leverage.** Leverage is the extent to which company relies on debt financing.
- **Profitability.** Profitability is the extent to which a company makes money.
- **Market value.** Market value is the perceived overall worth of the company.
- **Asset management.** Asset management is the ability of a company to properly control its investment in assets.

Let's take a closer look at some of the ratios that are used to provide insight into each of these five areas. Table 2.1 shows a chart of some of the more common financial ratios.

TABLE 2.1

Common Financial Ratios

Classification	Ratio	Formula	Industry Average
Liquidity	Current	$\dfrac{\text{Current assets}}{\text{Current liabilities}}$	4.2%
	Quick	$\dfrac{\text{Current assets–Inventories}}{\text{Current liabilities}}$	2.1%
Leverage	Debt-asset	$\dfrac{\text{Total debt}}{\text{Total assets}}$	40%
	Debt-equity	$\dfrac{\text{Total debt}}{\text{Shareholders equity}}$	67%
Profitability	Return on assets	$\dfrac{\text{Net income}}{\text{Total assets}}$	9%
	Return on equity	$\dfrac{\text{Net income}}{\text{Total common equity}}$	15%
Asset management	Total asset turnover	$\dfrac{\text{Sales}}{\text{Total assets}}$	1.8%
	Operating capital requirements	$\dfrac{\text{Operating capital}}{\text{Sales}}$	50.3%

Ratios of Liquidity

Ratios relating to the liquidity of a company measure its ability to pay its current bills. *Liquidity* actually refers to the speed and the certainty with which assets could be converted to cash. Assets that can be converted into cash quickly (and without any discount to their value) are referred to as *liquid assets*. To the extent the company has enough liquid resources, it will be able to avoid defaulting on its financial obligations, thus avoiding the associated economic difficulties.

Current Ratio

The current ratio is determined by dividing the current assets by the current liabilities. The term *current* refers to the ability to convert assets into cash or to pay off debts, within a relatively short period, generally assumed to be 1 year. The formula for current ratio is:

Current Ratio = Total Current Assets / Total Current Liabilities

If a company finds itself in the position of having poor liquidity, it may not be able to pay its debts and bills on time, which could precipitate an extension or an increase in its overall debt. No very strong connection exists between projects and the current ratio, because the assets that typically created a project are not current assets.

Quick Ratio

The quick ratio is calculated by removing inventory from current assets and then dividing the difference (called *quick assets*) by the current liabilities. The formula for quick ratio is:

Quick Ratio = Quick Assets / Total Current Liabilities

Quick assets are current assets that are considered to be particularly easily converted into cash; inventories generally are regarded as the least liquid of all current assets.

Ratios of liquidity can help us understand an overall business, but are not extremely relevant to project management. Other ratios, however, have a more direct influence on project management.

Ratios of Leverage

Ratios relating to leverage described the extent to which a company relies on debt financing versus equity financing. The higher a company's debt level, the more difficulty it may have in fulfilling its financial obligations. However, debt also can provide a significant tax advantage, because interest payments are tax deductible. Too much debt, however, can put a company in jeopardy of experiencing financial distress.

Debt Ratios

The debt-asset ratio (also called the debt-to-asset ratio) is determined by dividing the company's total debt by its total assets. The formula for the debt-asset ratio is:

$$\text{Debt-Asset Ratio} = \text{Total Debt} / \text{Total Assets}$$

This ratio offers some perspective on how much of a company's assets are yet to be paid for. A more direct method for understanding the application of debt financing versus equity financing may be to simply compare the two forms of financing directly. This direct comparison is called the *debt-equity ratio* and is expressed through the following formula:

$$\text{Debt-Equity Ratio} = \text{Total Debt} / \text{Total Equity}$$

Debt ratios can provide some sense of a company's ability to obtain additional financing for potentially attractive investment opportunities. This, of course, impacts the company's options on how much they may be able to invest in future projects (the capital budgeting decision). Obviously, project managers do not determine what the debt-equity ratio should be. They are affected by this ratio, however, because it is a major determinant in the calculation of WACC, which we discussed previously.

Ratios of Profitability

Ratios of profitability are important to understand, but can be misleading at times. For example, many business opportunities involve sacrificing current profits for future profits. As we discover in the later chapters, this certainly is true in the case of any project initiative to introduce a new product. Launching a new product line typically involves large startup costs and significantly delayed financial returns. As a consequence, this type of project investment usually produces very low initial profits and adversely affects profitability ratios—a seemingly poor reflection on a company.

The concept of profitability, however, can be a useful way to think about projects. It is actually quite consistent with the current principle of calculating NPV, which could be loosely interpreted as a variant of profit. The basic reason for doing projects—to make or save money—is consistent with the concepts of profitability ratios.

Return on Assets (ROA)

One very common measure of managerial performance comes in comparing the company's income to its average total assets. In very common terms, ROA represents the quantification of how a company is able to "make the most with what it's got." The ratio can be expressed by using either pretax (gross) or after tax (net) income values, as the following two formulas illustrate, respectively:

$$\text{Gross Return on Assets} = \text{Earnings Before Interest and Tax} / \text{Average Total Assets}$$

$$\text{Net Return on Assets} = \text{Net Income} / \text{Average Total Assets}$$

When we apply the ROA principle to project work, we can derive a very important principle: Very strong projects generate large earnings with a relatively small increase in the total asset base.

Return on Equity (ROE)

ROA and ROE are subsets of a broader concept called *return on investment* (ROI). ROE assumes a narrower view of financial return than ROA, because it focuses exclusively on the concerns of the equity owners in the business (i.e., the shareholders). The formula for ROE is:

$$\text{Return on Equity} = \text{Net Income} / \text{Owners Equity}$$

ROE is a very important financial metric. Net income is essentially the compensation for the use of equity capital during a given period. The most important measure of equity capital investment performance is not how much was paid in dividends, but how much income was generated from the use of the equity capital supplied.

The net income, expressed as a ratio to the equity capital supplied, really represents the rate of return to shareholders. A relatively high ROE (compared to other, similar investment opportunities) will satisfy shareholders and keep their confidence. If ROE falls short of shareholder expectations, problems could ensue.

Ratios of Market Value

A company's market value is one important measure of a company's value that cannot be directly found on a financial statement. The market value of the common equity of a company is the market price per share of common stock multiplied by the number of outstanding shares. Market pricing provides an assessment of how investors value the overall worth of a company's assets. The formula is:

$$\text{Market Value} = \text{Market Price per Share} \times \text{Number of Shares of Outstanding Stock}$$

Rising stock prices provide an important indication of investor confidence. When the company's management is viewed as having sound operating and investing policies, the result is an increase in market value, and growth in the market value added (MVA), as we discussed in Chapter 1.

Ratios of Asset Management

The final set of ratios that we examine have the most direct implication in the world of projects, project management, and capital investment. Ratios related to asset management are intended to express how effectively a company's assets are being utilized.

Total Asset Turnover

The total asset turnover ratio expresses the relationship between the total value of all assets owned by a company and the total revenue it is able to produce, given that asset base. The ratio itself is actually determined by dividing the total operating revenues in a given accounting period by the average of total assets owned by the company. The formula for total asset turnover is, therefore:

$$\text{Total Asset Turnover} = \text{Total Operating Revenues} / \text{Total Assets}$$

If a company's asset turnover ratio is high, it is using its assets very effectively to generate sales. If the ratio is low, it may not be using its assets efficiently, or it has too many assets that are simply not contributing to revenue generation. In either case, the company should consider eliminating some of the non–revenue producing assets it currently owns.

This was the case at the Eastman Kodak Company in Rochester, New York during the 1990s. Prior to this, Kodak had been pursuing a long-term plan to outsource a substantial portion of its support staff and in some cases, portions of its operations. Eventually, the company found itself in possession of a significant amount of assets, primarily in the form of property and buildings—some of which had long since been abandoned. Clearly, these assets were not being used to generate revenue. This led to a large-scale effort that included the demolition of several buildings and the selling off of a considerable amount of property. These actions allowed Kodak to significantly reduce its total asset base.

One problem with the interpretation of the total asset turnover ratio (and closely tied to capital investment practices) occurs when the ratio is enhanced through the use of old assets. In this case, the ratio improves because the value of old assets is reduced due to depreciation. Although this situation may yield a very favorable asset turnover ratio, it could signal significant problems ahead for at least two reasons.

First, it could be an indicator that the company is not investing a sufficient amount of capital in the application of state-of-the-art equipment and facilities. Second, the company could be wrestling with an operation that is highly inefficient (due to aging equipment), or it may be facing an impending disaster and/or a substantial reinvestment situation (due to the potential for breakdown failure or equipment obsolescence).

Operating Capital Requirements Ratio

From a capital investment and project standpoint, this ratio really gets at the heart of the matter. The operating capital requirements ratio answers the question, "How much capital must a company invest in operational assets to support a given level of sales?"

The answer to this question can be determined by using the following formula:

$$\text{Operating Capital Requirement Ratio} = \text{Operating Capital} / \text{Sales}$$

Operating capital is the sum of net operating working capital plus the net fixed assets. Together, these two quantities represent the funds that shareholders have provided to pay for the assets that directly support the company's operations.

The implication here is obvious. If we were to express this in common terms, we would say that it is desirable for a company to be able to generate high sales while "operating on a shoestring." This notion plays heavily into the process of determining the relative attractiveness of projects from a financial standpoint, because companies that have a low operating capital requirement ratio are perceived as being well-managed.

To illustrate this concept, I often digress from the world of large corporations as I discuss a situation that revolves around a pair of automobile repair shops on adjacent blocks. Because they are in the same neighborhood, both shop owners have about the same amount invested in their land and their facility. The owner of garage number one is able to generate annual revenue of $100,000, using tools and diagnostic equipment worth about $5,000 (fixed assets), and a parts inventory of $3,000 (net operating working capital).

The owner of the other repair shop generates exactly the same amount of revenue. To accomplish this, however, the owner requires tools and diagnostic equipment worth about $40,000, and carries an inventory of $10,000. Obviously, this represents a considerably larger initial capital outlay and considerably larger ongoing carrying costs.

While this scenario is simple, the principle behind it is profound. The owner of repair shop number one possesses the ability to generate the same amount of revenue with a significantly smaller investment. Most would consider that shop owner to be a better business manager.

FINANCIAL ACCOUNTING VERSUS MANAGERIAL ACCOUNTING

Although financial information can be displayed in many ways, the field of accounting often is viewed as dividing into two basic forms: financial accounting and managerial accounting. Most of the discussion to this point has been directly related to the world of financial accounting. To clarify the difference between these two forms of accounting, let's begin by describing some of the characteristics of each.

Financial accounting is concerned primarily with the gathering, recording, and reporting of economic data and activities for an entire business in a "bottom line" kind of way. Although financial accounting reports can provide useful insight for internal company managers, they are really directed more at those who are external to the organization. This group includes owners (shareholders), creditors, governmental agencies, and the general public. Financial accounting statements objectively and periodically report the results of past operations and the financial condition of a business in accordance with GAAP. Financial accounting information is typically seen in a company's annual report.

Managerial accounting (or *management accounting*) is used primarily by a company's management for the purpose of conducting daily operations, planning future operations, and in the ongoing development of business approaches and operational strategies. Managerial accounting practices are not obligated to conform to GAAP.

Another key difference between managerial accounting practices and financial accounting practices relates to time horizon and to the subjectivity of the data included in reports. Financial accounting reports typically are constructed using objective, actual, historical information. In contrast, managerial accounting reports typically provide both objective measures of past operations and subjective estimates about future possibilities. Table 2.2 summarizes and displays

TABLE 2.2

Comparing Accounting Systems

	Financial accounting	Managerial accounting
Users	External: Stockholders, creditors, government	Internal: Senior executives, middle managers, workers
Purpose	Convey the overall effects of the management decisions and process improvements to the outside world	Provide feedback and control process for business insiders, allowing them to make good tactical decisions
Content	Financial measures only	Economic, physical, and performance measurements on processes, personnel, technologies, suppliers, and competitors
Format	Prepared according to GAAP	Prepared according to the needs of company managers
Frequency	Prepared periodically	Prepared periodically or as needed
Scope	Aggregated and summarized for entire organization	Localized to specific work groups, departments, or divisions
Time focus	Delayed and historical	Current, timely, and oriented toward the future
Data quality	Precise, consistent, and objective	Subjective, variable, and customized; selectively relevant

some of the key differences between financial accounting and managerial accounting.

The Objectives of Managerial Accounting Systems

Managerial accounting systems are configured so that every manager in a given company can run her respective organization be it a department, a business unit, or major corporate division. The type of data that managerial systems provide allows for the proper management of budgets, workflow, resources, inventory, and a host of other elements critical to the operation of any organizational unit.

The design of managerial accounting systems is further influenced by some of the higher level functions that companies typically expect their corporate managers to perform. Figure 2.5 illustrates some of the more common functions, which include:

- **Continuous improvement.** Continuous improvement describes the never-ending quest that companies have for improving their

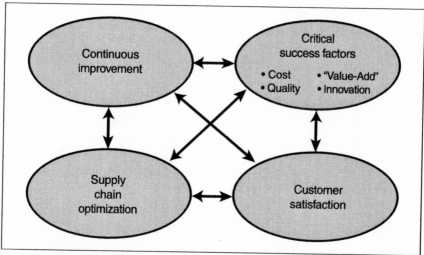

FIGURE 2.5

Some focus areas of managerial accounting systems.

existing systems, procedures, and processes. Continuous
improvement initiatives typically focus on the ongoing improvement of those most critical functions that a given organizational
unit performs. Naturally, the specific focus of continuous improvement initiatives will vary from company to company, and in some
cases, from department to department. For example, manufacturing units in most companies pursue continuous improvement initiatives that focus on reducing cycle time. Package delivery
companies and mail-order houses continuously seek to improve
their on-time delivery percentage. Airlines are on a constant quest
to improve their rate of on-time departures and arrivals.
- **Critical success factors.** Companies typically identify a set of
  key metrics that are used to evaluate the efficiency or effectiveness of their organizational units. Among the more commonly
  applied metrics are:
  - *Cost.* Regardless of whether it is stated explicitly, nearly all
    organizational units view themselves as being under a consid-
    erable amount of pressure to continuously reduce their oper-
    ating costs, their products, or their services.
  - *Quality.* Similar to cost, most organizational units are evalu-
    ated on the quality of their work outputs, which may not nec-
    essarily refer to a product or service.
  - *Value Add.* Although this particular metric may, at times, be
    a bit nebulous and difficult to define or measure in concrete

terms, organizational units frequently view themselves as required to demonstrate their contribution in terms of the value that they add to the overall success of the company.

- *Innovation*. In most companies today, a pervasive belief seems to exist that a continuous flow of new and different products and services is a necessary ingredient in the long-term success of any company.

- **Supply-chain optimization.** The term *supply chain* describes the flow of goods and services from cradle to grave, irrespective of whether any of the activities within the supply chain are performed by internal organizational units or outside entities. Companies typically encourage those internal organizational units that are part of the supply chain to improve the integration and/or coordination of all the steps within the overall supply chain.

- **Customer satisfaction.** In one form or another, most companies charge their organizational units with maintaining a customer-focused orientation, which is aimed primarily at the notion of enhancing the customer experience. In this case, the term "customer" is not restricted to those outside the company. Many organizational units, particularly in larger companies, may have a number of internal customers. As a strategy for maintaining inner harmony and a smoothly running operation, most organizational units are expected to please their internal customers as much as the company seeks to please its external customers.

Generally speaking, the type of information and data included in managerial accounting reports is of much greater value to project management professionals than the data included in financial accounting reports. Information shown in managerial accounting reports often is used to generate basic project objectives, develop project requirements, identify and quantify measures of project success, and even generate new project ideas.

CHAPTER 3

Fundamentals of Organizational Management

How do you eat an elephant? *Answer: One bite at a time.*

How do you manage a company? *Answer: One level of focus at a time.*

The business of managing an entire company is extremely broad and deep. It consists of addressing a wide range of critical issues, from the very large (What business should we be in?) to the very small (How should we categorize this particular item of cost?). Although these two questions pertain to dramatically different levels of detail and focus, both are valid questions within the broad spectrum of issues that comprise the world of *organizational management.*

In this chapter, we cover that spectrum and examine how companies are managed, from top to bottom. We begin by defining organizational management. We'll also review some of the historical perspectives and classic models that have gotten us to this stage in our collective understanding of organizational management. Finally, we'll look at some of the key principles and practices, from the highest-level strategic aspects to some of the ways costs are managed on a day-to-day basis.

As always, we focus our attention on issues that are most germane to projects and project management. As you read on, though, please keep in mind that this chapter will not necessarily be loaded with specific, direct references to ties between the worlds of organizational management and project management. In fact, organizational management may strike you as a knowledge area that is a considerable distance from cultivating the ability to manage projects in an effective manner.

It most definitely is not.

Possessing a general understanding of organizational management principles and practices is one of the most valuable components that project managers can have in their overall repository of business knowledge. The perspective and insights that a good working knowledge of organizational management provides will greatly enhance your ability to make sound project decisions. Understanding the principles and practices for your particular company is an absolute necessity, if you wish to function as an effective, business-savvy project manager within it. This chapter provides you with the structure and context needed to help you develop that understanding. Additionally, many of the principles embodied in organizational management are critical precursors in understanding topics such as portfolio management, which we will be exploring in Chapters 5 through 7.

WHAT IS ORGANIZATIONAL MANAGEMENT?

As the twentieth century unfolded, managers of companies slowly came to the realization that they did not necessarily have to be at the mercy of unpredictable forces within the complex and sometimes mysterious world of business. With this realization came the search for ways to manage their businesses so that success or failure was not dictated entirely by unforeseen events. As they came to understand that some of these events were actually predictable and quantifiable, managers began to use this information to their advantage. They also came to understand the essence of what we now appreciate as some of the basic principles of organizational management.

For some time, experts have emphasized that a preferred sequence of actions is associated with the practice of sound organizational management. First, managers need to understand their company's purpose and motivation for being in business. Once this understanding has been achieved, managers are able to develop meaningful objectives related to that motivation. Next, they must design and develop structures and methodologies needed to direct the company's activities towards these objectives. Finally, they must effectively implement and maintain those structures and methodologies.

While the above sequence of actions is unfolding, a parallel path normally is pursued, related to the development of a number of intermediate goals and plans needed to satisfy the company's objectives. In fact, level-by-level planning is what makes organizational management actionable.

Typically, the strategic planning process begins at the top, with the development of the company's *mission statement*. Supporting goals and plans then are developed one level at a time. Figure 3.1 represents the classic view of this process and illustrates how goals and plans are vertically segmented in many companies.

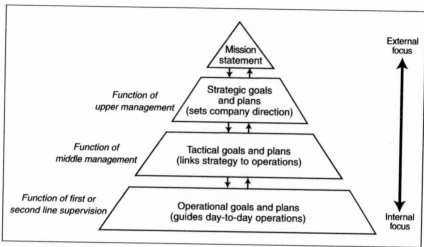

FIGURE 3.1

Hierarchy of plans and goals.

Before we examine the detail behind this process, let's take a short detour down memory lane, and take a look at how we reached our current understanding of organizational management.

HISTORICAL PERSPECTIVES

Throughout the twentieth century, countless researchers and management theorists have shaped our current understanding of organizational management. Among the more notable contributors are Frederick Taylor, Alfred Chandler, Michael Porter, and most recently, Gary Hamel and C.K. Prahalad.

Frederick Taylor

Although Frederick Taylor's influence dates back to the early twentieth century, some of the fundamental principles of *scientific management* he developed are as popular (and relevant) as ever in today's business environment. Prior to Taylor's emergence as an expert in management research, the belief was widely held that the management of a company was largely a soft, fuzzy, and unpredictable effort. The prevailing opinion was that some businesspeople were naturally talented managers, and others were not.

However, Taylor proposed the idea that every business activity could be broken down into measurable components, and each component could be reworked to achieve maximum efficiency. These molded components could then be combined into larger elements called business processes. The result was the notion that an entire business could be managed using measurable, manageable, and efficient subprocesses. Taylor's work was to become the driving concept behind several later works, such as those of W. Edwards Deming, the widely recognized guru of quality management.

Alfred Chandler

In the early 1960s, a noted researcher and management theorist, Alfred Chandler, promoted a straightforward yet powerful concept that *structure follows strategy*. According to Chandler, a company must focus attention on defining its strategy (Who are we, and what are we trying to do?) before it makes any effort toward developing its structure (How do we do it, and do it well?). If a strategy is not developed first, the structure is likely to be ineffective, if not useless. Conversely, Chandler asserted that if a company has taken the necessary time to develop a comprehensive, meaningful corporate strategy, the corresponding structure will follow with relative ease.

It's worth pointing out, however, that companies can sometimes have difficulty distinguishing strategy from structure, which can lead to problems. Take, for example, the practice of *decentralization*, which was a hot management trend in the 1970s. Decentralization was hailed as a brilliant corporate strategy by many at that time. In fact, the true strategy—at least the one that was often being attempted— was widespread product diversification. In reality, decentralization is a structural response to the desired strategy of product diversification. This is backward, according to Chandler and his opinion was often supported by reality. In far too many situations, widespread product diversification was not an appropriate strategy, and companies suffered; however, decentralization took the blame as a "poor strategy." This misclassification of strategy versus structure created a confusion that plagued some companies for years. Chandler's is a simple, but powerful lesson: Be sure you know what you want to do before trying to figure out how to set out to do it!

Michael Porter

A professor of strategic management at the Harvard Business School, Michael Porter is considered the guru of modern-day American business strategy. In one of his most notable works, *Competitive Strategy*, Porter provided a framework for guiding corporations through the process of developing an overall business strategy.

Although there is much more to Porter's framework, one of the key points that emerges from his model is the assertion that several elements are required for a company to be able to develop an effective competitive strategy:

- A company must clearly define itself in terms of its basis for competing, and its standards for measuring its success.
- Once it has defined itself, the company must develop a thorough understanding of its internal strengths and weaknesses.
- The company must then evaluate its strengths and weaknesses—with specific focus on its position relative to external competitive forces.
- Finally, the company must develop policies and methods that managers can use to communicate all of this information to all areas within the company.

Clearly, the power of Porter's work (still very vital in today's view of organizational management) comes from his recognition of the dual importance of strategic *and* tactical elements in defining a company's overall competitive strategy.

Gary Hamel and C.K. Prahalad

As the twentieth century drew to a close, further refinements in the views surrounding organizational management have come from Gary Hamel and C.K. Prahalad. These two strategy professors are probably best-known for their early 1990s *Harvard Business Review* articles, which identified and expounded on the concepts and principles of *strategic intent* and *core competence*. Many corporations have woven these principles into their organizational management fabric.

With respect to strategic intent, Hamel and Prahalad suggest that companies need more than just a model that defines the company's strategy. They also must define their desired leadership position within an industry—with a clear focus on the time frame required to reach that leadership position. Together, a well-defined leadership position and a time frame are combined to form what Hamel and Prahalad contend are a necessary component in a company's long-term success: *strategic intent*. Strategic intent adds value by providing a focal point for a company's stated strategies.

Perhaps one of the most illustrative and well-known examples of strategic intent came in the early 1960s, when President John F. Kennedy defined the United States' leadership position in the highly competitive "space race." Kennedy declared that the United States would be the first country to send a man to the moon and safely return him to earth. Additionally, he identified the time frame, specifically stating that this goal would be achieved by the end of the decade.

Why is the concept of strategic intent so important today? As much as anything, because of the message it communicates throughout the company. And the message of strategic intent is really this: The company has long-term goals that it intends to maintain, *even if the business environment changes along the way.*

According to Hamel and Prahalad, one of the key elements in the successful achievement of strategic intent in the face of a rapidly changing business environment is flexibility. Companies must maintain some amount of agility by engaging more in short-term planning. This approach leaves the company ample opportunity to periodically reevaluate its position and seize new opportunities as they become apparent.

This particular concept is huge, and it has enormous implications to us as managers of project efforts. It reinforces some of the concepts discussed in Chapter 1, such as the need to manage a project to a business objective, rather than to stationary, predetermined cost and schedule goals. And it reinforces Doug DeCarlo's contention that periodic reevaluation of the project position is warranted, driven by the notion that the answers to his Four Business Questions may change throughout the life of a project.

Finally, say Hamel and Prahalad, for strategic intent to take hold, it also must be communicated to all members of the company in a way that promotes their buy-in and enthusiastic support. The desired outcome is understanding and internalization, ultimately resulting in a sense of commitment in achieving strategic intent that becomes pervasive throughout the company.

Although their article on strategic intent pertains to overall company strategy, it has helped provide the foundation for today's emerging view of projects, and the growing sentiment that project management should be viewed more as an entrepreneurial, business-based discipline, and less as an exercise in the application of technology or logistics.

SOUND ORGANIZATIONAL MANAGEMENT THROUGH SOUND ORGANIZATIONAL PLANNING

Obviously, excellence in organizational management doesn't just happen—it comes about through careful planning. As Figure 3.1 suggests, once a company has identified its mission, a series of plans and goals must be developed to support that mission. This process is referred to as *organizational planning*.

Organizational planning is ordinarily performed by different groups at different levels within the company. Although there are certainly variations, Figure 3.1 serves as a good general model for the organizational planning process. As the model illustrates, planning is carried out at three levels of detail and focus: the *strategic level*, where upper management sets the direction of the company; the *operational level*, where the company's supervisory staff conducts the day-to-day business; and the *tactical level*, a kind of middle-ground, where mid-managers create goals and plans that are intended to link the company's strategy to its day-to-day operations.

Figure 3.2 reveals the elements that comprise each level. Let's take a closer look at some of these elements.

ELEMENTS OF STRATEGIC PLANNING

There is no single, "correct" methodology for coordinating and developing an overall strategic plan for a company. No matter what methodology is used, however, the objectives of any strategic planning initiative are generally the same, and these include:

- Identify corporate goals and objectives
- Identify high-level strategies for achieving goals and objectives
- Assess the industry and the marketplace within which the company functions
- Assess the general economic environment (macroeconomics)
- Benchmark against the competition ("external" metrics, such as financial strength)

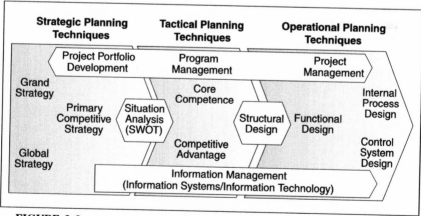

FIGURE 3.2

Elements of organizational planning.

- Determine how the company should orient itself toward the market and the competition
- Identify and track performance against high-level (corporate-wide) metrics

A company may use any of a number of specific techniques to formulate its overall strategic plan. The next sections detail some of the more common techniques.

Grand Strategy

A company's *grand strategy* is the highest level of a company's strategic positioning. In some circumstances, the choice of a grand strategy may be a purposeful decision made by upper management. But it also may be forced upon a company, as a result of the company's financial strength, competitive position, future growth potential, or even the general economy. Grand strategies tend to fall into three general categories.

Growth

A *growth strategy* is characterized by expansion. In some cases, the expansion may be internal, focused on making the existing company bigger from within. This could include activities such as developing new products, expanding existing product lines, or increasing sales of existing products. A second growth strategy, best described as internal/external, might be one of diversification. Here, a company acquires businesses that are related to a company's core business. Finally, a company might choose to pursue a growth strategy that is entirely external, in which it tries to acquire businesses that take the company into totally new areas.

Stability

Companies that pursue a *stability strategy* are those that wish to remain at their current size, or grow in a slow, controlled fashion. Company executives often pursue a strategy of stability after undergoing a tumultuous period of either rapid growth or forced decline. The objective in either case is to provide a period during which the company as a whole can adapt to the changes and reach of some sort of normalized state.

Retrenchment

A strategy of *retrenchment* ordinarily is precipitated by a forced decline in a company's overall position. Typical causes for retrenchment may include a reduction in the product demand, a general slowdown in the economy, or difficulties that may have been precipitated by management issues. The pursuit of a retrenchment strategy often includes budgetary reductions, workforce reductions, or in severe cases, liquidation of some of the company's existing assets or business units. A common term for retrenchment is *downsizing*.

Obviously, the grand strategy that a company pursues has a profound impact on the strategic planning processes that follow. Also, it is not uncommon for companies that do business internationally to have separate grand strategies for their domestic and global operations.

Global Strategy

Companies that conduct business internationally need to define their *global strategy*—a high level approach for how they will conduct business within and across national borders. The development of a global strategy can be tricky, because companies find themselves trying to satisfy a number of different objectives, such as:

- Promote synergistic relationships across organizations
- Pursue the company's overall goals in a unified manner
- Recognize geographically localized market influences
- Appropriately adapt to cultural influences
- Exploit large-scale business practices, such as economies of scale
- Seek to gain operational efficiencies, such as product standardization

At the core of trying to address all these objectives at once is the age-old decision of centralization versus decentralization. This decision could pertain to a large array of considerations related to products, services, operations, and in some cases, even management structures. Although many ways exist to configure a global strategy, three common variations are presented here.

Globalization

Companies that pursue a *globalization strategy* either assume—or are interested in promoting the idea—that a single global market exists for their products or services. In other words, no matter where in the world you are, the demand for your company's "standard" products will be virtually identical. For example, Kentucky Fried Chicken and McDonald's assume that people everywhere want to eat the same drumsticks and burgers. This approach can have tremendous value to a company, because it opens up vast opportunities for economies of scale. Key advantages of pursuing a globalization strategy may include standardization in product design and manufacture, leveraging of large-scale relationships with suppliers and materials, and interchangeability of operational components and personnel.

Multidomestic

Companies that pursue a *multidomestic strategy* either believe—or grow to recognize—that competitive environment is a localized phenomenon. Although the company is present in several different countries, subordinate strategies such as choice of product offerings, product design features, and approaches to marketing and advertising work best if they are adapted to the specific needs of each country or region.

> Many companies reject the idea of a single global market. They have found that the French do not drink orange juice for breakfast, that laundry detergent is used to wash dishes in parts of Mexico, and that people in the Middle East prefer toothpaste that tastes spicy. Procter & Gamble standardized diaper design across European markets, but discovered that Italian mothers preferred diapers that covered the baby's navel. This design feature was so important to the successful sale of diapers in Italy that the company eventually incorporated it specifically for the Italian market. Baskin-Robbins introduced a green-tea flavored ice cream in Japan, and Haagen-Dazs developed new flavor called dulce de leche primarily for sale in Argentina.

Transnational

Companies that pursue a *transnational strategy* attempt to reap the benefits of worldwide coordination that come from a globalization strategy, without forsaking the need for geographically localized flexibility that comes with a multidomestic strategy. A transnational strategy is primarily one of coordination, and—at times—compromise. It's really a balancing act between the quest to achieve a global efficiency and the pressure to meet local demands.

> One company that effectively uses a transnational strategy is Caterpillar Inc., a heavy equipment manufacturer. Caterpillar achieves global efficiencies by designing its products to use many identical components and by centralizing manufacturing of components in a few large-scale facilities. However, assembly plants located in each of Caterpillar's major markets add certain product features, tailored to meet local needs.

PRIMARY COMPETITIVE STRATEGY

Once a grand strategy and global strategy have been defined, companies turn their attention to the identification of their *primary competitive strategy*. A primary competitive strategy answers the question: What basic orientation will we assume with respect to the way we compete?

The concept of primary competitive strategy can be effectively illustrated by exploring a framework developed by Michael Treacy and Frederik Wiersema, in their book entitled *The Discipline of Market Leaders*.

The Treacy and Wiersema Framework for Competitive Strategy

A very popular framework for articulating competitive strategy emerged in the late 1990s. Introduced by Michael Treacy and Frederik Wiersema, this framework identifies three basic competitive strategies that a company could choose to pursue:

Product Leadership

The strategy of *product leadership* refers to a company's ability to offer products or services that are perceived by customers as superior and unique, relative to those of their competitors. This customer perception ordinarily is created through *product differentiation*, making this strategy similar in many regards to Porter's differentiation strategy.

Operational Excellence

The strategy of *operational excellence* refers to a company's ability to achieve low product cost through productivity and efficiency improvements, elimination of waste, and tight cost control. Once again, the strategy captures the essence of Porter's low-cost leadership strategy.

Customer Intimacy

The strategy of *customer intimacy* refers to a company's ability to provide a wide range of solutions aimed at specialized customer needs. The strategy normally is achieved by offering an extensive array of products or services which collectively provide total, unique, tailored solutions. Customers are willing to pay more, confident in the knowledge that the company will have the ability to solve their specific problem or satisfy their unique need. This strategy is a useful addition to Porter's two-dimensional framework.

It may be interesting, if not valuable, to imagine Porter's *focus* strategy overlaid onto Treacy and Wiersema's *customer intimacy* strategy. Specifically, I'm referring to the notion that perhaps another (unofficial) variation may exist, in which a company might assume a strategy of customer intimacy, but focus that strategy in specific segments of the consumer market.

SITUATION ANALYSIS

The development of a grand strategy, a global strategy, and to a certain extent a competitive strategy, really addresses questions such as: Who are we?, What business are we in?, and What is our framework for competing? These strategic considerations are largely proactive and directional in nature. They are really about the *what* of strategic planning, and they do not address the **how**. This is where *situation analysis* comes in. In effect, situation analysis forms a threshold, or linkage, between strategic planning and tactical planning (Fig. 3.2).

Often referred to as a SWOT analysis, situation analysis includes an examination of the Strengths, Weaknesses, Opportunities, and Threats that can affect a company's ability to achieve its strategic goals. No tremendous amount of mystery enshrouds the definition of these terms:

- **Strengths.** Positive, existing characteristics of a company, which it can rely on or exploit to achieve its strategic goals.
- **Weaknesses.** Unfavorable, existing characteristics of a company, which may inhibit or restrict its ability to achieve its strategic goals.
- **Opportunities.** Currently untapped areas that, if exploited, would enhance a company's ability to meet or exceed its strategic goals.
- **Threats.** Specific circumstances or conditions that may impede, preclude, or make it very difficult for a company to achieve its strategic goals.

Strengths and weaknesses tend to focus on factors that are internal to the company. Therefore, these elements of the SWOT analysis will be of much greater value when we discuss tactical planning techniques. Opportunities and threats are much more germane to our current discussion on strategic planning, because they traditionally focus more on factors external to the company. Table 3.1 offers some examples of various categories that could be used when performing a SWOT analysis.

TABLE 3.1

Some Common Areas of Focus in a SWOT Analysis

Strengths or Weaknesses	Opportunities	Threats
Senior management capability	Market size potential	Slow economy
Patent position	Unfulfilled customer needs	Rapid shift in technology
Research capability	Emerging markets	Shift in consumer preferences
Product quality	Rapidly expanding markets	Capability of competitors
Customer satisfaction	Void left by competitor	New government regulations
Marketing expertise	Relaxed government regulation	Scarcity of resources
Brand recognition/reputation	Technology immaturity	Supplier problems

ELEMENTS OF TACTICAL PLANNING

Tactical planning is the logical "how-to" extension of strategic planning. Largely structural in nature, it serves as a bridge between the high-level goals of a company and its business operations. Often formulated by those in the mid- to upper management ranks, tactical plans typically focus on the major activities or actions that the company (or major divisions within the company) must perform to fulfill the goals identified in the strategic plan. As was the case with strategic planning, no single recipe for success exists when it comes to developing tactical plans, but a number of typical elements are included.

Core Competence

In concept, *core competence*, *core business*, and *core products* are fairly straightforward principles. All the terms describe the same phenomenon: something that a company is good at. Although it may be best visualized as a threshold between tactical planning and operational planning (see Fig. 3.2), the concept of core competence actually translates into a singular mission: Determine what you are good at, and exploit it as much as possible. To many of us, this seems intuitively obvious, yet companies often are lured away from what they do best and begin to explore what often amounts to uncharted territory.

But what really is core competence? In a well-known *Harvard Business Review* article from the early 1990s, Hamel and Prahalad suggest that core competences are "complex harmonizations of individual technologies and production skills." Other less eloquent definitions have been offered for core competence; once again, though, all revolve around the simple notion that a core competence is an activity or set of activities that a company performs very well.

Experts suggest that, for a company's core competences to have maximum value, they should possess the following five characteristics:

1. They should provide the company with an opportunity to gain access to a wide variety of products and markets.
2. They should be capable of contributing—in a demonstrative way—to the benefits of end products, as perceived by customers (they are able to impact what customers care about).
3. They should make a company unique in comparison to competitors.
4. They should be difficult for competitors to imitate.
5. They are reasonably stable and sustainable.

Two common variants on this principle, core business and core products, are easy to understand. Core business is a collection of core competences directed at a particular segment of the product and/or consumer market. Core products, it follows, are outputs that stem from core competence, core business, or both.

Perhaps the most progressive and contemporary concepts related to organizational management theory comes from the same Hamel and Prahalad article identified above. Their view on core competence actually suggests that organizational managers should view their company not as a grouping of businesses, but as a portfolio of core competences. The authors further state that, to be successful, companies must be able to continually adjust to changes, such as technology advancements, new markets, and changes in customer preferences.

This is somewhat at odds with the Porter (and Treacy/ Wiersema) philosophy of choosing a single competitive strategy and running with it. Ironically, those companies that are most successful are able to find a harmonious marriage between the two philosophies.

Similar to our discussion about the relationship between structural design and project management, a strong connection also exists between the core competence concept and the project management function. The key issue here has much to do with the general acceptance of project management, buoyed by its widespread recognition as an important (if not critical), value-added competency.

Once again, in my observations, a pattern has emerged. In companies where project management has been embraced in part by being recognized as a core competency, the formal application of sound, valuable project management methodologies has ramped up relatively quickly. These companies have reaped the business benefits associated with such a transformation. This is not always the case, however.

One example of this can be seen in one particular major U.S. corporation. This company appeared to be serious about embracing project management. In fact, they were actually near the leading edge of what is now commonly recognized as a kind of project management boom, forming a project management office of substantial proportion in the mid-1980s. However, as the twenty-first century approached (some 15 years later), the company had not yet come to formally refer to project management as a "core competence." Instead, they continued to refer to it as an "enabling skill set."

Although this may seem like an exercise in semantics, the reality is that their reluctance to identify project management as a core competency sent a strong message rippling throughout the entire company: Project management is OK, but no big deal. The pervasive feeling, in fact, was that "doing project management" (again a revealing choice of wording) was more or less a discretionary activity—and something just about anyone could do. As a result, the overall value of the project management discipline had imposed limitations, and life for the company's full-time, professional project managers—who had to deal with largely nonsupportive team members—remained an uphill battle on a day-to-day basis.

COMPETITIVE ADVANTAGE

Once a company has defined what its competitive strategy will be, a very logical question becomes: How could we go about achieving an advantage with respect to our competitors? Certainly, the tactics required to establish competitive advantage are many and varied. But one thing is certain: The tactics must be directly aligned with competitive strategy.

Table 3.2 identifies some initiatives that a company could pursue in the quest to establish competitive advantage. You will undoubtedly recognize elements of the competitive strategies discussed earlier in this chapter.

STRUCTURAL DESIGN

As Figure 3.2 suggests, tactical planning is anchored by two basic elements: (1) core competence (What do we do well?); and (2) competitive advantage (How do we apply that competence to optimize our

TABLE 3.2

Tactics for Establishing a Competitive Advantage

Tactic	Rationale	Example
Reduce product pricing via lower operating costs	Selling more units at a lower cost can maintain or even increase profits, while also increasing market share.	FedEx automated much of its customer service operation by offering online parcel tracking.
Make it difficult for others to duplicate or "follow"	Use of expertise or technology that is not easily mimicked will reduce the number of competitors.	Microsoft has established a huge competitive advantage through the patenting of its software.
Create high switchover costs (called buyer lock-in)	Customer attrition can be reduced by making it difficult for customers to leave the company.	Verizon Wireless offers "deals" on two-year contracts, but makes it extremely costly to abandon them.
Introduce new products or services	Introducing new products or services often generates a period of time were these products or services are unique.	FedEx created a profitable niche in the late 1970s by introducing an "overnight delivery" service.
Differentiate existing products or services	Whether real or perceived, establishing a favorable differentiation in products or services will attract customers.	Kentucky Fried Chicken and Coca-Cola offer "recipes" that customers cannot find in similar products.
Improve product quality or develop enhancements	Customers naturally favor products or services that are better than the competition's.	For many years Kodak dominated the film industry, thanks to their exceptionally high product quality.
Establish business alliances	Combining the products or services of businesses results in lower cost and greater convenience for customers.	Credit card companies have aligned themselves with airlines and hotels through frequent flyer programs.
Supplier leveraging	Companies that purchase large quantities of materials can leverage that to create a pricing advantage.	Wal-Mart is well known for using its size to intimidate suppliers into agreeing to price reductions.

leverage in the marketplace?). Just as situation analysis links strategic planning to tactical planning, structural design links tactical planning to operational planning.

Structural design refers to the way that a company chooses to organize itself, as the process of organizing leads to the design and development of a formalized *organizational structure*. The purpose of a formalized organizational structure is to define job duties and effectively deploy human resources. This is done by addressing three things:

- Defining the formal tasks assigned to individuals and departments throughout the company
- Defining formal reporting relationships, including lines of authority, the number of the vertical "layers" within the company, decision-making responsibilities, and the span of control for each management level
- Designing methods and processes that ensure efficient coordination across workgroups

Companies must have a structural design that supports the company's overall strategic goals as well as its competitive positioning. Using the Treacy and Wiersema framework, for example, companies wishing to pursue a product leadership strategy are likely to have a structural design that is quite different from a company wishing to pursue an operational excellence strategy. Both of these designs look different from a company pursuing a strategy of customer intimacy.

For example, a company that has adopted a product leadership strategy must strive to develop a working environment that allows for—if not promotes—ongoing experimentation and learning. This type of organization values creativity and innovation, suggesting an organizational structure that is very flexible and characterized by efficient horizontal coordination.

However, if operational excellence is the company's primary competitive strategy, managers would be well served by an organization that is rigid, predictable, and efficient by design. In this environment, standardized procedures are valued over creativity. A strong sense of centralized authority is present, in which employees execute routine tasks under close supervision.

As you may have guessed, the organizational design of a company that pursues a strategy of customer intimacy is likely to be a combination of the preceding two structures. For these companies, some flexibility is needed to support an environment typified by unique customer solutions; however, the overall organization must be managed in a coordinated and efficient manner as well.

The implications related to the connection between a company's structural design and project management are enormous. However, the connection does not have all that much to do with the company's primary competitive strategy, as we discussed. It has much more to do with how the project management function is positioned within the company, and the message that any given position communicates to the company.

Specifically, I am referring to three different ways that project management is positioned on a given company's organizational chart and the related impact of those positionings. Let's take a look at these three variations.

Vertical Positioning

Companies that choose to position the manager of project management to report directly to a company CEO or senior VP send a very different message than those that choose to position that same manager as a first-line supervisor buried somewhere within one of the company's technical departments. And it's important to clarify that the issue here is not one of status, per se, as much as the message implied or perceived regarding the business-critical importance senior management places on the project management function. Lower-positioned project management groups often can have a harder time gaining cross-functional acceptance and respect.

Organizational Positioning

A reasonably strong relationship also appears to exist between the type of organizational unit that the project management function is associated with, and the perception of what project management actually is and what it can do for the company. This is certainly not an absolute phenomenon, but it holds true in a surprising number of circumstances.

Companies that perceive the project management function as having strategic and/or business value will often position the project management work group within an organization with a title such as Administration or Finance, for example. This kind of positioning allows for a more seamless integration of project management personnel with some of the higher-level business functions, such as strategic planning, budget preparation, and portfolio management.

Conversely, companies that continue to view project management as a technically focused, logistically based extension of the construction trades of years gone by will tend to connect the project management group with a technical organization, such as Engineering or Information Technology (IT). I have encountered many situations in which a Project Management Office (PMO) exists within a company's IT organization, but is not invited to participate anywhere else. To me, this is quite sad, and it represents a significant lost opportunity for the companies that choose to operate that way.

Centralized versus Decentralized

The centralized versus decentralized phenomenon also is tied to perceptions of project management value. Companies that believe that project management has potential long-term value often form a centralized project management group, incorporating (at least) a few key staff functions, such as process development experts. These companies recognize a simple fact: Without such a dedicated group, no one is paying attention to the care and feeding of the project management discipline; that is, no one is charged with advancing the state-of-the-art of the craft within the company.

In many other companies, project management personnel are dispersed across the entire company. Very often, these people are "owned" by a non–project management department, and are charged with leading projects in addition to performing their so-called "real job" (this is actually a commonly used phrase!). This decentralized structure often is seen in companies where project management is viewed as an enabling skill set, not as a free-standing, value-added function that can contribute to the company's business success. This is sad.

ELEMENTS OF OPERATIONAL PLANNING

The term *operations* refers to the conduct of day-to-day business. Operational plans are generally developed at lower levels within a company, and specify those activities required to achieve operational goals and support tactical planning outputs. The process of operational planning includes activities such as:

- Determining the functions that should be performed within different departments
- Establishing policies in support of strategic and tactical initiatives
- Establishing work processes, procedures, and controls
- Addressing issues of employee development and employee satisfaction
- Identifying and tracking against local (departmental) standards of performance

Although specific operational planning approaches may vary from company to company, many utilize the following techniques in the development of operational plans.

Functional Design

Within the context of the organizational structure identified as part of tactical planning, individual operating units (let's call them departments) must be designed and organized so that the functions that they perform: (1) support the company's strategic goals, and (2) are properly coordinated with the functions performed by other departments within the company.

For example, let's consider a company that has adopted the strategy of product leadership, in which new, differentiated products constantly are being developed. In a company such as this, technical departments (such as engineering) would seek to acquire employees who are more oriented to a research and development environment and outfit them with the tools, equipment, and facilities needed to perform functions such as conducting experiments and building prototype models. The human resources department of this company would develop strategies to facilitate frequent and continual interdepartmental movement. The marketing department would prepare themselves for activities such as test marketing studies, aggressive advertising campaigns, and product trials. Meanwhile, the finance department would adopt methods to secure increased financing, deal with large asset investments, and develop processes for authorizing the building of new research or production facilities.

A company that has adopted a strategy of operational excellence would take quite a different approach to functional design. In this case, the engineering department might consist of a core group of engineers, supported by outsourced engineering services on an as-needed basis. The human resources department would adopt strategies for retaining and developing a stable workforce. The marketing department would promote brand loyalty throughout their customer base and focus on developing efficient product distribution methods. Finally, the finance department would stress the importance of—and adherence to—the practice of approving only those projects having the highest net present value.

Internal Process Design

One of the most basic elements of conducting day-to-day business is the *process*. Simple term—big concept. Companies develop processes for doing just about everything, and essentially, all work in a company is performed through some kind of process. A process may be defined as a set of steps or procedures that define how a function is to be performed and what results may be expected. A process also may be defined as a set of interrelated resources and activities that transform inputs into outputs. I think these definitions work well when put together.

Internal process design is the foundation of operational planning. By definition, it consists of the development of approaches, methods, and guidelines for guiding virtually every activity performed within the company. Process design is likely to affect nearly every aspect of a company's overall business, and may include detailed prescriptions for issues such as behavior, methods, and documentation around business functions such as:

- Preparation of drawings by the engineering department
- Interviewing of potential new hires by the human resources department
- Preparation of invoices by the finance department
- Assembly of products by the manufacturing department
- Performance appraisal conducted by the first-line supervision
- Ordering of parts and materials by the purchasing department

And let's not forget project management! A project schedule is actually an excellent example of internal process design, albeit a one-time process.

Undoubtedly quite obvious from this list is the notion that internal process design is performed by many different groups throughout the company. By definition, each group cares primarily about the processes that are used in their organizational subgroup. This leads to another common practice that many companies have adopted—the identification of a *process owner*. Process owners are typically accountable for all aspects of a given process, including process design, process improvement, and ultimately the performance capability of the process itself. Identifying a process owner helps ensure that someone is responsible for managing that process and for optimizing its effectiveness.

To ensure continuous improvement in project results, every company that executes a significant number of projects should identify a process owner for the project management process. In many cases, this role is served by the Project Office (or Project Management Office).

This critical concept ties directly back to our discussion regarding the implication of having a centralized versus decentralized project management function.

Control System Design

The purpose of control systems is to establish (and impose) the boundaries by which a company's day-to-day business processes are conducted. It is an extension of internal process design, with an added element of checks and balances. *Control system design* is the mechanism by which managers may be assured that processes are being applied in an appropriate manner in accomplishing the company's strategic objectives. A secondary, more detailed, function of control system design is to ensure that specific tasks are being carried out and resources are being applied effectively and efficiently.

A classic example of control systems design is the process and methods a company uses to establish the size of next year's departmental budgets. To further reinforce the perceived importance of maintaining control for some, consider the fact that many companies impose considerable regulatory control over the process by which a given organization is permitted to use the monies that have already been allocated to them. Many companies, for example, require a large number of signatures before a project is considered formally approved.

Control systems typically possess these characteristics:

- Well-defined procedures
- Rules and/or guidelines
- Exact, quantifiable data
- Strict monitoring and measurement
- Expectations of specific performance against predetermined standards

Control systems are likely to be prevalent—and often quite rigid—in functional areas such as manufacturing, production, and assembly. Examples of control systems in these areas include procedures relating to inventory control, order processing and billing, and production scheduling.

Some typical examples of activities normally associated with control system design include:

- Approvals and authorizations
- Verifications and reconciliations
- Job descriptions and performance reviews
- Security of physical assets and proprietary information

Although all companies perform some form of control system design, the needs of companies may differ considerably. Consequently, control systems must be specifically designed for each individual company, making these systems unique.

OVERARCHING LINKAGES IN ORGANIZATIONAL PLANNING

Some organizational design elements can be viewed as spanning all three phases of organizational planning. Among these design elements are project management (naturally), information management, capital asset infrastructure, human asset infrastructure, and technology infrastructure, to name a few. Let's take a closer look at two of the more relevant of these overarching organizational design elements, project management and information management.

The Project Management Continuum

From a "big picture" standpoint, the discipline and practices of project management actually exist at different levels within a company. As Figure 3.2 attempts to illustrate, project portfolio management is largely a strategic element, program management is essentially a tactical element, and project management is an operational element. Together, these elements form linkages that span the entire spectrum of organizational planning techniques. This is a critical point, and one that is not well understood (or appreciated) today.

In fact, developing and implementing a solid project portfolio development process is undoubtedly one of today's most important business-based issues, relative to the discipline of project management.

Why? Because one of the greatest opportunities that many of today's companies have for effectively linking corporate strategy to business operations comes in the form of adopting a top-down approach to the process of identifying new initiatives. This process begins with project-portfolio development. Regrettably, not all companies do a good job of this.

Project-portfolio development can be very powerful, easy, and effective, when implemented as a top-down process. This process starts much like the process of organizational management itself: by listing and quantifying the strategic goals of the company. This can be done easily and effectively by using approaches such as the *Balanced Scorecard* (refer to the discussion on Balanced Scorecard in Chapter 5). Through a process of progressive elaboration (much like a process of developing a work breakdown structure), goals and performance metrics are identified in increasing levels of detail. The endpoint is a list of proposed projects that are obviously and inarguably connected to the company's strategic goals.

Unfortunately, I have observed in far too many situations a process in which one group within the company formulates strategic goals, and an entirely different group (ordinarily at or near the operational level in the organization) strives to develop projects that they hope will "fit the company strategy." In effect, the two groups use the middle ground (the tactical planning arena illustrated in Figure 3.2) as a kind of awkward meeting place, rather than using this area as part of a continuous pathway to purposefully link strategy development with project development. At best, the "bottom-up meets top-down" approach leads to a situation in which the company has identified a set of projects that may be *compliant* with strategy. This is not the same as identifying the *optimum* set of projects needed to advance the strategy. At worst, this approach can lead to a potentially significant disconnect between projects and company strategy.

In many cases, the disconnect occurs because those who are responsible for originating project ideas are not intimately familiar with the details of their company's strategic intent. Accordingly, their project ideas spring from a combination of:

- What they believe is "within the spirit" of the company's strategic directive
- Local (department) problems that are causing them immediate pain
- How much money is in their department budget (which was determined as an independent activity)

The application of a sound, top-down approach for identifying project initiatives is imperative. Once the optimum set of projects has been identified, much is to be gained by managing them in a coordinated fashion. This is the focus of *program management*. Program management can include combining small projects to tackle a major organizational issue. However, it also includes routine activities such as enterprise-wide resource management. In short, program management reduces the amount of independent, random motion that occurs when large quantities of individual projects are simply "cut loose." Excellence in program management requires excellence in managing individual projects. This is the third element in the project management continuum shown in Figure 3.2.

In Chapters 5 through 7, we explore a variety of techniques for identifying projects using a top-down approach and managing them as a program. For now, it's important to note that project management should be viewed as a critical link—and an integral component—of the overall organizational planning process.

INFORMATION MANAGEMENT CONFIGURATION

As Figure 3.2 suggests, organizational design elements related to the area called information management planning may be viewed as spanning all three phases of organizational planning. Determining how the information management "system" should be configured may actually begin during the latter stages of the strategic planning process.

Before going too much farther, let's clarify the terms shown in Figure 3.2. Here are three definitions that I would like to use for the purposes of our discussion:

- **Information Systems.** Computer-based sets of software, hardware, and telecommunications components that are supported by people and procedures, and that are used for the purpose of processing data and turning it into useful information.
- **Information Technology.** The full set of technological methods and approaches that collectively facilitate the construction and maintenance of information systems.

For our purposes, I'd like to express the combination of these two elements as simply *information management*.

In the so-called "early days" (circa late 1970s), information management was treated as more of a reactive support function. Many companies had departments with names like "data processing," which often collected and manipulated data at a relatively low level of application, typically relating to localized, day-to-day operations. Eventually, company managers came to realize two things about this function: (1) In the absence of forethought, information management costs easily could become a ballooning and potentially uncontrollable expense for the company; and (2) the information management function could be more effectively applied by recognizing its potential as a core business process, one that can effectively facilitate the effectiveness and efficiency across the company.

These realizations led to the existence of a new planning function—*information management planning* (called information systems planning by some). Referring once again to Figure 3.2, information management planning can effectively allow for the design and development of information management needs that effectively span the transition between strategic planning and tactical planning.

For example, consider Pep Boys, the American auto service chain. The operations of such an organization may seem simple enough not to warrant the integration of information systems into its business planning. However, management does consider information systems in its plans, which has resulted in the development of a data warehouse of close to 2 TB (terabytes), one of the country's largest data warehouses. This warehouse is a major part of the company's long-range business plan. Among other activities, top management can use the data warehouse to find out which services are most popular with customers—information that serves a strategic purpose. The company can also use the data warehouse to continue to minimize customer returns due to car problems that were not fixed well the first time.

In this example, the use of data warehousing as a method for enhancing Pep Boys' understanding of customer preferences touches on the organizational planning techniques of competitive strategy and competitive advantage. However, it is also easy to see how this type of activity could readily play into other organizational planning techniques such as project-portfolio development, core confidence analysis, internal process design, and functional design. It's clear from this example that information management planning truly does span the entire spectrum of organizational planning.

Even though information management is highly integrated within the overall organizational management planning cycle, information management planning actually exists as a somewhat distinct planning function unto itself. Figure 3.3 illustrates the steps required to carry out information management planning, and shows how the steps are remarkably similar in nature to the overall organizational management planning process.

As an information management configuration is being developed, planners must pay attention to a number of critical design factors:

- **Flexibility.** Refers to the extent to which a company can use (or reuse) the same components (hardware and software) for different functions, in different locations, and by different people over an extended period time.
- **Scalability.** Refers to the ease with which a given system or subsystem can be enlarged without degrading overall functionality, capability, or other measures of effectiveness and efficiency.
- **Compatibility.** Refers to the extent to which different components of hardware and software are able to interact with one another. Interaction might refer to information flow, data file swapping, or communications.

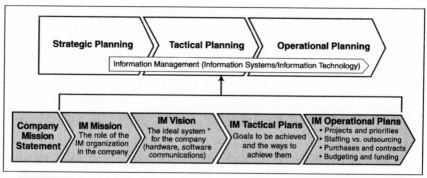

FIGURE 3.3

Information management planning mirrors organizational planning.

- **Standardization.** Refers to the extent to which literally identical components of hardware and software are used throughout the company. Standardization can be attractive from the standpoint of purchasing advantages, maintenance efficiencies, and compatibility.
- **Financial justification.** Refers to whether a given information management project represents the sound financial investment. This can be a difficult question to answer, because it often is difficult to accurately assess the cash inflows and outflows relating to information management projects. Very often, many hidden benefits or hidden costs are associated with installations relating to information management. At times, this can make the process of performing a financial justification somewhat tricky, uncertain, and difficult. Unfortunately, this prompts some companies to simply give up and justify information management projects solely on the basis of a perceived need. This particular point is debated in the outset of Chapter 10.

BUSINESS PROCESS MANAGEMENT

Up to this point in the chapter, nearly all our discussion on organizational planning more or less assumed an orientation of initial startup; that is, how a company might go about organizing itself for business success.

But what about a company that has been in operation for a while? What does the concept of organizational management mean to these companies? For many, the answer comes in the form of three words: *business process management.*

Actually, the term "management" in business process management may be a bit misleading, because it sounds like a reference to maintaining the status quo. But for most successful companies, the term business process management actually has a strong orientation toward the ongoing improvement of business processes. This ongoing improvement that companies make may be gradual or not so gradual, as illustrated by three different approaches to process management: business process improvement, business process reengineering, and business process redesign.

To provide context to the discussion on these three approaches, it can be very helpful to first have a discussion on what is commonly viewed as a baseline for the analysis of business processes, the value chain of business functions.

THE VALUE CHAIN OF BUSINESS FUNCTIONS

Decisions related to organizational planning and control often focus on the performance of several different business functions within the company. One of the most common ways of displaying these business functions is through the value chain. The term *value chain* refers to the sequence of business functions within which usefulness is added to the products and services of a company.

Figure 3.4 suggests that the value chain is comprised of all specific organizational departments. Although some overlap obviously exists in terms of nomenclature, it's vital that you look at and think of the value chain in terms of business functions rather than departments.

The value chain of business functions includes the following elements:

- **Research and development functions.** Includes the identification of new ideas and concepts and the experimentation and testing of those new ideas and concepts (research). Research activities commonly relate to new products, services, or processes. It also includes a variety of development activities that are undertaken to answer questions regarding whether a new product should be produced in large quantities (called scale-up), whether it can be produced in a cost-effective manner, and even whether the new product will have sales appeal (market research).

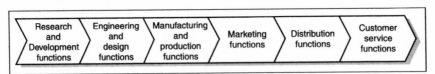

FIGURE 3.4

The value chain of business functions.

- **Engineering and design functions.** Includes the detailed design, engineering, and planning functions required to get new products, service, or process launched. This segment of the value chain is often the central focus of most projects executed by the company. Design and engineering functions may be applied to salable products, manufacturing equipment and machinery, or process development.
- **Manufacturing and production functions.** Includes the acquisition and set up, as well as the ongoing operation and maintenance, of resources, materials, and facilities required to produce a product or deliver a service.
- **Marketing functions.** Includes all the functions and approaches that companies use to advertise, promote, and (hopefully) sell their products or services to customers, prospective customers, or users.
- **Distribution functions.** Includes a broad range of activities required to deliver products, materials, or services to customers or users. Comprised of activities such as shipping, retail delivery, and warehousing.
- **Customer service functions.** Includes the post-sales support activities required to maintain an acceptable level of long-term customer satisfaction. Comprised of several activities, from help desk support to warranty repair work.

Although Figure 3.4 appears to show the value chain as a sequence of operations, it's important to note that significant gains can be realized by reconfiguring the relationship between functions within the value chain. Cycle-time improvements, for example, are a common manifestation of project opportunities in which value chain functions can be addressed concurrently with minimal disruption.

HOW ORGANIZATIONS IMPROVE THEIR BUSINESS PROCESSES

Over time, most companies seek to improve the way they conduct their external business or their internal operations; in short, they use many of the elements described in this chapter. Three of the more common methods that organizations employ for improving their business processes are: (1) business process improvement (often referred to as *continuous improvement*); (2) business process reengineering; and (3) business process redesign. Each of these methods commonly use the value chain of business functions as an integral part of their analytical framework.

Business Process Improvement

The term *business process improvement* refers to the concept of continuous improvement, applied to all processes within a company. In the past, "traditional" improvement programs tended to concentrate at the lowest levels within a company, often focusing on the dimensions of day-to-day business such as work efficiency, productivity, and cost reduction. A focus on improving the quality of all business processes is a relatively recent change in philosophy, stimulated primarily by the success of Japanese companies.

One of the more notable forms of ongoing business process improvement is *kaizen*, a Japanese term that means "gradual and orderly continuous improvement." The *Strategy of Kaizen* is intended to pertain to all activities and all employees in a given company. In the *kaizen* philosophy, improvement in all areas of business—cost control, data management, supply chain management, employee development, supplier relations, product development, and manufacturing productivity—serve to enhance the quality of the company.

Business Process Reengineering

Business process reengineering is a somewhat more radical approach to business process management, compared to continuous improvement. A good working definition for business process reengineering might be "the fundamental rethinking of business processes, aimed at achieving dramatic improvements in critical measures of performance, such as cost, quality, efficiency, and service."

The reengineering approach consists of asking deep and basic questions about all business processes, questions such as: Why do we do this?, Why is this process done in this manner?, and Is this process necessary? These types of questions are intended to reveal inappropriate, obsolete, or incorrect methods and assumptions. In contrast to continuous improvement, which involves changes to existing processes, reengineering often involves throwing out, dramatically revamping, or eliminating existing processes and reinventing new ones. The objective is to achieve very large improvements in performance, not the small, incremental improvements that an approach like *kaizen* would yield.

Success in business process reengineering requires four critical elements: (1) a deep understanding of existing processes; (2) an ability to think creatively; (3) the courage to challenge existing beliefs and assumptions; and (4) the effective use of new technology, if required.

Business Process Redesign

Although the result is frequently the same dramatic revision to existing process, business process redesign is somewhat different from business process reengineering. While reengineering consists of systematically examining the process or set of processes, business process redesign often is precipitated when a problem or opportunity is identified. Generally speaking, the customer or user (either internal or external) is the driving force behind the redesign process. Often, business process redesign has a specific focus or goal, such as increased sales, higher profits, or improved level of service.

Business process redesign initiatives often have a broad impact across a company. For example, it would not be uncommon for a single effort to affect a company's organizational structure, its existing governance of procedures and policies, and even its organizational culture.

It's not uncommon for this kind of approach to precipitate a short-term dip in output and/or efficiency. One possible explanation for this short-term efficiency loss may relate to the fact that, in contrast to the other two business improvement processes, business process redesign occasionally comes as a bit of a surprise and typically has a more far-reaching impact on the overall company.

CHAPTER 4

Cost Management in Organizations

"Cost" is probably the single most important term (and concept) in the entire field of business. An enormous number of concepts and meanings are tied to the term cost. Developing a solid understanding and strong working knowledge of the many interpretations, applications, definitions, and methods for managing costs will prove invaluable to you. It will significantly enhance your ability to survive—if not excel—in the world of projects and business.

The ideal starting point for an elaborate discussion on the many aspects of cash would be at the place that costs call home: a budget.

ORGANIZATIONAL BUDGETING AND CONTROL

The process of budgeting forms the basis of cost management and is one of the most widely used tools used in the planning and controlling of any company's future. One of the most powerful aspects of the entire budgeting process comes from the way in which it serves to focus the attention of management directly on the future of the company.

Although in this book, we will be examining budgeting from the perspective of for-profit companies, it's important to note that the budgeting also plays a very important role in the management and control of government entities and the nonprofit sector. For example, budgets are important elements in managing school districts, towns, and villages as well as government agencies. Budgeting is an equally important process in managing the operations of hospitals, churches, charities, and other nonprofit organizations.

THE BASIC PROCESS OF BUDGETING

The budgeting process used by most companies is remarkably similar to the process many of us use to manage and control costs on projects. Both processes rely heavily on the basic planning-directing-controlling-feedback model, though the length of the cycle and the dollar amounts associated with company-level (or organizational-level) budgeting are much larger than that of projects.

At the company level, the budgeting process typically consists of a number of elements, typically performed on an annual basis, and collectively referred to as the *budgeting cycle*. In many companies, the budgeting cycle is a very straightforward form of a standard feedback-control process; it consists of five elements: planning, performance expectations, directing, comparing performance to expectations, and controlling.

Planning

During the planning phase of the budgeting cycle, the performance of the company as a whole, as well as its individual operating units, is considered. Many options are discussed with regard to the way the ongoing company operations will be conducted, and potential opportunities for improvement are identified. Typically, this portion of the budgeting cycle is closely aligned with the annual process of establishing goals for the company and its organizational units. Many companies refer to this as their *strategic planning process*.

Setting Specific Performance Expectations

In this phase of the budgeting cycle, a set of specific goals and performance expectations is developed. These expectations should support the plan identified in phase one, and serve to guide and focus the activities of individual organizational units, such as business units or operating departments. Examples of performance expectations may include statements such as "increase the company's gross margin on product XYZ by 5%," or "reduce the number of lost time incidents in department ABC to one per 75,000 labor hours."

It will become quite apparent how closely this phase of the budgeting cycle is (or should be!) tied to the identification of organizational goals that are best addressed through the identification and execution of project efforts. We also discover that one of the key methods used by companies in determining the relative attractiveness of projects relates directly to a given project's ability to satisfy budgetary expectations.

Directing

Once specific budget plans have been identified, they can be used to coordinate and direct the efforts of everyone in the company in achieving the desired goals. Ordinarily, the company's overall budget (called the *master budget*) is constructed in a way that clearly identifies how each unit of the company is integrated into the overall budget. Breaking down the company's overall budget in this way provides one of the most useful tools in directing and coordinating the activities of individual business units and operating departments. Each organizational unit within the company fully understands the obligation it has in supporting the achievement of the company's goals during the forthcoming budgeting cycle. In this regard, individual budgetary units of an organization are referred to as *responsibility centers*. Activities within each responsibility center are directed by a manager who has authority over and responsibility for that unit's contribution to the achievement of the company's overall budget goals.

Comparing Actual Performance to Expectations

Once the budget cycle is underway, the actual performance of an operating unit should be continuously measured and compared against planned budgetary goals. The difference between these two points is referred to as the *budget variance*. When variances are identified, managers should determine the cause for the variance. At the macro level, a determination must be made with regard to whether the correct course of action is to modify performance or to modify the expectation. At the micro level, the existence of current or forecasted variances may require specific actions to ensure that the integrity of budget goals is maintained.

Controlling

The actions taken in comparing actual performance to expectations refer to the processes of *feedback* and *corrective action*, which are common components of any budget-related cost management process. Midyear corrections often may be needed if budget limits appear to be in jeopardy. For example, many operating units set up travel budgets at the beginning of their budget cycle. If they are doing their job properly, these operating units will track travel expenditures through the course of the budget cycle. As actual expenditures begin to approach the budget limits, it is not uncommon to see controls imposed, such as a policy declaration mandating the discontinuance of nonessential travel.

THE MASTER BUDGET

A budget is the quantified representation of a company's proposed plan of action. It can include financial as well as nonfinancial components. Developed both directly and indirectly by management, budgets typically focus on the future. In many companies, this future perspective frequently is subdivided into elements of *short-term planning budget* (typically a 1-year horizon), and *long-term planning budget* (typically a 3- to 5-year horizon).

The 1-year version, or short-term planning budget, is referred to as the *master budget*. Master budgets often appear as a set of budgeted financial statements. The same financial statements we examined in Chapter 2: The Core of Business Knowledge: Finance and Accounting. It includes all the impacts of running the business, including operating decisions, investing decisions, and financing decisions. Operating decisions are focused on the efficient use of the resources required to run the business. Investment decisions are focused on where and how to apply cash so as to achieve the maximum return. Financing decisions are focused on methods for obtaining the funds to pay for the required resources and future improvements investment.

As you may have observed, this discussion parallels some of our previous discussions. The key difference here is we are focusing on the budgeting implications of finance and accounting. Financial statements that are expressed as budgets are sometimes called *pro forma statements*.

The pro forma statements mirror the financial statements discussed in Chapter 2, and include the *budgeted income statement*, the *budgeted balance sheet*, and the *budgeted statement of cash flows*. These statements tie finance and accounting concepts to the process of budgeting, which is important, because the budgeting process allows the release of funds to company activities such as production operations, marketing and advertising, and yes, even to project execution!

Figure 4.1 illustrates all of the various budgets that comprise the master budget, and how they relate to one another.

Income Statement Budgets

For companies that conduct any type of business operations (which are most companies), the overall budgeting process begins by predicting the anticipated level of sales and revenue for the upcoming budget cycle.

The sales information is provided to the company's production units for the purpose of estimating the budgets required to support production operations (materials usage, direct labor requirement, and overhead costs), as well as selling and administration expenses. Together, all these budgets are combined with the estimates of sales revenue in a way that allows for the calculation of the *gross margin from sales*.

Understanding what the gross margin from sales figures will be helps companies understand how much they can budget to support

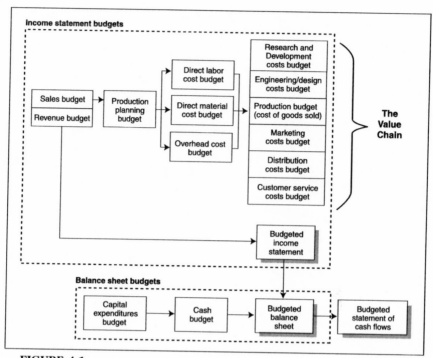

FIGURE 4.1

Components of the master budget.

functions. The support functions are often grouped together into an entity called the *value chain*. The value chain has significant implications in the world of projects and project management.

Everything that is left over after all these calculations have been made is the budgeted income statement. The budgeted income statement summarizes the estimated budgets for all phases of a company's sales and operations. Hence, all the individual budgets that feed into the budgeted income statement are collectively referred to as the *operating budget*.

Balance Sheet Budgets

Balance sheet budgets are used by company managers to build specific plans around the financing, investing, and cash management objectives of the company. Luckily, the balance sheet budgets are referred to as the financial budgets, because they directly relate to the three basic financial statements discussed in Chapter 2. In fact, as Figure 4.1 illustrates, the budgeted income statement combines with

the budgeted balance sheet to allow for the preparation of the budgeted statement of cash flows.

But where does the budgeted balance sheet come from?

Here, the connection with projects, specifically the financial
aspects of project justification, really comes into focus. Why?
Because two of the main components that make up the budgeted balance sheet and, ultimately, the budgeted statement of cash flows, are
directly affected through project economics.

The first major element is the *capital expenditures budget*. As
we examine in detail in Chapter 5, the capital expenditures budget
summarizes the company's plans for acquiring assets, specifically
those assets required to run the business. In some cases, new assets
are required to expand the scope and therefore the income potential
of the business. In other cases, as machinery, equipment, and other
assets required to keep the business running begin to wear out or
become obsolete, they must be replaced. In either case, an outlay of
cash, or cash outflow, is required to keep the asset base at the level
necessary to keep the operation running.

The cash budget is one of the most important elements of the
budgeted balance sheet. It includes all the estimated receipts
(inflows) and payments (outflows) of cash over a specific period.
Naturally, the wisdom that a company demonstrates in its capital
investment strategy has a direct and potentially profound impact on
the cash budget. It is, therefore, incumbent on the project management community to identify those project opportunities that will
have a sustained and positive impact on the cash budget. This only
can be done through the application of some of the rigorous financial
and analysis techniques that we will review in Chapter 10, Project
Economics, Part III: Performing a Project Financial Analysis.

RELATING THE MASTER BUDGET TO PROJECTS

A strong and specific relationship exists between the projects the
company pursues and that company's master budget, as illustrated in
Figure 4.2. And as we will see in Chapter 10, Project Economics, Part
3: Performing a Project Financial Analysis, projects ordinarily have
an effect on the steady-state cash flows of several functional departments within any company.

But rather than using an organizational chart to illustrate this,
Figure 4.2 offers an excellent way to visualize this point from the
standpoint of business operations by displaying this effect on cash
flows in terms of the company's value chain. These relationships
become much clearer in Chapter 6, when we discuss the identification and estimation of project cash flows.

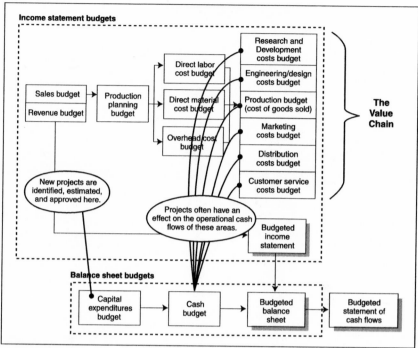

FIGURE 4.2

Relating projects to the master budget.

THE RESPONSIBILITY CENTER: CONCEPT AND PRACTICE

Although it can be very useful to look at budgets from the standpoint of cash flow effects on business functions, a more practical concern is related to the development, management, and control of budgets.

In a decentralized company (which many companies are today), a large number of individual operating budgets are likely to exist. Obviously, this begs questions such as: Who estimates these budgets?, Who monitors and controls these budgets?, and, in short, Who is responsible for these individual budgets?

All these questions can be answered by discussing the concept of *responsibility centers* and *responsibility accounting*.

In one form or another, every manager in a company is viewed as being in charge of a responsibility center. The responsibility center is any portion of an organization whose manager is accountable for a specified set of activities.

Responsibility accounting is directly tied to any and all financial considerations related to a responsibility center. Responsibility accounting is a process that measures and reports the plans (through budgets) and the actions (by tracking actual results) of every responsibility center. Four common types of responsibility centers existing in companies today are:

- Cost centers (managers are accountable for costs only)
- Revenue centers (managers are accountable for revenues only)
- Profit centers (managers are accountable for revenues and costs)
- Investment centers (managers are accountable for investments, revenues, and costs)

Each one has a dramatically different focus, responsibility, and managerial approach. Characteristic of any company's organizational structure, higher-level managers typically have broader and deeper responsibilities. As a result, their perspective relative to responsibility accounting is also quite different.

For example, consider the case of a hotel chain, such as Embassy Suites. The maintenance department in any given Embassy Suites hotel would be a *cost center*, because the manager of the maintenance department is responsible primarily for costs incurred in maintaining the hotel. The sales department within the hotel would be a *revenue center*, because the sales manager has primary responsibility for generating revenues. A manager of an individual Embassy Suites hotel would be considered to be managing a *profit center*, because the hotel manager assumes accountability for both revenues as well as costs. Finally, one of the Embassy Suites' district managers would have *investment center* responsibility. In this capacity, the district manager would focus on, and make decisions around, management issues such as new hotel projects and district-wide hotel upgrades. He also would assume the overall responsibility for revenues and costs at the district level.

The responsibility center approach is closely tied to the concepts of controllable versus noncontrollable costs.

ABOUT COST ACCOUNTING SYSTEMS

Cost accounting is an important subset of managerial accounting. Much of the information and data that appear in managerial accounting reports is derived by using customary cost accounting methods. Therefore, it is crucial that you understand the various concepts, terms, and definitions related to cost. And although there is no formal regulation of cost accounting methods, considerable similarity exists in this field across organizations.

The primary objective of most cost accounting systems is to accumulate costs relative to the company's products or services. Product or service cost information is used by company management for several purposes, including the establishment of product price points, to control ongoing operations, and in the development of financial statements.

Cost accounting systems may assume one of two basic forms. The first is the *job order cost system*, which provides unique records for the cost of each quantity of product that is produced by company. The job order cost system is, by far, the most common cost accounting system, and it is best suited to companies that manufacture products that fill special orders from customers or companies that produce a wide variety of products or stock for eventual resale. Many companies in the service industry also use a job order cost system so that they may accumulate and collect cost data related to specific client services or client engagements. This approach can help service companies better estimate the cost of future client engagements as well as aid in determining client billing and profitability values.

The second type of cost accounting system is called the *process cost system*. In this system, costs are recorded and accumulated for each department or process within the company. A process cost system ordinarily is used by companies that manufacture, produce, or deliver products that are not unique and distinguishable from one another. Typically, this includes companies that have a continuous manufacturing or production process, such as food processors, chemical processors, or oil refineries.

General Cost Terminology

Accountants define *cost* as "a resource sacrificed or forgone to achieve a specific objective." It is usually measured by the monetary amount (dollars and cents) that must be paid to acquire goods and services. An *actual cost* is the cost incurred as part of a real transaction, as opposed to budgeted or forecasted costs. As an aid to decision-making, people must know how much something costs. That "something" is referred to as a *cost object*, or anything for which a unique measurement of cost is desired.

Cost management, cost accounting, and the cost control systems are ordinarily concerned with two basic aspects related to cost: cost accumulation and cost assignment. *Cost accumulation* refers to the process and methods used to collect cost data in an organized manner. This is typically accomplished through the managerial accounting methods described in Chapter 2, The Core of Business Knowledge: Finance and Accounting.

Because the information included in managerial accounting systems is relied on so heavily for management decision-making, it's important to ensure that the costs associated with any given cost object are as accurate and valid as possible. To accomplish this, all costs must be properly assigned. *Cost assignment* consists of tracing or allocating the appropriate type of accumulated costs to a cost object. Whether a cost is traced or allocated relates directly to whether it is a direct cost or an indirect cost.

Direct Costs and Indirect Costs

The distinction between direct and indirect costs has widespread application in the world of manufacturing and production. It also relates directly to projects and project management, particularly with respect to the methods you should use to correctly estimate project costs. In turn, proper project cost estimation has an even broader implication to the company, because project costs directly influence the estimated value of the assets created through project execution and used by the company to conduct business.

Direct costs can be reasonably measured and directly attributed to a work activity or a specific output. This statement can be applied to either company operations or project work. An example of a direct cost in the context of manufacturing operations would be the cost of the motherboard used in a specific model of laptop computer. The cost of the motherboard is easily traced to the cost of the laptop; hence, the term *cost tracing* is used to describe the assignment of direct costs to a specific cost object. In a project context, a direct cost is the hourly pay rate earned by an engineer who designs the equipment that automatically assembles the laptop computer.

Indirect costs cannot be reasonably attributed to a specific output, but they are still considered part of doing business. In the case of a laptop computer scenario, an example of an indirect cost is the cost of quality-control personnel who conduct tests on all types of computers released for distribution. In this case, it is difficult to trace the exact amount of quality-control support to a specific cost object (the specific laptop computer model in question). Instead, a calculated, proportional amount of additional cost is allocated to the final cost of that laptop product.

This practice is very consistent with the job order cost system. It is also consistent with a relatively new product costing approach that many companies use today called *activity-based costing*. Activity-based costing is a method of tracking and allocating overhead costs to products and services using a variety of overhead rates. It also is used to determine charge rates for project personnel, thus allowing for the more accurate and appropriate valuation of the assets created by projects and owned by the company. Using activity-based costing methods allows accountants to be able to properly reconcile (or balance) financial accounting records with managerial accounting records.

In aggregate, all indirect costs tend to break down into two major categories: overhead costs and fringe benefit costs. *Overhead costs* include labor-related expenditures required: (1) to support the company's operations (or the execution of a project), such as a centralized purchasing department, or to provide the environment in which operations (or project work) are carried out, such as the staff needed to perform facilities maintenance activities. Overhead costs may also include a certain nonlabor support, such as office supplies and utility costs. *Fringe benefit costs* are additional nonsalary, employee-based expenditures incurred by the company as an ordinary part of maintaining a workforce. These may include the company's payments toward employee health insurance, stock options, pension plans, or tuition-aid programs.

The term commonly used to describe all additional indirect costs is *overhead costs* or *burden costs*. The most common application of indirect costing occurs when organizations add these burden costs to worker salaries to establish a *fully-burdened charge-out rate*. This is how companies allocate their overhead costs to project work. Therefore, the fully-burdened charge-out rate (typically a per hour figure) is used whenever you are estimating the cost associated with the use of any internal resources on projects. If this is not done, the financial accounting and the managerial accounting system will not properly reconcile.

The calculation of a predetermined overhead rate is determined as follows:

$$\text{Burden Rate} = \text{Estimated Total Company Overhead Costs} / \text{Estimated Activity Base}$$

Now let's assume that the sum of all overhead costs incurred by a company in a given year is estimated at $960,000. Further, let's assume that the activity base, which is the sum total of all direct labor used to produce the company's products, is estimated at 64,000 hours (about 32 full-time employees). These assumptions yield the following calculation for burden rate:

$$\text{Burden Rate} = \$960,000 / 64,000 \text{ Direct Labor Hours}$$

$$\text{Burden Rate} = \$15/\text{hour}$$

Although the actual calculation of the burden rate is more complex than this, the principle is essentially the same.

Now don't get nervous … you won't be asked to make this calculation. The fully burdened charge-out rate is a figure that is ordinarily given to you by your financial department. Conceptually, however, the value this figure provides you for each resource is easy to understand.

Let's say for example, a senior software programmer (a formal wage grade title) is working on your project. Further, let's assume that the average hourly salary for senior software programmers is $35. Given that the burden rate is $15, you would be instructed to use an hourly rate of $50 when estimating the cost of having this particular software programmer (or any software programmer in the same wage rate) work on your project. By doing this, you have allowed for the assets created by your projects and project to be properly evaluated, and you have allowed the financial and managerial accounting systems to properly reconcile.

FIXED COSTS, VARIABLE COSTS, AND MIXED COSTS

The proper accumulation, measurement, and control of costs is also related to the concept of *cost behavior patterns*. Understanding how certain costs behave allows for improved cost management. The most commonly analyzed form of cost behavior patterns found in most managerial accounting systems are fixed costs and variable costs. Both of these cost types are characterized with respect to a specific cost object, and for a prescribed period.

Fixed costs are unaffected by reasonably large changes in activity or volume over some feasible range of operation and period. Typical fixed costs could include:

- Interest on borrowed capital
- Insurance and taxes
- General management and administrative salaries
- Facility leasing arrangements

Variable costs change with the quantity of output, volume, or other measure of activity. Typical variable costs include:

- Material usage
- Waste
- Fuel consumption
- Sales commissions

It may be useful to consider and visualize how the dimensions of cost assignment and cost behavior interact with one another. Figure

Cost object: laptop computer model AZ-16		Cost behavior pattern	
		Fixed cost	Variable cost
Cost assignment type	Direct cost	Test equipment used to perform QC tests on motherboards	Motherboards used in assembly of product
	Indirect cost	Annual fire insurance policy for the entire assembly facility	Salaries of all QC personnel who test laptops (they also test all other types of computers)

FIGURE 4.3

The combinations of cost assignment and cost behavior.

4.3 illustrates this, revealing that four possible cost classifications exist. This structure frequently is used in analyzing costs and in making decisions relating to cost management.

Finally, *mixed costs* are a combination of fixed and variable costs, often expressed in conjunction with a single entity. As an example, consider how some telephone billing plans are structured. Many telephone customers actually are charged a mixed cost. They must pay a monthly connection charge (fixed), plus an additional fee related to actual usage (variable).

COSTS RELATED TO MANAGEMENT AND OPERATIONS

Several cost terms are tied to general business management and the management of operations.

Allowable versus Unallowable Costs

Allowable and unallowable costs relate most often to the world of contracts and contracting, but it can also be applicable to a wide range of internal costs, primarily expenses.

An *allowable cost* is a cost that the parties of a contract agree to include in the costs that will be reimbursed. Some contracts also specify how allowable costs are to be determined. An example of this is the stipulation that "airline travel will be reimbursed only up to the cost of economy class fares."

Conversely, some contracts identify costs that are *unallowable*, that is, not reimbursable. For example, the costs of alcoholic beverages as a subset of travel costs are sometimes specifically identified as an unallowable cost.

Controllable versus Noncontrollable Costs

Although nearly all types of costs can be controlled by someone, all are not controllable at the same level of management. For any given level of management, *controllable costs* are costs that can be influenced by the manager at that level. For example, department managers often have significant control over the expenses associated with office supplies. However, they have virtually no control over the insurance or taxes associated with the facility in which their department works. These are referred to as *noncontrollable costs*. This distinction is particularly relevant to the concept of responsibility centers, discussed previously.

Recurring Costs versus Nonrecurring Costs

Recurring costs are repetitive in nature, and occur when a company produces or provides similar goods and services on an ongoing, but discrete, basis.

Nonrecurring costs do not repeat. They are sometimes referred to as "one-time costs." Nonrecurring costs often involve the development or establishment of a capability or capacity to operate. For example, the purchase of land on which an operating facility will be built is a nonrecurring cost.

Standard Costs

Standard costs are those costs of a unit of physical output that is estimated and developed in advance of any actual production or delivery of services. The practice of developing standard costs is commonly applied in operational settings. Standard costs are developed by combining direct labor costs, material costs, and overhead costs. Standard costs serve a useful role in cost control and other management functions, particularly related to operations. They can be used to evaluate operating performance levels, prepare bids, and establish inventory values.

COSTS RELATED TO QUALITY MANAGEMENT

These types of costs focus on a wide variety of efforts aimed at trying to ensure that a company's products conform to predetermined quality standards. Costs can be incurred in virtually all business functions within a company. For the purpose of identifying exactly where and how money is being spent to achieve a given level of conformance, costs related to quality are typically subdivided into four categories.

Prevention Costs

Prevention costs are incurred to preclude the production or manufacture of products that do not conform to product specifications. This often equates to costs associated with the design and planning of a quality control (QC) program, such as quality training programs or the design of quality measurement equipment.

Appraisal Costs

Appraisal costs are incurred to detect when individual units of products do not conform to product specifications. This may include activities such as testing, inspection, or maintenance and calibration of testing equipment.

Internal Failure Costs

Internal failure costs are incurred by a nonconforming product before it is shipped to customers. This may include costs such as waste, rework, or investigations of quality failures.

External Failure Costs

External failure costs are incurred by a nonconforming product after it has been shipped to customers. Classic examples of external failure costs include warranty costs, service calls, and loss of customer goodwill.

COSTS RELATED TO BUYING AND SELLING

Several types of costs are associated with the practice of selling goods and managing inventory. *Purchasing costs* are the actual costs of goods acquired from suppliers, including freight and transportation costs. Ordering costs include expenditures related to preparing, issuing, and paying the purchase orders needed to acquire the goods. *Ordering costs* also include expenses related to receiving and inspecting the items included in orders. *Carrying costs* occur whenever a company maintains an inventory of goods for sale; carrying costs includes two basic components. First, an obvious cost is associated with the storage of the goods, such as space rental, insurance, and spoilage. However, an opportunity cost also is related to inventory, because the money invested in inventory could be used for other investments.

The last type of cost associated with goods for sale are *stockout costs*. A stockout occurs when a company runs out of a specific item for which demand exists. This may result in the need to expedite a special order from a supplier, which frequently results in added expenditures. A stockout situation could also result in lost sales, and even lost future sales, as a result of customer dissatisfaction caused by the stockout situation.

COSTS RELATED TO PROJECT ECONOMICS

Many of the cost types described in this section have broad application. However, what sets these costs items apart from other general terms is that these cost types are particularly relevant to projects and project management. In fact, several of these terms will reappear later in the book, as we explore how to perform a financial analysis on a project.

Capital Costs versus Expense Costs

Perhaps one of the most important (yet not well understood) cost issues on projects is the practice of determining whether a given project expenditure is a *capital cost* or an *expense cost*. It is an extremely important, yet tricky, area related to asset management. To help you sort this issue out, let's define each of these terms.

Capital Costs

Capital costs are clearly and directly assignable to the creation of an asset. The sum of all capital costs gets recorded as the value of the asset. The asset value is then capitalized, or amortized (written off) slowly over a period of several years. A classic example of capital costs is the direct purchase of buildings and equipment, plus any modifications needed to make them usable for production or resale. The second part of the previous sentence, the part that says "plus any modifications needed to make them usable," is worth a special note. It's important to understand that the application of a company's *internal resources* (a.k.a. employees) should be included in the overall valuation of the capital assets produced as a result of executing a project.

Generally speaking, capital costs comprise the bulk of the costs that you will be required to estimate and include in any project financial analysis you perform. This is covered in detail in Chapters 9 and 10.

Expense Costs

Project-related *expense costs* are expenditures associated with the supporting environment of the project, but not directly attributable to the creation of a specific asset. Cost items that fall in the expense category may include items such as travel, secretarial staff assigned to support the project, computer usage time (data gathering, labor charging, etc.).

A number of issues add significant concern to the question of correctly categorizing items as capital or expense costs. First, considerable confusion and a lack of knowledge often exists on the part of project personnel regarding the rules on how to classify some kinds of project expenditures. Second, as Figure 4.4 suggests, different people within a company frequently can have different motivations for classifying a given project cost as capital or expense. Third, it's very important to classify project costs correctly, because the practice directly impacts the proper valuation of the company's asset base and enables compliance with corporate income tax regulations, both of which are important to the government. To further complicate matters, the rules of capitalization versus expense can sometimes be a bit fuzzy.

Consider, for example, a scenario in which you are managing a project that involves the delivery of a large piece of equipment. You have just purchased a significant quantity of materials that you must run through the equipment to ensure that it is running properly and reliably. Clearly, you would not have been able to successfully complete the project without these materials, but they are not part of the final project deliverables (i.e., not part of assets you are creating). The materials were purchased with project funds, and they are worth nearly $3,000.

Life in the trenches

Accountants would like to see as many project costs as possible categorized as items of *expense*, as this offers the company an immediate tax shelter in the current year.

Operations and Business Unit Managers want to capitalize as much of the project as possible, as expense items detract from the perception of their organization's profitability.

FIGURE 4.4

The proper classification of project costs can be tricky.

Should the materials be capitalized or expensed? You may need to work closely with your financial department to properly answer this question. If your financial department is concerned with the categorization of costs, you may be required to assist them in determining whether certain project expenditures can be capitalized (written off against the bottom line over the course of several years), or whether they should be expensed (written off against the bottom line in the current calendar year). Even though rules govern cost categorization, situations frequently arise that require a certain amount of judgment in making the capital versus expense determination.

In practice, categorizing project costs often boils down to identifying all the items of expense encountered during the course of a project. All other costs are then considered part of the value of the assets being created, and they are therefore capitalized. Guidelines for identifying expense items may vary somewhat from company to company. Table 4.1 provides a sample set of guidelines for identifying expense costs.

TABLE 4.1

Sample List of Project Expense Items

- Business and concept investigation of new projects
- Problem definition
- Determining initial requirements
- Creation of new, stand-alone assets valued at less than $2,500
- Improvements to existing assets costing less than $2,500
- Rotating spare parts costing less than $2,500
- Discarded equipment (book value)
- Cosmetic changes (generally related to facilities and equipment)
- Extended maintenance warranties and service contracts
- Software
- Relocation of human resources
- Relocation of existing assets to make room for new assets
- Miscellaneous supplies (special clothing, expendable tools, etc.)
- Rewards and recognition awards given to the project team
- Training
- Travel
- Operating and maintenance manuals
- Debug, testing, and certification
- Quality control procedures
- Shipping and mailing
- All costs incurred on a project that has been cancelled

The information shown in Table 4.1 is not intended to reflect hard and fast categorization rules, and the situation is likely to be somewhat different for your company. With this in mind, I urge you to consult your financial department before making determinations of capital versus expense.

Total Cost, Incremental Cost, and Differential Cost

As the name suggests, *total cost* is merely the overall, bottom-line expression of an item of cost. Total costs primarily are used in reference to other cost forms, such as incremental costs and differential costs.

An *incremental cost* represents a change in costs—typically a change in a company's cash flows—that occurs as a direct result of accepting a certain decision. Typically, this decision relates to either selecting a particular alternative solution to a problem or to the approval of one project over another. As we discover in Chapters 9 and 10, every item of costs included in a project financial analysis is expressed in terms of incremental costs. These costs represent the difference in every existing cash flow within the company that comes as a result of approving that project.

Differential cost ordinarily relates to the comparison of two or more competing alternatives or projects. In most of these cases, the difference in incremental costs is what's being compared.

For example, imagine that a company is considering a significant upgrade to their production equipment, which currently requires an annual expenditure of $375,000 in maintenance costs to keep the equipment running. This expenditure represents the current *total cost* of maintenance.

One of the project alternatives under consideration, Alternative A, promises significant overall improvement in the efficiency of this operation. However, if Alternative A is accepted, it would precipitate a $35,000 increase in the annual cost of maintenance for this department. The additional $35,000 represents the *incremental cost* associated with the decision to accept Alternative A.

Meanwhile, Alternative B also promises an improvement in the overall efficiency of the operation, but will use a different approach. If Alternative B was accepted, one of the many effects would be an increase of $45,000 in the annual cost of maintenance for the department. In this case, $45,000 represents the *incremental cost* associated with the decision to accept Alternative B.

However, a side-by-side comparison of the two alternatives would reveal that that a *differential cost* of $10,000 exists between these two alternatives, at least in terms of their impact on the overall annual cost for equipment maintenance.

Cash Costs, Noncash Costs, and Book Costs

Any cost tied to the actual payment of money is the *cash cost*. Cash costs are represented as cash flows, a term we will be using a little later in the book, when we calculate project financials.

A cost that does not actually involve a cash transaction is a *noncash cost*. Also referred to as *book costs*, these costs represent the recovery of past expenditures over a given period of time, and they are reflected only within a company's accounting system. In the world of projects and project management, the most common example of a book cost is the *depreciation* applied to those assets produced by the project that are typically used over long periods of time. As we will see later, adjustments in the accounting system and noncash costs are not cash flows. However, these types of costs are utilized in our calculations of project financials, because they affect income taxes, which are actual cash flows. This is covered in great detail in Chapter 10, Project Economics, Part 3: Performing a Project Financial Analysis.

Sunk Costs

Sunk costs are cash outlays that have already occurred or have been committed. The concept of sunk costs is particularly relevant when making a decision regarding a future investment, such as the decision on whether to approve a project. The rule is quite simple: Sunk costs must not be included in any financial analysis.

For example, let's say you hired a consulting firm to do market research on whether a new product idea had promise. If the prospects for this new product were favorable, and a project was proposed, the financial analysis on this project must not include the prior cost of hiring the consulting firm. The key here is recognizing that the only decision being made at the time of project approval is whether to spend future dollars. The company will never be able to recover the cost incurred by hiring the consulting firm, regardless of whether the project is approved. We revisit this topic in Chapter 9, Project Economics, Part 3: Preparing for a Project Financial Analysis, when we discuss what costs should and should not be included as part of a project's cash flow chart.

Opportunity Cost

As with sunk costs, *opportunity costs* are another unusual, but important cost concept. Opportunity costs are defined as cash flows that could be generated from assets the company already owns, provided they are not used for the project in question. Let's say, for example, a company already owns a property that would be suitable for constructing a new facility. When evaluating a project to build the new facility on that piece of land, it's tempting to disregard the cost of the land in the project's financial analysis because no future outlay of funds is required. However, a price to be paid actually is associated with the use of this piece of land. It comes in recognizing that the property could be sold on the open market for an estimated $175,000. Therefore, an opportunity cost of $175,000 exists, which must be charged against the project. This cost represents what the company is giving up by building the facility on that particular piece of land.

PART 2

APPLYING SOUND BUSINESS PRACTICES AT THE ENTERPRISE LEVEL

CHAPTER 5

Project Portfolio Management, Phase I: Identifying the "Right" Business Initiatives

Over the next three chapters, we will review the topic of project portfolio management in great detail. We begin in this chapter, as we examine the first and most strategic phase of portfolio management— the phase in which specific business initiatives are identified. Before proceeding, however, I'd like to offer a few qualifying remarks about the way the topic of portfolio management is presented in this book.

Most topics covered in this book are addressed in an authoritative manner—that is, more or less trying to simply describe "the way things are."

We will not be addressing the topic of project portfolio management in that way. Project portfolio management is still in its formative stage as a "business-centric" discipline related to the practice of project management. Because of this, different opinions exist regarding how project portfolio management is defined, what it is supposed to accomplish, how it should be conducted—even its rightful domain within companies.

In some ways, views on how the portfolio management process should be practiced in companies mirror the views (and controversy) that surround the role that project management should play. On one end of the spectrum are those who believe that many of the higher level activities that are currently identified as part of project portfolio management (i.e., ensuring strategic alignment, identifying business objectives, conducting business analyses) lie exclusively within the domain of traditional strategic planning, and should be of little or no concern to those in the project management community.

On the other end of the spectrum are those who believe that these high-level activities represent an appropriate and meaningful avenue to expand the positive influences that project management methodologies can bring to a company. This group believes that project managers (and the Project Management Office, if one exists) can contribute much, given a chance to play an expanded role in corporate governance and including some amount of participation within the strategic planning arena. After all, this group contends, this is really where projects are born.

As you might expect, my beliefs are aligned with the latter of these two groups. Consistent with the objectives of this book, I contend that even if you are not currently (or do not even expect to be) an active participant in the process of project portfolio development, it is imperative that you understand the process. This will enable you to be fully effective in your role as project manager.

We begin this quest for understanding with a look at the process of *capital budgeting*—in many regards, the predecessor to current project portfolio management practices. We discuss some of the issues and problems that have historically surrounded the capital budgeting process. Undoubtedly, these are among the factors that have contributed to the emerging popularity of project portfolio management.

But as we venture through the next three chapters, keep in mind that the information offered on project portfolio management is not intended to be authoritative or prescriptive in nature. Currently, no universal agreement or consistency stands with regard to the way it should be practiced. The main objective of Chapters 5 through 7 is simply to build awareness around the common elements that form the basis of project portfolio management, as practiced by some companies today.

ABOUT THE PROCESS OF CAPITAL BUDGETING

Budgeting is an important element of organizational planning and control. The *capital budget* is one of many types of budgets that companies prepare each year. The capital budget deals with planned investments in major assets such as buildings, equipment and machinery, facilities, and information technology systems. These investments typically involve long-term expenditures (greater than one year).

Capital budgeting refers to a variety of techniques and approaches used to analyze project ideas and decide which are worthy of being funded, often based upon their attractiveness as a financial investment. Although companies that are now steeped in the practices of project portfolio management may not use the term explicitly, what they are doing is actually a form of capital budgeting.

Several factors combine to make capital budgeting decisions one of the most important decisions that financial managers must make. Perhaps the biggest factor comes in the recognition that most capital budgeting decisions are long-term in nature. For example, when a company invests in an asset with a 10-year economic life, its business operations are impacted for 10 years. In essence, the company is "locked in" to that investment for that period. Furthermore, a decision to invest in a 10-year fixed asset involves an analysis that relies on a 10-year future forecast. This can be difficult to do, inducing decision-makers to shy away from using pure financial criteria, supplementing it with other criteria for establishing project justification and approval.

The process of capital budget preparation is also an important business function. The company must be capable of accurately forecasting all its needs for capital assets in advance, thus ensuring that these assets are ready to go when needed. If this is not done well, opportunities can be lost. The acquisition of fixed assets typically involves a substantial outlay of funds, and so, sufficient monies must be made available at the right time as well. Traditionally, companies have relied on the capital budgeting process to predict future needs, identify projects to address those needs, verify that the projects represent sound investments, and make provisions that ensure that funds will be available to execute the projects when needed. This can be tough.

Capital Budgeting: A Classic Tale

Many companies, particularly large companies, still build their capital budgets and project lists through a process that lies somewhere between *levitation* and *percolation*. Typically, managers at the operational level are asked to identify project suggestions that they think are necessary, useful, or sometimes even "interesting." Unfortunately, project opportunities identified at the operational level often are aimed at addressing relatively parochial problems, issues, needs, or pain points. Although the concept of the strategic alignment of projects is a goal, the reality is that many project proposals are aimed at alleviating immediate, localized distress, and often do not incorporate a broad, visionary perspective.

Many times, in the process of classic, operationally driven capital budgeting, proposed operational initiatives, which should be stated in terms of performance gaps and needs, are frequently phrased in terms of *solutions* when initially documented. This stems from a practice called *solution jumping*. Solution jumping occurs when those who are charged with uncovering needs simply go too far and identify a set of solutions. This can be a tough habit to kick, because most minds are wired in a way that compels them to come up with solutions to problems. This issue is not unique to the capital budgeting process; in fact, we discuss it as a portfolio management issue later in this chapter.

So, a list of specific project solutions emerges from the operational level of the company. After spending some time trying to determine which of these project solutions are worthwhile, the survivors are put into the form of proposals and submitted to divisional managers for further review. Some of the project proposals coming from operational managers will fail to "make the cut" while other, often larger, project efforts may be added to the list by divisional managers. These efforts are likely to be a bit more strategic in nature, but will still have a parochial perspective that focuses on what's best for a given organizational unit.

The divisional project listings are collectively submitted to senior management who—in conjunction with the company's financial managers—determine which projects will survive and become included in the forthcoming year's capital budget. Before that list is finalized, however, a series of negotiations may occur between the company's senior management and various divisional managers.

Meanwhile, other projects may be identified from the top down, as a result of the company's strategic planning sessions (assuming the company has a strategic planning process). During these sessions, senior managers identify strategically oriented initiatives to be pursued in the forthcoming year (and beyond, in many cases). But even at this level, the specter of solution jumping often appears.

Ideally, strategic planning outputs should be limited to the identification and quantification of strategic goals (the "what"). Then, using these goals as inputs, project teams can perform a thoughtful, data-driven analysis of alternatives and identify the best all-around solution (the "how"). Instead, human nature takes over, and strategic planners often go too far, identifying specific methods for achieving those strategic goals (the "how"). This is really just another form of solution jumping done at a higher level in the company. This is often worse, though, because project teams often are unable to gain a full understanding of the business leads that may have led to a given solution. Furthermore, if it is later determined that the solution determined by strategic planners is not the best way to satisfy the true need, issues of organizational politics and power can make it difficult for project teams to undo the original set of marching orders.

As the capital budgeting cycle finally draws to a close, projects identified using a top-down approach are merged with projects identified by using a bottom-up approach. After some final reconciliation, a capital budget for the forthcoming year emerges. For some companies, one additional step is necessary, because the proposed annual capital budget is not considered official until it has been approved by company's the Board of Directors.

PROJECT PORTFOLIO MANAGEMENT: MOVING IN THE DIRECTION OF BUSINESS

It's clear that classic capital budgeting techniques can be problematic. In response to this, a growing amount of attention is being given to the area of *project portfolio management*. I'm not aware of any universally agreed-upon definitions for project portfolio management, but its focus is more or less around the coordinated shepherding of often unrelated project investments across an entire organization or company throughout their entire life as an investment. Generally, portfolio development is carried out in a linear, top-down fashion, with a strong emphasis being placed on the principle of strategic alignment. Once this has been accomplished, the focus shifts to portfolio coordination, the management of many projects that are being executed during the same period of time.

THE BENEFITS OF USING A PROJECT PORTFOLIO MANAGEMENT APPROACH

Much of the appeal in using a project portfolio management approach comes in recognizing that, by definition, it assumes a comprehensive, strategically oriented, and holistic perspective to the process of project identification. This, in turn and to a certain extent, leads directly to an ability to leverage concepts such as optimization, coordination, and even economies of scale.

This process become more apparent by examining some of the key benefits of project portfolio management listed below:

- Ensures a direct link between company strategy and project identification
- Facilitates a balanced approach to project investments
- Establishes a sense of relative importance (priority) of different projects
- Clearly articulates the business value of every project
- Enables the optimization of a varied collection of projects
- Enables a broader application of project management methods—particularly resource allocation
- Facilitates the effective management of project interactions

GUIDING PRINCIPLES OF THE PROJECT PORTFOLIO MANAGEMENT APPROACH

At the core of the project portfolio management process is project classification: the establishment of well-defined and appropriate project investment categories, or *project portfolios*. The value in establishing portfolio groupings can be characterized by examining the four basic objectives of the overall portfolio management approach: *value maximization*, *balance*, *strategic alignment*, and *feasibility*. Each must be considered to ensure that the portfolio categorization scheme will have the maximum possible utility. It also can be helpful to think of these objectives as guiding principles when developing your own portfolio management process.

Value Maximization

Although the very concept of value may be somewhat subjective and controversial, few would argue that the underlying objective of any portfolio of projects must be to position a company to maximize its future business success. For many (including me), the concept of value maximization generally equates to the notion of profitability and economic growth. In this way, company managers remain faithful to the primary objective of maximizing market value added (refer to Chapter 1, Project Management as a Business Function).

Balance

Perhaps the single most important premise behind the entire portfolio management concept is balance. The primary design consideration behind portfolio configuration is achieving some measure of balance within the total project investment strategy. For example, if a company was to simply force rank a large group of projects appearing on some sort of master project list, it is quite possible that one particular aspect of the company—or one type of project—would continually win out in the competition for project funding. Over time, this would manifest itself as an obvious imbalance in the company's approach toward asset management and investment strategy. This would be neither healthy nor good for the company's image.

Strategic Alignment

The concept of strategic alignment is not just a buzz word or passing management fad. Many aspects of corporate planning and control discussed in Chapter 3, Fundamentals of Organizational Management, are at risk of being undermined or severely compromised if the company's portfolio of projects does not align well with mission, vision, and high-level business strategies. For example, imagine the devastating effects that a misaligned group of projects would have on management issues such as grand strategy, global strategy, primary competitive strategy, competitive advantage, and core competency. Not a pretty sight. In addition, a group of projects that are not well-aligned with strategic goals is likely to lead to a suboptimized application of the overall project budget. This concept was unveiled way back in Chapter 1, when we revealed Revelation #5: A portfolio of projects that all generate a positive cash flow may not represent an organization's best opportunities for investment! This, as much as anything else, makes strategic alignment a portfolio management imperative.

Feasibility

The principle of feasibility is directly tied to a practice which, regrettably, is quite common in companies today: the tendency to pursue many more projects than they can effectively support with resources. In most cases, this refers to human resources. However, the term resources can also refer to financial resources, technology resources, and other types of resources. To sustain the desired forward movement of individual projects, the overall size of the project portfolio must take into account the supply of available resources. If this is not done, plans developed at the project level are rendered invalid, and projects begin backing up. This only serves to complicate future cycles of project portfolio construction.

THE BASIC BUILDING BLOCKS OF THE PROJECT PORTFOLIO MANAGEMENT PROCESSES

Because portfolio management is still somewhat of an evolving art form, a wide variety of approaches have been developed by different companies to address the overall process of project portfolio management. And although individual differences may exist, many of the approaches used by companies today contain most—if not all—these basic components:

- **Characterization of strategic intent.** This entails the development of a company's highest-level strategies for business success. Key components include mission, values, and vision, all of which lead to an expression of corporate strategy. Technically, this is not part of portfolio management, but represents its logical starting point. Also, the development of strategic intent is not done in conjunction with the project portfolio management process; it exists as a separate business planning function performed by the company's senior executives.

- **Development of long-range goals.** As the measurable, logical outgrowth of strategic intent, long-range goals are composed of reasonably specific objectives that a company hopes to achieve in a few years. The time frame usually is vague, because the desired horizon for long-range goals can vary from company to company; some define *long-range* as 3 years in the future, while others may define it as 10 years or more. Long-range goal development is typically done by senior executives and/or business unit managers. It is not done exclusively in service of the project portfolio management process, but can be viewed logically as the first step in the project identification process.
- **Identification of targeted business initiatives.** This entails the identification of a set of specific, near-term, quantified goals that, if achieved, will demonstrate incremental progress toward satisfying long-term goals, and in turn, toward the achievement of strategic intent. It is actually a subset of long-range goal development in terms of scope and time horizon. Normally, a new set of business initiatives is identified each year, as part of a company's annual strategic planning sessions. Initiatives often are expressed in terms of hitting a specific set of performance targets in a particular area of the company (department, product line, or process) within a specified, short-term time frame.
- **Project development.** This includes those processes aimed at the identification of solutions (i.e., projects) aimed at addressing the decided-upon business initiatives. Over time, successfully executed projects allow the company to meet its prescribed goals. A key element of project development is a rigorous evaluation of alternatives, leading to a proposed best solution in satisfying a given business initiative. Projects, then, are really the "how to" response to targeted business initiatives.
- **Project classification.** These methods identify a logical set of project investment categories, also referred to as portfolios. Project classification also includes the process of placing specific project proposals into the appropriate portfolios.
- **Project financing and allocation strategy.** This entails securing the cash required to fund projects and determining how that cash will be distributed across portfolio categories and how it then will be allocated to individual projects.
- **Project evaluation and prioritization.** These techniques assess the relative attractiveness of projects; the process often com-

prises a combination of absolute attractiveness (using financial models) and comparative attractiveness (using attribute scoring models).

- **Project selection, approval, and launch.** This process establishes criteria for identifying which projects the company will pursue, the procedure by which project funding will be released, and the coordination of individual project initiation.
- **Project coordination.** These methods analyze the interrelationships that exist between all projects in the portfolio—particularly during project execution—with specific emphasis on resource management.

The key difference between the classic capital budgeting approach and the portfolio management approach lies in the project development and project classification steps.

PROJECT PORTFOLIO MANAGEMENT: A THREE-PHASE PROCESS

For me, what brings the most clarity to the practice of project portfolio management is considering it as subdividing into three distinct efforts, or "phases" (and corresponding methodologies). Figure 5.1 illustrates these phases, which are briefly described in the next sections below.

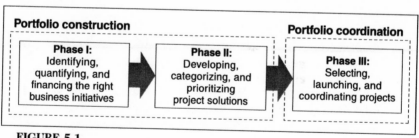

FIGURE 5.1

The three phases of portfolio management.

Phase I: Identifying, Quantifying, and Financing the Right Business Initiatives

In essence, this is the strategic phase of portfolio management. As part of the normal course of running the business, most companies develop and communicate their long-term strategic intent. Using this as a starting point, a quantified set of strategic (externally focused) as well as operational (internally focused) objectives and goals are identified. These objectives and goals then are made actionable through the identification of a number of targeted initiatives (focused, quantified statements of business needs). This marks the genesis of project development.

Phase II: Identifying, Categorizing, and Prioritizing Project Solutions

This is the tactical phase of portfolio management. Here, specific solutions (projects) are identified that will satisfy the targeted business initiatives. They then are placed into the appropriate groupings (portfolio categories). Portfolio categories should have been identified in advance, and should be configured in a way that reflects how projects are thought of as investments. Finally, projects are prioritized within portfolio categories, using criteria that strives to reflect the relative value or importance of a given project to the company.

Phase III: Selecting, Launching, and Coordinating Projects

This is best described as the operational phase of portfolio management, because it is more about project execution than portfolio construction. Final selections are made regarding which specific projects the company should pursue. A launch sequence is developed, establishing the date when each individual project should begin. Finally, this phase includes coordination across projects.

A very strong linkage exists between project portfolio construction (Phases I and II) and the world of business. Many of the steps required to build a strong project portfolio rely heavily on processes, methods, and decision-making frameworks that are grounded in sound business practices. Portfolio construction is essentially capital budgeting—but with more of a company-wide perspective and a much stronger emphasis on guaranteeing the alignment of projects with the company's strategic direction. Accordingly, we devote a considerable amount of detailed attention to these aspects of portfolio management, throughout this chapter and Chapter 6.

In contrast, Phase III, which is covered in Chapter 7, relates primarily to portfolio coordination. This part of the portfolio management process involves a substantial number of logistical methods, but not a particularly large element of business-based methodology and decision-making. One might almost be tempted to describe portfolio coordination as the science of managing complex logistics and project interactions. In reality, it employs many of the same skills and techniques used to manage individual projects or programs, simply applied at a higher level.

For example, one of the more critical elements of effective project portfolio coordination is the practice of resolving resource conflicts across all projects in the company. In many ways, this is similar to resolving resource conflicts across all activities on a single project. The coordination of project portfolios is a valuable organizational practice, and I urge you to learn as much as possible about it. And although we touch on this subject in Chapter 7, be aware that it is not as strongly tied to the "business" focus of this book as other subjects are.

PROJECT PORTFOLIO MANAGEMENT: STEP BY STEP

So, how exactly a does company go about constructing and coordinating a portfolio of projects?

The model shown in Figure 5.2 certainly represents one approach. Once again, however, it's critical to note that this is only one of many possible models for implementing project portfolio management. Instead of concerning ourselves with the design of the model per se, we will undoubtedly get more value by examining the component techniques, using the model in Figure 5.2 as a general guide.

The terms *goals*, *plans*, and *initiatives* have become very common in today's business jargon. But what do these terms really mean, and how do they relate to the process of project portfolio development?

First, *goals* serve to describe the desired future state that a company is attempting to achieve. They mark the starting point of strategy formulation. By definition, goals are *end points*—or in some cases, incremental end points en route to some greater or more meaningful set of end points. Stated another way, strategic goals define the place where we expect company strategy to lead, but do not specify how to get there.

Long-range goals define an end point that is "out there" in time—typically, a minimum of three years into the future (this time horizon varies across companies). Developing a set of long-range goals is one of the logical extensions of the development of strategic intent for many companies.

It is vital to our overall understanding of the portfolio development process to recognize that the support of strategic intent is not limited to strategic goals alone.

The development (and achievement) of operational goals can be equally helpful in enabling a company to fulfill its overall strategic intent. This concept is illustrated by the existence of a dual pathway of goals emanating from the "Strategic Intent" step shown in Figure 5.2.

To me, this top-down dual pathway represents the most meaningful departure from the classic capital budgeting approach described at the outset of this chapter. Using this approach, operational project proposals are no longer dominated by local (depart-

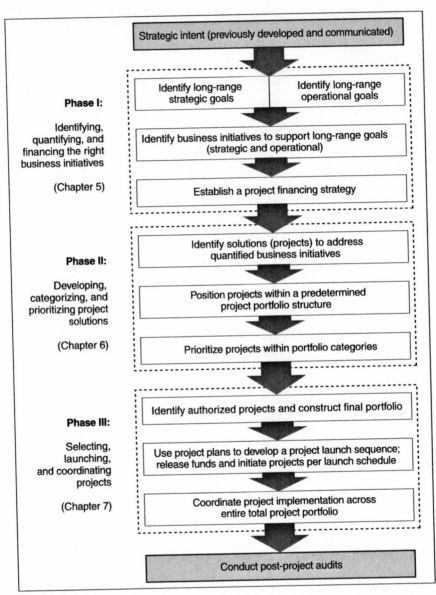

FIGURE 5.2

The phases and steps of project portfolio management.

mental) issues, concerns, opportunities, or pain points. Instead, they are identified using a methodology that strives to ensure that the motivation for their existence is based primarily on what the company truly needs to achieve overall business success.

Meanwhile, plans are at the other end of strategy formulation. Plans describe, sometimes in detail, the blueprint for *how* a stated goal is to be achieved. Taken to the logical end of project portfolio development, this ultimately refers to the detailed project plans and schedules that accompany specific project proposals.

To smooth out the project portfolio development process, something must span the distance between goals (which strategic planners develop) and plans (which the project management community should develop). This brings us to our third term, *initiatives*—more specifically, business initiatives. We explore this term in more detail in the next section.

These steps can be logically grouped into three distinct phases of portfolio development. The remainder of this chapter addresses the first of those three phases.

PHASE I: IDENTIFYING, QUANTIFYING, AND FINANCING THE RIGHT BUSINESS INITIATIVES

Project portfolio development begins at the very top. Most companies develop high-level strategic statements and publish sets of guidelines that serve to guide the course of the company. Typically, these guidelines consist of a number of principles, concepts, and statements that address a wide range of considerations, such as the company's mission, values, vision, and high-level strategy. Collectively, this group of statements and plans is sometimes referred to as an expression of a company's strategic intent. As Figure 5.2 shows, Phase I of the project portfolio development process can only begin in earnest once a clear understanding of strategic intent has been established. From there, strategic intent is decomposed—much like the overall scope of a project is decomposed through the development of a work breakdown structure until a specific set of tasks eventually is identified.

The first major milestone in this decomposition process occurs at the end of Phase I, marked by the identification of a set of focused, short-term, quantified business initiatives, and a clear understanding of the level of financing (funding) that will be available to tackle those initiatives. Before beginning our study of Phase I, however, we must understand what it takes to get prepared.

Defining Strategic Intent: The Precursor to Portfolio Development

The process of defining and communicating a company's strategic intent is typically done by senior executives without any real consideration for project portfolio management. Nonetheless, a well-defined corporate strategy serves as the foundation for project portfolio development. Projects, after all, represent one of the key enablers in converting strategy into tangible business results.

So, given that strategy will serve as our foundation, let's take a close look at how strategic intent is developed.

The Development of Strategic Intent: A Generic View

Figure 5.3 illustrates the basic components that might comprise a company's overall expression of strategic intent. Note that the combination of strategic intent elements named "Values, Vision, and Strategy" are equivalent to the segment of the hierarchy shown in Figure 3.1 named "Strategic Goals and Plans." As shown in Figure 3.1 (and discussed earlier), these elements are developed by upper management as part of their job of setting basic company direction. The next sections briefly describe those basic components shown in Figure 5.3.

Mission

The mission is the overarching goal for a company. It is the company's reason for existence and the basic purpose toward which it directs all its goals, plans, and activities. Sometimes referred to as a

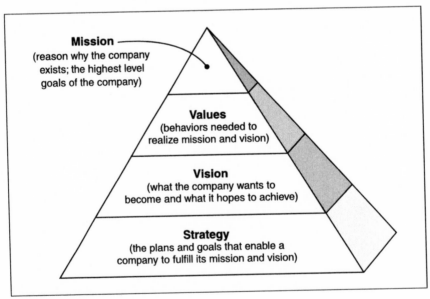

FIGURE 5.3

Adopting a total life cycle focus.

mission statement, it is the formally stated definition of a company's business scope and the highest level outcome(s) it is trying to achieve. Among other places, the mission often appears in a company's policy manuals and/or their annual reports, and is, by far, the most stable element of strategic intent.

Values

Values are the basic principles that guide an organization. Often expressed as attitudes, behaviors, or beliefs, *value statements* serve as an open proclamation of how the company expects to conduct itself—as a corporate entity as well as through the conduct of each of its employees. Adherence to this code of conduct, referred to by some companies as *core values*, are viewed by many as a necessary component in the perception of overall business success. Many companies tend to identify a relatively small set of core values that represent the sentiments of senior executives, and are therefore unlikely to change over time, barring any dramatic corporate metamorphosis.

Vision

A *vision statement* (or group of statements) defines what a company wants to become and what it hopes to achieve in the future. A well written vision statement, while straightforward in appearance, often serves a broad range of important functions. First, it provides everyone in the company with a shared mental model that helps employees understand future direction. It also serves to enable employees understanding of why and how they should support the organization, and what they may expect if they do so. Finally, it provides the foundation for the formulation of strategies and goals, thus serving as a point of transition between the picture of the future, colored by the mission and values, and the action required to get there.

Strategy

The term *strategy* is open to a wide range of interpretations. Some equate strategy with the high-level plans and objectives that senior managers develop to lead the company in the desired direction. Some define strategy as a set of specific, reasonably detailed actions that must be taken to enable a company to achieve the desired outcomes. Still others equate strategy with the act of consistently applying a comprehensive set of best practices over an extended period of time. Considering how frequently the term strategy is used, it is a surprisingly difficult term to define in detail. This is because strategy is not so much an entity unto itself, as it is the collection of things that comprise it—irrespective of whether they're plans and objectives, detailed actions, or best practices.

From the perspective of project portfolio management, this actually makes sense, because by the time we have completed our study of project portfolio management, we will have identified everything from high-level plans and objectives (i.e., the strategic and operational goals illustrated in Figure 5.2) all the way down to reasonably detailed actions (i.e., project proposals). So, in reality, project portfolio development, if done well, is really just a logical extension of a company's strategic intent.

Frameworks for Expressing Strategic Intent (and Strategy)

Most companies use some combination of mission, values, and vision as the grounding for the development of strategic intent. In many respects, they tend to look similar from company to company—not necessarily in content, but in form. However, the way in which companies articulate the actual strategy component of strategic intent can take on a variety of different forms, depending on the company.

Articulating strategy is primarily an issue of structure and organization. In effect, it comes down to how a company wishes to partition its overall corporate strategy into major areas of strategic focus—sometimes referred to as *strategic thrusts*.

Here again, a strong analogy exists between this process and the process of developing a work breakdown structure (WBS). One of the first steps in WBS development consists of deciding how Level 2 of the WBS should be configured by major deliverable, functional work group, process phase, or any of a number of other potential categorization schemes. This is quite similar to the kind of decision that senior executives make when trying to determine the best way to articulate their company's strategy.

The next sections detail a few examples of how companies can orient their strategy. Although they may assume different forms, each of these methods of modeling strategic thrust feeds off the mission, values, and vision developed by the respective company.

The Strategic Buckets Model

This structure identifies a number of very high-level strategic groupings that simply represent areas of focused attention. A few examples of strategic buckets include:

- Cost reduction
- Competitive advantage
- Competitive response
- Supply chain management

- Cycle time reduction
- Six Sigma (and/or other special initiatives)

These designations tend to be stable, because they represent the basic focus of the company. Obviously, they must be further broken down before a strong sense of strategy would emerge.

The Stated Goals Model

This model is similar to strategic buckets, but considerably more detailed, more goal-oriented, and therefore, more readily actionable. Accordingly, many more categories are likely to exist in this model than in the strategic thrusts model. Examples include:

- Reduce the asset base
- Maximize use of existing assets
- Expand market penetration
- Achieve process excellence
- Grow product lines
- Achieve a worldwide market presence
- Achieve customer service excellence
- Obtain ISO certification (and/or other special goals)

This model obliges strategic planners to provide much more focus than the strategic buckets approach does, which is generally a good thing. However, because this approach is focused in its nature, it also is subject to a higher level of change over time, as company goals may be subjected to some amount of refocusing through the years.

Investment Category Model

Similar to the stated goals model, the investment category model is more inclusive of everything needed to run the company. It takes a more holistic view, including aspects of the company related to operational and support functions.

- Develop new products/markets
- Expand existing products/markets
- Reduce cost of operations (and/or many other functions)
- Maintain asset infrastructure
- Research and development
- Address legal and regulatory requirements
- Enhance workforce satisfaction

Essentially, this model comes at strategic planning more from the standpoint of where and how money should be invested in managerial initiatives rather than what it takes to compete. Accordingly (and as we'll soon see), this is actually a pretty good model for configuring portfolio categories.

Strategic Partitioning: Organizational Units

Obviously, this model starts with segmentation of overall strategy into organizational units. It could assume any number of forms, depending upon how the company is structured; for example:

- Develop business unit A strategy
- Develop business unit B strategy
- Develop support organization C strategy
- Develop support organization D strategy
- Develop operational division E strategy
- Develop operational division F strategy

This is a popular format, and it really makes sense in those cases where organizational level strategy is actually a logical extension of well-defined cause-and-effect strategic linkages to the company's overall strategy. Unfortunately, though, I have observed many cases in which the starting point is simply a pot of money that has been allocated to a given organizational unit, implicitly entrusting them to "do right by the corporation." Unfortunately, the temptation to do what's best for one's organizational unit can be overwhelming, opening the door for potential suboptimization of overall strategic intent.

One other format that companies use is similar to this model. In this case, though, partitioning is done according to product lines rather than organizational units.

The Balanced Scorecard Model

This approach has gained considerable attention over the past several years as the tool of choice in strategy formulation. It is simple, yet powerful—and quite adaptable to the needs of individual companies.

The *balanced scorecard* is a comprehensive management control system that merges traditional financial and strategic measures with operational measures, all which can be tied back to a series of critical success factors (as defined by upper management). It is designed to reveal the underlying nonfinancial drivers, or causes, of financial performance. For example, if a business improves customer satisfaction, it is likely that this will lead to improved financial performance. Specifically, it is a set of financial and nonfinancial measures that reflect the multiple performance dimensions of a company and its business results.

The balanced scorecard methodology consists of four major perspectives:

1. **The financial perspective.** This perspective evaluates the profitability of a company's strategic direction or current operations. It serves as a framework for measuring a company's pursuit of both short-term as well as long-term financial performance. Typically, the financial perspective includes traditional business measures such as net income and return on investment.
2. **The customer perspective.** As the name suggests, this area focuses on the relationship between a company and its overall customer base. Indicators of success in the customer perspective may include relatively hard measures, such as market share and customer retention, or soft metrics, such as customer satisfaction and customer perception. The principle is that success in this arena will have direct impact on the financial perspective.
3. **The internal business process perspective.** This area views the company from the inside and focuses on the functional, organizational, and procedural elements of the company's internal operations. The intent of the internal business process perspective is to focus on operationally focused activities that will further the customer perspective (by creating value for customers) as well as the financial perspective (by contributing to shareholder wealth). Opportunities for improvement in this perspective frequently come from benchmarking the performance of other companies. The internal business process perspective typically focuses on performance dimensions such as quality, efficiency, and cycle time, and it is comprised of three subprocesses:
   - *The operations process.* This relates to how a company produces and delivers existing products and services to existing customers.
   - *The innovation process.* This relates to how a company creates new products and services that will better meet the needs of existing customers, or better position the company to meet the needs of future customers.
   - *The post sales service process.* This relates to how a company provides service and support to customers after the sale or after the delivery of a product or service.
4. **The learning and growth perspective.** The learning and growth perspective identifies the capabilities in which a company must excel to achieve superior internal business processes. The improvement in internal processes translates into improvements in both the customer and financial perspectives. Also an internally focused area, this perspective focuses on how well resources and human capital are managed, with a distinct eye

toward the future. Metrics in this area typically include items such as new product innovation, research and development capability, and employee retention.

Figure 5.4 displays the four balanced scorecard perspectives and the high-level measures that are commonly used to gauge performance within a given perspective. It's very important to note the cause-and-effect within these four perspectives. As the arrows in Figure 5.4 suggest, the gains that a company achieves in the learning and growth perspective will lead to improvements in the company's internal business processes. Improvements in processes will, in turn, lead to improvements in the customer interface. Eventually, the entire progression leads back to superior financial performance, characterized by the financial perspective.

The recognition of this progression—in which everything leads back to the financial perspective—is consistent with our earlier assertion that the fundamental purpose for all projects is to make or save money.

To me, one of the strengths of the balanced scorecard approach is the way in which it is able to effectively combine elements of strategic goals and its operational goals, as indicated in Figure 5.4. Although it's not explicitly stated in most of the literature about the balanced

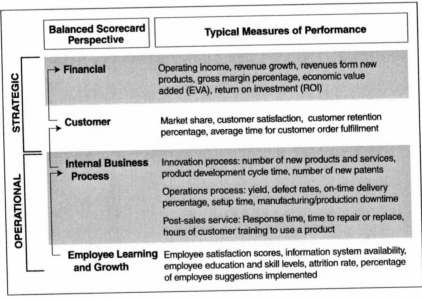

FIGURE 5.4

Balanced scorecard perspectives and some high-level measures.

scorecard, I tend to view the financial perspective and the customer perspective as primarily externally focused elements, and therefore strategic in nature. Similarly, I view the internal business process perspective and the learning and growth perspective as being internally focused elements, and therefore operational in nature. Again, this is just my interpretation. To me, this orientation is helpful in enabling management decision-makers to make a reasonably clear, comprehensive, and fundamental decision about their desired balance in allocating resources between strategy and operations within the overall project portfolio.

Although the balanced scorecard model is a useful construct for identifying the company strategy, the reality is that several of the approaches identified above are utilized successfully. In keeping with the purposes of this book, Table 5.1 offers a number of examples of strategy statements. Note that this list is not intended to be a set; that is, some pairs of strategy statements may be mutually exclusive, and some obviously are specific to a given industry segment.

TABLE 5.1

Examples of Corporate Strategies

Strategically Focused	Operationally Focused
• Expand revenue opportunities	• Optimize fixed asset utilization
• Maximize customer loyalty	• Attract and retain the best people
• Be a reliable source of credit	• Enhance employees' cross-functional knowledge
• Provide speedy and accurate service	• Optimize asset utilization
• Sell solutions, not just products	• Improve manufacturing yields
• Maintain a global marketing presence	• Optimize employees' knowledge of products
• Increase availability of products	• Create customer-focused culture
• Offer lowest prices to consumers	• Use only the highest quality input materials
• Assure rapid launch of new products	• Achieve excellence within core competencies
• Extend current products to new markets	• Execute just-in-time delivery channels
• Provide customers with total solutions	• Apply technology to optimize process excellence
• Deliver cost-efficient health care	• Enable employees to make meaningful decisions
• Provide outstanding customer service	• Optimize collaboration within supply chain
• Align research with growth areas	• Deliver only relevant and timely internal data
• Minimize market risks	• Develop a continuous improvement culture

THE START OF PORTFOLIO DEVELOPMENT: IDENTIFYING LONG-RANGE GOALS

OK, so we've identified the many ways in which a company can express a strategic intent and identify the strategies that will lead it to long-term business success. Now, we are (finally) ready to begin the project portfolio process!

The first major step in the project portfolio development process consists of identifying a set of long-range strategic goals and long-range operational goals (remember the dual pathway?). Figure 5.5 reveals the steps needed to accomplish this. It also provides a description of each step, along with three hypothetical examples.

The first step is to identify *key indicators of performance*. Generally, these are the areas in which the company wishes to excel,

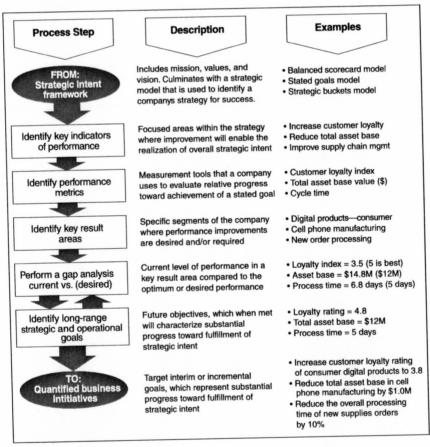

FIGURE 5.5

Process for identifying long-range goals.

as identified in its strategy statements. Once this is done, *perform-ance metrics* can be identified. These are quantified measurement scales that will be used to evaluate progress toward the stated goal. Next, *key result areas* identify the places within the company where improvement is desired. These "places" could be anything, including the name of a department, a product or product line, or a process. For many companies, *gap analysis* is the next step. Ordinarily, a gap analysis is performed for three reasons: first, to determine the current level of performance; second, to assist in the process of identifying long-range goals; and third, as a tool to demonstrate steady progress toward a goal over time. A few iterations may be required before a reasonable and achievable long-term goal can be established (note that the arrows between gap analysis and long-range goals shown in Figure 5.5 run in two directions). Inputs for reasonable long-range goals can come from a variety of sources, including executive opinion, industry averages, benchmarking, and customer feedback. The gap analysis can also be used. Although not explicitly shown through a dual pathway, the steps illustrated in Figure 5.5 are used to identify long-range operational goals as well as strategic goals. As mentioned previously, this process normally is performed by senior managers, and probably remains reasonably fixed over time. However, as a nor-mal part of a company's annual strategic planning process, long-term goals undoubtedly are reviewed and occasionally revised, as fluctuat-ing business conditions warrant. Table 5.2 offers several examples of possible long-range goals.

TABLE 5.2

Examples of Long-Range Goals

Strategically Focused	Operationally Focused
• Gross margin = 11%	• Average project schedule variance = 4 weeks
• 18 offshore (non-U.S.) district sales offices	• Total fixed asset base = $10.6 M
• Customer loyalty rating of 4.8	• Department ABC manufacturing yield = 94%
• 20% new products leveraged from existing	• Internal communications index = 4.0
• Customer return rate = 6%	• Maintenance costs = 8% of manufacturing cost
• 70% of product launches on time	• Process cycle time = 5.5 days (process-specific)
• Average age of receivables = 24 days	• Employee satisfaction index = 4.5
• 10% growth in existing customer sales	• Average days in inventory = 1.4
• Annualized customer complaints = 1,200	• Annual waste product line A = $130,000
• 15% gross revenue from new customers	• 12% cross-trained employee
• 22% market share (product-specific)	• Inventory turnover ratio = 12
• Customer service rating = 90%	• Accuracy of market planning = 90%

IDENTIFYING QUANTIFIED BUSINESS INITIATIVES (STRATEGIC AND OPERATIONAL)

As mentioned, business initiatives are really a subset of long-range strategic and operational goals. They are much more focused in nature than long-range goals, and are one of the key outputs of annual strategic planning sessions. Ideally, a business initiative should identify some sort of quantified, focused objective, but should not define a solution. In most cases, that job is best left to the project management community through a rigorous process that analyzes and compares a set of alternative solutions.

Quantified business initiatives represent the logical handoff between senior executives and the project management community.

Having said that, however, I would strongly urge companies to invite key project management personnel (such as a Project Management Office director, for example) to participate in strategic planning sessions—at least when project initiatives are being identified.

Figure 5.5 shows three typical examples of quantified business initiatives that are developed from three different sets of long-term goals. Table 5.3 offers a number of additional examples to help clarify how quantified business initiatives might be expressed.

TABLE 5.3

Examples of Quantified Business Initiatives

Strategically Focused	Operationally Focused
Increase gross margin on sales of household products at least 2% by 20XX	Reduce average schedule variance on capital projects to 5 weeks in 20XX
Open 3 new non-U.S. district sales offices next year (not Canada and Mexico)	Reduce total fixed asset base in overseas transportation segment to $11.6 M while maintaining the current level of service
Achieve customer loyalty rating of propane customers by 4.2 by 20XX	Improve internal communications index to 3.6 by year-end 20XX
Reduce average customer return rate on amateur digital cameras to 8% by 20XX	Reduce cost of equipment maintenance to 9% of asset value by 20XX
Reduce average age of receivables to Tier 1 suppliers to 24 days by 20XX	Reduce the average response time in the blood testing lab to 5.5 days next year
Reduce three-year composite average for customer complaints by Northeast U.S. cell phone subscribers to 1,600 in 20XX	Reduce the average age of perishable goods in storage by 4 hours next year
Establish a 20% share of the home office scanner market next year	10% of warehouse staff will be capable of performing two functions by 2nd Qtr 20XX

ESTABLISHING A PROJECT FINANCING STRATEGY

This issue is common to both portfolio management as well as capital budgeting. Obviously, no projects (and therefore no portfolio or capital budget listing) are possible without money.

But where does the money come from? To some extent, we addressed this question back in the early part of Chapter 2 (see the section, How Are Projects Financed?).

As you may recall, projects generally are funded through a combination of debt financing (what the company has borrowed from financial institutions) and equity financing (what shareholders have invested in the company, plus the cash that has been set aside for the purpose of reinvestment—retained earnings).

When we discussed how projects are tied to a company's bottom line in Chapter 1, we touched on the concept of net present value (NPV). The point was made that NPV is simply an estimation of the amount of wealth that a given project is expected to return to a company. We further noted that any project having a positive NPV (an NPV that is greater than zero) represented a sound financial investment, because it was able to generate wealth in excess of the financing costs.

Thinking about this from the standpoint of pure financial theory, this might lead us to believe that if a company had a list of positive NPV projects—but didn't have enough cash on hand to cover them all—it would make good business sense for management to reach out to financial institutions or shareholders and raise whatever monies were necessary to support all these "solid" investments.

That's theory.

The reality is that most companies set limits on the amount of funds that they're willing to raise, thereby limiting the size of their capital budget in any given year. The practice of placing limits on project spending is referred to as *capital rationing*. Faced with the knowledge that funds are limited, companies are strongly motivated to identify the set of projects that will provide the greatest business impact, yet remain within the imposed spending limit. Two basic types of capital rationing are practiced: soft rationing and hard rationing.

Soft Rationing

Soft rationing refers to the practice of placing limits on the amount of funds available for the execution of projects, based on the judgment of senior managers. Company managers normally view this practice as one method they can use to exercise financial control over the company. Typically, the practice of soft rationing also includes a placement of limits at the divisional or departmental level, commonly referred to as *capital budget allocation*. A company's management may be motivated to limit capital spending for a variety of reasons, including:

- **To promote the need to establish relative priority.** Recognizing that the supply of project money is not endless, managers across the company will naturally seek to ensure that they apply the funds they have to only the most valuable initiatives. As a result, they are driven to develop and apply intelligent, business-based methodologies to the practice of project prioritization and financial justification.
- **To control estimating bias.** For a variety of reasons, it is not uncommon for those preparing a financial analysis of a project (which could include project managers, project sponsors, and even department managers) to be overly optimistic in their projections of projects cash flows. This just seems to be a fact of life.

Some companies attempt to hedge against estimating bias by simply limiting available capital spending—soft rationing. Other companies attempt to control this phenomenon by increasing the required return for all projects (called the *hurdle rate*). Although we will re-examine the practice of increasing the hurdle rate as a strategy for managing risk, here it is used as a throttle on spending.

Neither one of these approaches has much long-term effectiveness, because it doesn't take very long to figure out the rules of the game and manipulate the estimating data accordingly. Obviously, this serves no useful purpose and often promotes further distortion in project estimates. More important, both approaches do very little to ensure that only the best projects are pursued.

Hard Rationing

Hard rationing refers to the existence of *real constraints*, often tied to serious considerations such as sound financial judgment or legal concerns. Here are some examples where hard rationing might come into play:

- **The marginal cost of capital is excessively high.** In Chapter 2, we discussed weighted average cost of capital (WACC). As you may recall, WACC is a blended combination of debt financing and equity financing and represents the current interest rate associated with financing projects using cash from the company's existing financial reserves. If the demand for project funding exceeds the current supply, management must go out and secure additional monies. The interest expense associated with these additional monies is referred to as the *marginal cost of capital*. Sometimes, particularly in situations in which the economy is doing poorly, the financing costs associated with securing these incremental funds are excessively high when compared to the current weighted average cost of capital. This discourages management from securing these funds.

- **Stock issuance would have serious drawbacks.** In cases in which company management might be considering funding the projects via equity financing (issuing new stocks), they may also recognize some potential associated problems. For example, investors might perceive new stock offerings as a signal that the company's equity is overvalued, even though this perception may be quite incorrect. Another concern would be whether a company would have to reveal strategic information (to attract potential investors), which may compromise the company's competitive advantages.

- **Constraints on nonfinancial resources.** Sometimes a company simply does not have the resources needed to pursue all the projects it would like. In many cases, this comes in the form of a shortage in human resources, because the pursuit of a large number of projects would stretch existing resources too thin. I once worked with a client company that was attempting to execute over 50 projects at once, although it really only had enough resources to adequately pursue about 12 projects! This is, of course, a clear violation of the portfolio principle of feasibility described earlier in this chapter.

HOW CAN YOU BE SURE YOU HAVE A SOUND APPROACH TO IDENTIFYING THE "RIGHT" INITIATIVES?

The key deliverable in Phase I of portfolio management is a set of quantified business initiatives. But I'm sure you noticed that I included the term "right" in the Phase I title. This term is aimed squarely at the concept of *strategic alignment*. The reason for this is simple: I tend to think of projects as being a logical extension of the way in which a company is run. In other words, projects are actually agents of a company's basic business strategy. In this regard, then, strategic alignment is not simply a nicety—it is a business imperative. But developing a structure and process that yields the best possible set of business initiatives (which leads to the "right" projects) is not as easy as it may appear. Here are a few criteria to evaluate whether your company has done a good job in developing the right set of business initiatives:

- **The process leading to initiatives communicates strategic linkages in a clear and unambiguous fashion.** An appropriately developed and well-defined strategic formulation process can have enormous value as a communication device. It can serve as a vehicle for showing how projects are connected to a company's high-level strategic intent. This puts the project management community in a much better position to identify appropriate project solutions and make better project decisions. The often missing piece of the puzzle is the clear articulation of the intermediate goals and objectives that create a stream of consciousness between the highest-level strategy and the individual project effort.
- **The process utilizes only the most critical performance factors.** A well-designed and effective process limits the quantity of measures used and identifies only the most critical ones. Typically, the term "critical" means those areas of the company in which: (1) good performance is essential to fulfilling strategic intent, and (2) current performance is significantly less than desirable. An appropriate set of business initiatives directs the attention of everyone in the company to those issues that need to be addressed *right now* to keep the company moving in the desired direction.
- **The set of business initiatives clearly reflects the company's basic competitive strategy.** The extent to which business initiatives truly reflect a company's competitive strategy is directly tied to the existence of cause-and-effect relationships. For example, if the company's primary competitive strategy is operational excellence (using the Treacy and Wiersema model), business initiatives are biased toward fulfilling its operational strategy. Also, long-range goals, performance measures, and business initiatives are directed more toward improving internal business processes.

THE BIGGEST CHALLENGE IN IDENTIFYING THE "RIGHT" INITIATIVES: KNOWING WHEN TO STOP

This topic is addressed at those charged with actually carrying out Phase I of the portfolio management process. Typically, this group performs the annual strategic planning function.

One of the most critical aspects of identifying the "right" business initiatives is ensuring that strategic planners know when to stop. In far too many companies, those charged with identifying critical business needs (i.e., quantified business initiatives) simply go too far.

They identify solutions rather than quantified business initiatives. Referring to Figure 5.2, this really means that strategic planners have jumped ahead to Phase II.

This is a difficult situation to overcome. It's human nature. It relates to the way our brains are wired—and we all suffer from it.

For example, consider this: You're in a situation where you are faced with a problem. Once you grasp the nature and extent of that problem what's normally the next thing that happens?

You either think (or blurt out) this statement: "I know how to solve that!" In many companies, strategic planners do the same thing. As the saying goes, they're only human.

But how can strategic planners know when to stop? How far is too far? One way of answering this question is to consider the desired attributes of business initiatives, all of which are embodied in the initiatives listed in Table 5.3 (it may be helpful to refer to them as we review the list of attributes below).

To be of optimum value to the overall portfolio development process, business initiatives should:

- **Describe a quantified, measurable end point.** This is a rather obvious set of attributes. It's literally impossible to know whether a given business initiative has been accomplished without verifiable metrics.
- **Be time bound.** Business initiatives are not goals the company would like to reach some day. They refer to the achievement of specific results within a given period of time.
- **Be feasible.** Remember, these are not vision statements. A clear and inarguable expectation should exist that the objective stated in the business initiatives is realistically achievable.
- **Provide focus, but not specific direction.** Note that nearly every entry in Table 5.3 identifies a particular part of the business, such as a product or product line, market segment, organizational unit, or process.
- **Provide specific limits, constraints, or conditions, as appropriate.** Two examples of this attribute are illustrated in Table 5.3. In the list of strategic initiatives, note that the term non–U.S. specifically excludes district sales offices in Canada and Mexico. In the list of operational initiatives, note that the total asset base of the transportation segment must be reduced while maintaining the current level of service.
- **Leave the door open for alternative solutions.** This attribute describes the crux of the entire solution-jumping situation. To be fair, it really is difficult to define the exact moment when a solution emerges. One way that I try to reconcile this dilemma

is by looking at a given initiative and asking a very simple question: How many different types of approaches exist for satisfying this initiative?

Bearing in mind that we are not talking about *design alternatives*—if the answer to that question is "One," you probably have gone too far.

Unfortunately, the practice of going "too far" during Phase I can severely compromise the remainder of the overall portfolio development process. Gone forever is a thoughtful, data-driven analysis of alternatives—the primary vehicle for ensuring the identification of the best possible method for addressing the true need. All that remains is a title that prescribes a specific action (design and build a machine, develop a new process, purchase a piece of equipment).

To make matters worse, the true need may not be well understood by the project management community: the very group charged with effectively managing the project's implementation. When a project manager is assigned to lead a project, but not provided with a clear understanding of a project's true need, she is thrust into a very bad situation. Wishing to be perceived as a good corporate citizen, the project manager may be afraid to question the process or the decisions that have led to this point. As a result, the project manager simply accepts whatever is handed to her as "the project" and immediately moves into project planning.

Therefore, a specific solution—which may literally have been developed in matter of moments—begins to take on a life of its own. The question of whether the chosen course of action represents the best way to satisfy the original need may never be addressed in a meaningful way.

Only by following a systematic, rational, and analytical process, in which strategic planners identify the right business needs and project practitioners identify the right solutions to those needs, can a company be assured that it is working on real problems, identifying the most critical issues, and pursuing optimal solutions (projects). To put it in business terms, the process flow illustrated in Figure 5.2 offers some level of assurance to a company that it is investing its money as wisely as possible. Unfortunately, solution jumping can severely compromise that process.

When that happens, the die has been cast for Revelation #1 (referring back to Chapter 1, Project Management as a Business Function): It really doesn't matter how well you execute a project, if you're working on the wrong project!

Identifying the right projects starts by identifying the right business initiatives.

CHAPTER 6

Project Portfolio Management, Phase II: Identifying, Categorizing, and Prioritizing Project Solutions

At this stage in the portfolio management process, a list of quantified business initiatives has been identified. This is an excellent starting point for Phase II of the project portfolio management process.

Much work lies ahead. First, we need to identify a set of solutions (i.e., projects) to satisfy the quantified business initiatives. We also must bring some structure to this list of projects. We then must determine which projects are worth pursuing, which are really marginal investments, and which are simply not worth pursuing—even though they may have seemed like good ideas at the outset. Finally, we must find a way to verify that the projects we intend to pursue represent a balanced approach with regard to our overall project investment portfolio.

Phase II of the project-portfolio management process addresses all these needs. As Figure 5.2 showed, it begins by determining the best way to satisfy all the business initiatives that had been identified in Phase I.

IDENTIFYING SOLUTIONS TO
ADDRESS BUSINESS INITIATIVES

Ideally, we would like to begin constructing a portfolio *right now*, using the list of business initiatives from Phase I. The next logical question then would be, "which business initiatives should we be working on first?"

We can't do that. Yet.

Why? Because (as of this point in the portfolio construction process) we normally can estimate the financial benefits associated with addressing a given business initiative, but have not yet estimated the cost of addressing that initiative. In other words, we know how much money we will make or save by tackling a given initiative—but we don't know what it will cost to make it happen, because we have not yet identified a specific solution. In fact, we can't be absolutely certain that a cost-effective solution even exists!

To estimate the cost of satisfying a business initiative with any kind of reasonable precision, a solution must be identified and sufficiently defined.

This is the point at which "projects" are born.

The process for bringing a project into the world centers on the identification and thorough analysis of alternatives.

INTRODUCTION TO THE ALTERNATIVE IDENTIFICATION AND ANALYSIS PROCESS

The *alternative identification and analysis process* is a rational, systematic, data-driven, analytical methodology, whose ultimate deliverable is a recommendation on the best way to satisfy a given business initiative. The trick, though, is to identify a solution that key stakeholders can agree is "best." This is not always easy, for at least four good reasons.

First, different solutions appeal to different people in different ways. Some alternatives, for example, often may benefit one department or organization while adversely affecting another.

Second, different alternatives require the investment of different sums of money—and generate different benefits streams. The cost versus benefit question can get quite convoluted.

Third, most proposed alternatives do not simply pass or fail with respect to addressing a set of needs; ordinarily, alternatives will address these needs with varying degrees of effectiveness. This can make judging goodness and badness quite messy. To complicate matters even more, different, complex, and varied sets of advantages and disadvantages frequently are associated with different alternatives.

And finally, let's not forget about risk. Different alternatives likely are to be associated with different types and different levels of risk. Some solutions are considered ideal—if nothing bad happens. But what are the chances of that?

ALTERNATIVE IDENTIFICATION AND ANALYSIS: STEP BY STEP

All this leads to the need to develop a rational, easy-to-use, well-understood and agreed-upon process that project teams can use to identify and evaluate alternative solutions to business initiatives. Figure 6.1 illustrates the following five-step process for alternative identification and analysis:

1. **Start with a well-defined problem statement.** In this case, I am using the term "problem" as a generic way of referring to the existence of a problem, a need, or an opportunity. Typically, the business initiatives identified in Phase I will assume one of these forms. As described in Chapter 5, business initiatives must be well-defined, but not dictate a specific solution.

   Sometimes, taking the time and trouble to further clarify a business initiative can lead to the recognition of a situation that

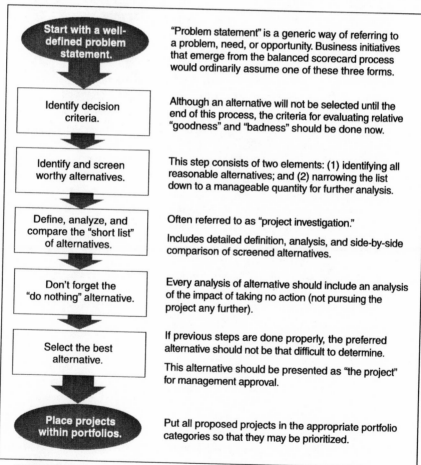

FIGURE 6.1

Using alternative analysis to identify project solutions.

is either much better or much worse than originally had been suspected. This can be valuable input when it comes to the point of determining the relative attractiveness of projects within the portfolio.

2. **Identify the decision criteria.** Although the actual decision on which alternative is "best" will not actually be made until the end of this process, it can be useful to develop the evaluation criteria early—ideally, before any specific alternatives are even identified. One big reason for identifying decision criteria in advance is the concern over bias. Nearly as insidious as solution jumping is the phenomenon of the *pet project*—or in this case, the *pet alternative*. If the evaluation criteria are developed after several alternatives have surfaced, the door is open for some decision-makers to design (or to be blunt, manipulate) the evaluation criteria in a way that allows their favorite alternative to "win out." The factors commonly used to evaluate alternatives often will use a combination of financial and nonfinancial criteria.

3. **Identify and screen worthy alternatives.** This step actually consists of two basic elements: (1) Identifying all reasonable alternatives; and (2) narrowing the list down to a manageable quantity for detailed investigation and analysis.

    The process of identifying reasonable alternatives is best done in a large group. At the very least, the step calls for full team participation—if not a larger group that would include potential stakeholders. It's critical that the project manager solicits and understands everyone's perspective. Once assembled, a list of alternatives may be generated through the use of classic facilitation approaches such as brainstorming.

    Since limits often exist on the available time and money to analyze alternatives, it's necessary to generate a "short list" of potential alternatives (typically three or four) before proceeding to the next step. This can be accomplished by using a simplified version of any *attribute scoring* method you wish. The topic of attribute scoring is covered later in this chapter.

4. **Define, analyze, and compare the short list of alternatives.** Some companies refer to this step as *project investigation*. As the title suggests, project investigation has three components:
    - *Definition.* To be capable of determining the best alternative, decision-makers must develop a good understanding of what's required to execute a given alternative. It's likely that this definition will eventually become the *statement of work* for that project. Basic planning functions also are performed, including schedule development, cost estimating, and identification

of key deliverables. Finally, a comprehensive list of results and outcomes should be defined.

– *Analysis.* This step focuses on the identification of attributes, characteristics, and other relevant factors that enable a determination of the best alternative. To that end, these items tie directly to the decision criteria identified in Step 2. Although the analysis should focus on financial criteria, other considerations must be considered, such as:

- Assumptions
- Risks, uncertainties, and unknowns
- Rules, responsibilities, and resource requirements
- Advantages and disadvantages
- Key enablers and inhibitors of success
- Critical success factors
- Interface, integration, and compatibility issues
- Effect on other projects or organizational units

This information should be compiled and placed with a structured matrix (Excel spreadsheet is fine) in a way that allows for a clear comparison of alternatives.

– *Side-by-side comparison.* This commonly is referred to as *mutually exclusive decision-making*, which simply means that only one alternative can survive the analysis. Mutually exclusive decision-making is most effective when the analysis focuses on contrasting and comparing one alternative to another, specifically comparing incremental benefits to be gained by choosing one over another.

Ideally, all comparisons of alternatives should focus primarily on financial considerations, and a rigorous financial analysis should be performed for each alternative. The financial analysis methods used to evaluate competing alternatives is virtually identical to the methods used to compare a group of projects within a portfolio category. These methods are described later in this chapter, and examined in detail in Chapter 10, Project Economics, Part III: Performing a Project Financial Analysis.

The extent to which decision-makers will be able of make sound judgments depends highly on the structuring of the analysis and the quality of data within the analysis. Recognizing that analysis takes time and money, it's prudent to recognize that the amount of time and money spent performing alternative analysis should be somewhat proportional to the magnitude of the decision. It may not make a great deal of sense, for example, for a team of five people to spend many weeks performing analysis on a relatively small project. Conversely, selecting the best alternative on a multimillion dollar project may be worth a considerable investment on the part of the team performing the investigation.

– *Don't forget the "do-nothing" alternative.* Every once in awhile, I encounter someone who argues against the need to perform an alternative analysis.

"There's really only one way to do this project," they assert.

This is not true. In all cases, two possible choices exist: Do something or do nothing.

The so-called *do-nothing scenario* should always be part of any alternative analysis that you perform. Several possible reasons exist for why it makes good sense to evaluate do-nothing as a legitimate alternative:

- It reinforces the need to take action. Sometimes, we are so busy comparing alternatives—and anguishing over their slight differences—that we may lose sight of the fact that a significant inherent value is present in taking *any* sort of action. Understanding the impact of inaction helps us appreciate that.

- There really are times when doing nothing may yield the best overall result. If you fail to perform an analysis of the do-nothing alternative, you may never learn this.

- If you don't think of it, your management probably will. The last thing you want to happen is to get halfway through your well-rehearsed, polished, professional presentation, and have one of the managers in the audience raise their hands and ask: "Gee...what would happen if we didn't do anything right now?" And you don't have a snappy comeback. It is a perfectly valid question, and one you should expect to receive when delivering your project proposal to management. Instead of sitting back and waiting for the question to be asked, bring it out into the open.

5. **Select best alternative (but keep the others on the back burner).** I cannot stress enough the notion that if the first five steps of this process have been done well, selecting the preferred alternative will not be very hard at all. The soundness of your analytical framework, the selection of agreed-upon decision criteria, and the quality of the input data are key contributors to making this step relatively painless.

One useful method for structuring the final comparison and preparing for final decision-making revolves around understanding and applying the concept of *base alternative*. The base alternative is that alternative requiring the smallest possible capital outlay, while achieving the minimum acceptable performance results (which, in this situation, means closing the "performance gap" identified on the balanced scorecard). The alternative that has these characteristics is the one that management decision-makers often use as their basis of comparison.

So, what does this mean to you (particularly if you are going to present this analysis to your management)? It means that a useful and intelligent way to structure your analysis may be to start by explicitly acknowledging the base alternative. Then, if more attractive alternatives arise (based on criteria other than minimum cash outlay), you will need to justify them by identifying the incremental increase in cash outlay versus the incremental benefits to be gained.

You also should identify any qualitative criteria that led you to making a recommendation other than the base alternative.

CONFIGURING THE PORTFOLIO CATEGORIES

Configuring the portfolio categories is an activity that ordinarily is done once and modified infrequently over time (note that Figure 6.2 refers to the existence of "predetermined" project portfolio categories). Portfolio categories fundamentally should reflect the way a company wishes to invest in projects, and the categories, therefore, are not something subject to much change.

As we now begin to shift our focus to project portfolio categories, it's important to note that a significant transformation is taking place relative to our perspective on portfolio development. In Phase I, we thought exclusively in terms of corporate strategy and business initiatives. As we now begin to think in terms of implementing projects—

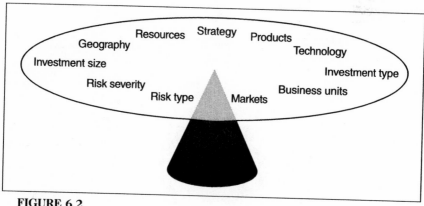

FIGURE 6.2

Portfolio construction is a balancing act.

and the sum total of the effects they will exert on the company—we must begin thinking in several dimensions. What we really need is something that will allow us to think beyond whether a given project supports our company's strategy. If we've done our job in Phase I, strategic alignment can be assumed. We now must develop an intelligent, well-balanced methodology that considers all aspects of how the business is run. That methodology comes in the form of project portfolio categorization.

What Is the Function of Project Categories?

On the surface, the answer to this question is easy: To ensure that some sort of relative balance exists across the portfolio.

Now there's the tricky part...what exactly is being balanced?

Actually, the business of balancing a project portfolio might be considerably more complex (and difficult) than you might think. Why? Simply because so many things must be kept in balance. Figure 6.2 graphically depicts the difficulty in achieving all of these balances at once.

Project portfolios may be visualized as being composed of many different dimensions, each of which should be maintained in some sort of relative balance, if the collective effect of the entire project portfolio is to be optimized. The following list provides some examples of these dimensions, and the types of balances that must be considered as part of portfolio construction:

- Strategic balance. Considers the relative balance in any number of areas of strategy, for example, the competitive strategies of product leadership, operational excellence, and customer intimacy (from the Treacy and Wiersema model). Although companies ordinarily identify one of these as a primary strategy, the reality is that their business—to some extent—will exist in each area. This dimension also refers to achieving an appropriate balance between strategic projects and operational projects.
- Product balance. Considers the relative balance in providing financial support to the company's various products or product lines.
- Market balance. Similar to product balance, but viewed from a higher level. Examples could include market categories such as the consumer market, the professional market, and the commercial/industrial market.
- Business unit balance. Similar (and in some cases identical) to product balance and/or market balance. Considers the relative balance in financial support across business units, assuming the company is structured this way.

- Geographic balance. Considers the relative balance across a pre-defined geographic region. For example, a company operating domestically could choose to focus its attention on the "Northeast," "Southeast," "Midwest," or "Pacific Coast" regions of the United States. Similarly, a company that conducts business globally could choose to focus its attention on the "North American," "Latin American," or "European" regions.
- Technology balance. Considers the relative balance in supporting research and development across a broad range of advanced technology applications. Examples may include laser technology, optical technology, or software development technology.
- Risk balance (severity). Considers the relative balance between high- and low-risk projects.
- Risk balance (type). Considers the balancing of risk types, such as financial risk, technical risk, operational risk, market risk, and others.
- Resource balance. Considers the relative balance in involvement of all project-dedicated resources within the company in project efforts. This could refer to either organizational units or functional competencies.
- Investment balance (size). Considers the relative balance between projects requiring large capital investments versus those requiring a relatively small outlay of cash.
- Investment balance (type). Also called *project type*, this approach considers the relative balance across category types that generally align with the way many businesses are managed. Examples of investment types may include new product development, process improvement, cost reduction, equipment maintenance, and employee satisfaction.

As you can see, certainly a number of ways exist for orienting portfolio categories. Ultimately, though, it's necessary to select a single, dominant scheme that can be used as a primary portfolio categorization scheme. You may have your favorite scheme—I know I have mine! And here it is...

Using Project Investment Type as Portfolio Categories

My personal favorite for portfolio categorization is *investment type*—as illustrated in Figure 6.3. It's my favorite for a few different reasons.

First, it's one of the only categorization schemes that probably is not already being monitored by someone in the company. In most companies, managers often are concerned with issues such as product balance, business unit balance, technology balance, and geo-

Portfolio type	Description	Key characteristics
Expansion into new product, service, or market areas	Investments to prepare for production of new products or new product lines, or for expansion into geographic areas not currently served.	Involves strategic judgment. Requires large expenditures with relatively slow payback.
Expansion of existing products, services, or markets	Expenditures to increase output of existing products, or to expand sales and/or distribution outlets in markets currently being served.	Requires accurate forecasts of growth.
Cost reduction	Expenditures aimed at reducing ongoing operational costs, such as labor, material and waste, or inputs, such as electricity or fuel.	Discretionary; involves competing internal projects; relies heavily on calculations of financial returns.
Maintenance and protection	Expenditures to replace worn out, damaged, or obsolete equipment or facilities used in the production of profitable products (maintenance), or to reduce the probability of catastrophic failures (protection).	Nondiscretionary (assuming the company wishes to continue in that business). Questions that should always be asked are: • *Should operation be continued?* • *Should process be modified?*
Regulatory (e.g., legal, safety, environmental)	Expenditures required to comply with government regulations, labor agreements, insurance policy terms, etc.	Often called "mandatory projects." Normally comprised of non-revenue-producing projects and financial "losers."
Research and development	Expenditures made for purposes such as investigating feasibility, gathering information, testing concepts, or promoting innovation.	Cash flows produced are highly uncertain, and significantly delayed. Decisions to stop or proceed often made in "stages." R&D expenditures can be "written off" as expense.
Infrastructure and "other"	Expenditures that support a wide variety of needs within the company. Examples include office buildings, parking lots, information systems.	Methods for funding and justifying tend to vary widely from company to company.

FIGURE 6.3

Constructing a project portfolio using investment type.

graphic balance—a natural byproduct of the way companies are structured. The same cannot be said for investment type.

Second, as we have discussed many times, projects are investments. So, it only seems logical to orient project portfolio categories according to investment type.

And finally, as mentioned before, the kind of balance represented by using investment type as the primary categorization scheme really mirrors the balance that many companies seek to achieve in the way they operate their business. Most companies try to strike a balance between addressing their immediate needs, achieving their short-range goals, and achieving their long-range goals, while continuously preserving their infrastructure.

Figure 6.3 illustrates just one way of categorizing projects that capture the essence of the investment type approach. In fact, many variations to this basic design are possible. This approach, however, is similar to many I have seen used.

PRIORITIZING PROJECTS WITHIN PORTFOLIO CATEGORIES: WHY AND HOW

It is common for companies to identify many more project opportunities than they are able to execute. Limitations are likely to exist that will preclude the company from doing all the projects that they'd like to do. Naturally, this trickles down to the portfolio level. Consequently, a limit is likely to exist on the number of projects that can be pursued within each portfolio category. So, the projects listed in each portfolio category must be prioritized.

Prioritization refers to the act of evaluating which projects are the most urgent, of greatest importance, or of greatest value to the company. If this evaluation could somehow be restricted to purely financial considerations, prioritization would be reasonably straightforward. In the real world, however, many reasons exist to include the so-called nonfinancial factors.

We'll examine a number of frameworks for prioritizing projects—financial as well as nonfinancial. You may wish to refer to Figure 6.4 as we move forward. Let's begin by examining the financially based framework.

Using a Financial Framework for Project Prioritization

While I will be one of the first to admit that performing a rigorous, thorough, high-quality financial analysis on a project is not an easy task, I remain a staunch believer in the inherent righteousness of relying primarily upon financial criteria in project prioritization, selection, and approval. It simply makes a lot of sense from a business standpoint.

But some project management practitioners (and managers) are very critical of financially based decision-making. Some even disregard it entirely, claiming that financial approaches are "poor predictors of business success," "unreliable," or "don't tell the whole story."

In my observations, the criticism that some people level at financially based approaches to project decision-making is not so much a case of concern over accuracy or a penchant for good storytelling, but often is related to other factors, some of which they are either unaware of or unwilling to admit, such as:

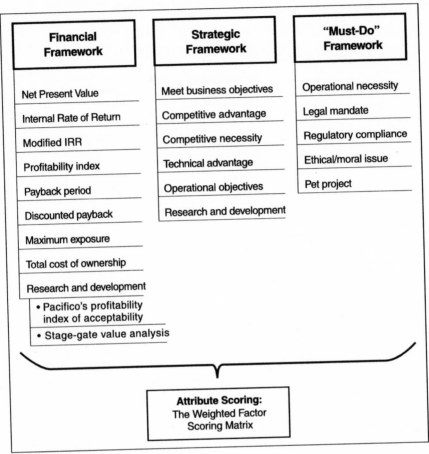

FIGURE 6.4

Attribute frameworks used in project prioritization.

- Inability to properly identify and model all relevant cash flows
- Reluctance to commit to (or get others to commit to) specific financial goals
- Unwillingness to put in the required effort (it is a lot of work!)
- Desire to accelerate the overall process
- Lack of knowledge or understanding about a project or a given situation
- Fear that their "pet project" will not survive a rigorous financial analysis

We'll touch on this sensitive subject again in Chapter 10. Meanwhile, I strongly urge you and your company to begin applying some of the financially based approaches we're about to examine as the foundation for your approach to project prioritization, selection, and approval. Economic considerations should not be your sole decision-making criterion—but they should be the dominant one.

Several methods can be used to evaluate projects from an economic standpoint. Of the many methods described here, some are expressed as measures of financial return (net present value), some are expressed as performance indicators (profitability index), while some are simply limits or guides to aid the decision-making process (maximum exposure). Again, all are shown in Figure 6.4.

Net Present Value

One of the most popular approaches that companies use to establish financial justification is the net present value (NPV) method. Net present value calculates the amount of wealth that a project is expected to return to the company.

The rationale for using the NPV method is surprisingly straightforward and is directly tied to concepts we discussed in Chapter 1, in the section called "connecting the dots." As you may recall (and as illustrated in Figure 1.5), we discussed how the NPV of each individual project directly contributes to a company's annual calculation of the economic value added (EVA), which in turn contributes to the company's long-term market value added (MVA).

Expressing this concept from the standpoint of finance theory, the rationale for the NPV method is equally straightforward. Having an NPV of zero signifies a project whose total cash inflows (all the money it is expected to make or save) are just enough to repay the invested capital and to service the debt. The term *servicing the debt* refers to providing the required rate of return expected by those whose capital we used, namely financial institutions and shareholders (as you'll recall, this required rate of return is referred to as the *weighted average cost of capital*).

So, if a project is determined to have a positive NPV, it is generating a financial return that is greater than what is needed to pay for the funds provided by investors, and this excess is returned to the firm—which leads to EVA (i.e., shareholder wealth). As we discussed in Chapter 1, the underlying premise of good business is to maximize shareholder wealth. This train of thought has led to the considerable popularity of the NPV method.

Internal Rate of Return

The internal rate of return (IRR) method uses many of the same underlying financial principles (and calculations) used in the NPV method, but seeks to evaluate the economic strength of a project from a slightly different angle. It is expressed as a percentage, the rate at which the company expects to recover its initial investment in a given project. This calculated rate of return is then compared to the required rate of return, which is often the weighted average cost of capital (WACC). If the IRR exceeds the cost of financing the project, then a surplus will remain after paying off the borrowed funds and all financing costs. As with NPV, this surplus accrues solely to the firm's shareholders. Therefore, if a project's IRR exceeds the WACC, the project is viewed as a sound investment from a strictly financial standpoint.

Although the IRR method traditionally has been quite popular, it has one significant drawback worth mentioning. Inherent in the way that it's calculated is the assumption that all the cash flows generated by the project under consideration will be reinvested at the project's own IRR. This generally is not a very accurate assumption. Generally, the cash flows generated by a project are returned to the company's overall pool of cash reserves. Some of the funds returned to this pool will be distributed to shareholders. However, some of the funds will be reinvested in future projects at the WACC (or something close to it), not at the project's own IRR.

Modified Internal Rate of Return

Recognized as an improvement over IRR, the modified IRR calculation (MIRR) assumes that cash flows from projects are reinvested at some predetermined rate—normally assumed to be the WACC. Since reinvestment at the WACC is generally closer to the truth, MIRR is a better indicator of projects actual profitability.

Even though MIRR represents an improvement over IRR, both methods suffer from the same shortcoming. Neither MIRR nor IRR provided any specific insight on *how much money* will be returned to the company. It would be quite possible, for example, for a project to have a very high MIRR (say 50%), while only returning $10,000 of wealth to the firm—not a lot of cash. In fact, that project would be less desirable than a project with a much lower MIRR (say 15%) that returns $100,000 of wealth.

Profitability Index

The profitability index also is referred to as the benefit cost ratio, because it is a simple comparison of all the benefits and costs associated with executing a project. Specifically, it is defined as ratio of the *equivalent worth* of benefits to the equivalent worth of costs. The concept of equivalence is discussed in detail in Chapter 8, Project Economics, Part I: Foundational Principles. It should be noted, however, that some companies using the profitability index as a measure of economic strength do not consider the time value of money (also discussed in Chapter 8).

The profitability index rule states that a project whose profitability index is greater than 1.0 should be viewed as a favorable investment from a financial standpoint. Although the profitability index can be applied effectively as an initial screening tool, it suffers from the same drawback as the IRR method: It does not explicitly state the amount of wealth that a given project is expected to return to the company.

Payback Period

All the above methods for calculating economic strength are intended to express the *profitability* of a proposed project. The *payback period* (also called the *time-to-money*), is intended to serve as an indication of a project's liquidity, rather than its profitability. Simply stated, the payback period method describes the amount of time it will take to recover the initial project investment. This payback period also is referred to as the *break-even life* of a project, and the point in time when it occurs is referred to as the *break-even point*; both are ordinarily expressed in terms of months or years. When comparing two projects, the one that has a shorter payback period (or break-even life) is considered relatively more desirable.

Figure 6.5 provides a pictorial representation of the payback period and how it relates to the overall cash flow of a typical project. The initiation of a project immediately thrusts the company into a cash hole. This is quite normal and to be expected. As the project draws to a close, the company begins to reap the benefits of the project in the form of positive cash flows, and the curve takes a definite turn upward.

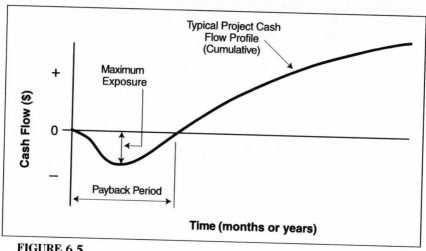

FIGURE 6.5

Payback period and maximum exposure.

When the curve crosses the zero line, the initial investment has been recovered. This point in time defines the payback period.

Discounted Payback

Some companies use a variation of the payback period, the discounted payback period, which is virtually identical to the payback period, except that the expected future cash flows are discounted—or devalued—by the WACC. Naturally, discounting future cash flows will have the effect of lengthening the break-even life of a project.

It should be noted that neither the payback period nor the discounted payback provide any specific information about a project, except the speed with which its investment amount will be recovered. In addition, the serious drawback of both methods is that they ignore cash flows that are either paid or received after the end of the break-even life. Once again, this precludes a company from understanding exactly how much wealth a given project will return to the company. However, either of these methods can be a useful supplement to decision-making, when applied in conjunction with other methods used for calculating economic strength.

For example, the payback period method tells decision-makers exactly how long funds will be tied up in a given project. And, because cash flows expected in the distant future are generally riskier (less certain) than the near-term cash flows, the payback period method can be used as a relative indicator of riskiness.

Maximum Exposure

The maximum exposure of a project investment is another expression of riskiness, and it serves as an excellent corollary to the payback period. While the payback period describes how long a company's money will be tied up in a project, maximum exposure describes how much will be tied up. As the name suggests, maximum exposure refers specifically to the largest amount of money that will be tied up in a given project at any given point in time. This is represented by the lowest point in the cumulative cash flow profile shown in Figure 6.4.

Once again, this type of metric can be effectively applied as a kind of tiebreaker. For example, if two projects are equal in all other respects, but one project exposes less money, that project would be the favored choice.

Total Cost of Ownership

Total cost of ownership (TCO) is an approach intended to ensure that all costs associated with a capital investment over a given period are accounted for in the value assessment. The approach is used as a tool for sound decision-making as well as for optimizing asset ownership.

Its main intent is to find the best value between several competing alternatives (or several competing projects).

The TCO methodology was originally developed in the late 1980s, by Bill Kirwin, vice president and research director for the Gartner Group, Inc., as a way to express the cost of owning and deploying personal computers. It has been applied subsequently in a variety of arenas, most notably in information technology implementations.

A variety of direct and indirect elements of cost are typically included in the TOC, including acquisition costs (capital purchase or project execution), modification or customization costs, installation and commissioning costs, operating costs, maintenance and repair costs, disposal costs, and of course, financing costs. Even costs such as downtime and overhead are included in calculating TCO.

Although it is most commonly associated with purchasing decisions and with information-technology implementations, the TCO approach epitomizes the philosophy behind the procedure for making calculations such as NPV. As we will see in Chapter 10, Project Economics, Part III: Performing a Project Financial Analysis, the key to making high-quality calculations of NPV and IRR depend entirely on the project team's ability to identify all elements of cost, both favorable and unfavorable, throughout the life of the project.

Economic Evaluation of Research and Development Projects

Ideally, financial evaluations should follow the TOC philosophy and include all costs associated with a proposed project investment. But obtaining precise estimates on the value of future cash flows is not easy to do. This is one of the driving forces behind the use of nonfinancial factors in project analysis.

In the case of research and development (R&D) projects, it can be virtually impossible to model future cash flow streams with any kind of precision or accuracy, because they have an excessive amount of uncertainty associated with them. R&D projects frequently require major course corrections, multiple decision nodes, and a very high level of unpredictability related to future outcomes.

This has led to the development of an application of methods that seek to evaluate the economic strength of an R&D project. Here are a few of the more popular approaches.

Pacifico's profitability index of acceptability. Proposed over 30 years ago, *Pacifico's method* serves as a good example of how any approach—if applied consistently—can be used to evaluate relative attractiveness of investments. This method is oriented towards new product development or product line extension projects. It calculates a *profitability index of acceptability* (PI):

$$PI = rdpc \; (SP[L]^{0.5})/ \; C$$

where:
r = probability or research success
d = probability of development success, given research success
p = probability of process implementation success, given development success
c = probability of commercial success, given process success

The project's total anticipated cash flow is represented by the term:

$$[SP(L)^{0.5}] \; / \; C$$

where:
S = estimated annual sales volume
P = estimated profit per unit
L = estimated life of the product, in years
C = estimated total cost of the R&D effort

Although this method does not predict the amount of wealth that a given project will return to the company, it can be used as an effective tool for using financial criteria to prioritize the relative attractiveness of a group of R&D projects.

Stage-gate value analysis.   Projects involving R&D work are characterized by extremely high levels of unknowns, uncertainties, and risk. This pertains not only to the achievement of technical results, but to the ability to make accurate and definitive predictions regarding potential costs and benefits. It is very difficult, if not impossible, to cost-justify R&D projects at the outset, due to the inherent inability to make direct comparisons between costs and benefits.

Consequently, it's extremely difficult to make the approval decision for an entire project at the outset of the initiative. Some companies address this situation by integrating a stage-gate process with the value analysis approach first popularized by Peter Keen in 1981.

Keen recognized that the rationalization of projects requiring innovation, invention, or breakthrough must be value-driven in a step-wise fashion. Figure 6.6 shows a model of a basic three-step approach, consisting of a research stage, a development stage, and a pilot stage.

Obviously, this basic process is different for different companies, but the basic thoughtware that occurs in each major process step would be the same. A company's ability to perform step-wise prioriti-

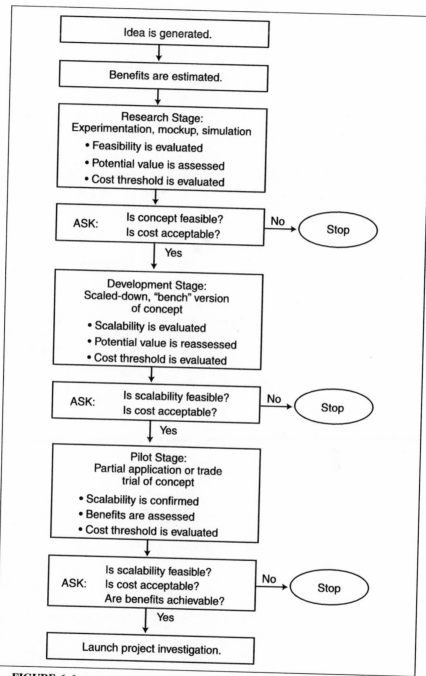

FIGURE 6.6

Stage-gate value analysis.

zation, selection, and approval for R&D projects consists of asking these three basic questions at each stage:

- What kind of positive outcomes can we expect by pursuing this stage?
- If we are successful, what potential benefits could be realized by continuing?
- How much are we willing to pay to take this process to the next level?

Performing these steps as part of a formal management review process can provide benefits to the company, such as enhanced communication, the ability to examine alternatives at several points during the project, and ongoing stimulation of new ideas.

Using Nonfinancial Criteria and Attribute Scoring for Project Prioritization

Most of the financial methods described above rely on making calculations using specific dollar amounts. By definition, only one attribute is being used in this process—economic strength. For anyone who wishes to paint a more complete picture of projects, using a variety of project attributes can be a very good idea. Attribute scoring methods enable the prioritization of projects based on a host of factors beyond pure financials. At times, this kind of approach can definitely add value to the prioritization process.

The Value in Going Beyond Pure Financials

At the risk of repeating myself, let me once again contend that utilizing financial considerations as the dominant criterion in the evaluation and prioritization of projects makes a great deal of sense. However, several valid arguments also exist for including nonfinancial criteria—project attributes other than economic strength—in this process. Among these arguments are the following:

- **Financial methods are definitely not perfect.** All the financial methods described earlier rely heavily on someone's ability to use the appropriate estimating methods in predicting future outcomes and to accurately translate those outcomes into expressions of cost or value. These are not easy things to do, and many companies may not be well-equipped to do them without professional estimating support.
- **It may be very difficult to place a precise value on some factors.** This is particularly true of *project benefits*. For example, how

would you go about assigning a specific dollar amount to benefits such as an improvement in the workforce output due to a process enhancement, an increase in sales resulting from enhancements in user comfort or convenience, or a reduction in potential legal action against the company?

- **Financial models do not display assumptions explicitly.** Although a number of assumptions are typically embedded within a rigorous financial analysis, they often are buried in the background details, and therefore tend to go unnoticed, as everyone tends to focus on the bottom-line results of the analysis. By explicitly bringing key characteristics to the surface, models that identify a project's nonfinancial attributes do an excellent job of enhancing everyone's understanding of what is actually involved in a given project.
- **Consideration of the intangibles can be a healthy process.** I often hear the word *intangibles* used to describe so-called *soft benefits*. Soft benefits are project attributes that are not easily translated into cash terms—nor even easily quantified at all. I have often observed that management decision-makers appreciate the opportunity to consider these intangibles when making judgments related to project prioritization and selection. Making an allowance for these intangibles to be surfaced and discussed through attribute scoring can aid in improving everyone's understanding of projects, while enhancing management's support and buy-in of the projects that are ultimately selected.
- **Nonfinancial criteria can serve as an excellent tiebreaker.** To me, this is the greatest value of attribute scoring models. It is quite possible to develop a list of proposed project opportunities in which a number of projects have similar NPVs. Acknowledging that the potential for estimating inaccuracies exists, a question must be asked: Does it really make sense to select a project with an NPV of $200,000 over a project with an NPV of $190,000 without considering other mitigating factors (namely, the intangibles we just discussed)?

Using a Strategic Framework to Identify Prioritization Attributes

A word of caution is in order here. Allowing for strategic considerations to play into the process of project evaluation and prioritization makes perfect sense. However, simply because a given project is considered to be "very consistent with company strategy," "well aligned with company strategy," or even does a commendable job in "advancing company strategy," this alone should not automatically trigger project approval. It's crucial to note that arguments such as this are qualitative, not evaluative.

And the quotation marks used above were put in there for a good reason. I have heard phrases like these used to many, many times to characterize projects. There is nothing wrong with that.

Unfortunately, I have also heard phrases such as this used many, many times to literally launch project efforts—with no additional analysis! There is something wrong with that.

I have observed that strategically based arguments on behalf of projects seem to have a certain amount of emotion attached to them. In other words, if the project is strategically aligned, it is therefore deemed to be a good thing by definition. I have seen situations where arguing in opposition to a strategic project is tantamount to heresy.

Don't get me wrong: There is nothing wrong with strategic projects—they are good and necessary things. However, for any project portfolio to be as strong as it can be, all projects should undergo a rigorous analysis using the models we discussed.

Strategic models, such as those we're about to discuss, can and should be used to trigger project ideas—this is quite consistent with the entire strategic planning process we covered in Chapter 3. However, a truly business-centric project prioritization and selection process must not include strategic considerations alone: It should always include financial considerations, tactical considerations, and operational considerations. And these should be melded together in one logical, consistent, and agreed-upon methodology.

The approaches described here are best utilized in the context of project rationale. They should be used as the impetus to trigger business needs and potential project ideas, but should not be used as the sole criterion for initiating projects.

Meets Business Objectives

Classifying a project as one that meets business objectives is surely one of the most fundamental and powerful arguments for justifying a project. This category could take on any number of forms. For example, let's say you are in the business of assembling sophisticated computer systems and that a significant amount of your company's image is based on the advertising and marketing claim that your company "can assemble and deliver entire systems with lightning fast speed."

If a project were to come along that could dramatically reduce the assembly process cycle time, it would clearly be given strong consideration because of the way it meets business objectives.

Competitive Advantage

Using the competitive advantage model, the company identifies where they might be able to create a competitive edge that will leapfrog them ahead of rival companies. The opportunity could exist within the new products arena, or it might simply be an extension or exploitation of an existing competitive advantage. Sometimes, these opportunities are born from an entirely unique set of circumstances, and are not an outgrowth of the company's strategic planning process. For example, a manufacturer of cellular phones may consider the ultra small size of their phones to have mass appeal, thereby creating a competitive advantage. Certainly, a project proposal touted as having the ability to further reduce the size of cell phones would be a strong contender in the context of this strategic model.

Competitive Necessity

This justification model is similar to competitive advantage, except that it comes at the issue from a defensive posture rather than an offensive one. The notion here is that this category of projects is mandatory if the company is to keep up with the competition. As much as any, this model underscores the need to apply a clear-headed, logical, and analytical approach. Project decisions identified in this category frequently are buoyed by fear or panic, leading to hasty or irrational judgments relative to project prioritization, selection, and approval.

Technical Necessity

Projects that fall into this model frequently include efforts that are either *enablers* or *prerequisites* to other desirable undertakings. Consider a large-scale furniture manufacturer that wishes to reduce their manufacturing costs by automating their protective-coating operation using a dozen robotic sprayers. Unfortunately, the existing computer systems are unable to support this kind of operation, particularly with regard to guiding and tracking the flow of components through this part of the manufacturing and assembly process.

Ideally, the company wishes it could simply purchase a dozen robots, plug them in the wall, and go! Obviously it's not that simple. A new computer system would have to be purchased and installed before the vision of having a fully robotic spraying operation could be realized.

Here, financial justifications can get a bit tricky. The company cannot have a robotic spraying operation without the computers, but including a computer upgrade in the business case of the robotic project might kill it. And as a stand-alone project, installing a new computer system has no direct, intrinsic financial benefits stream.

At this point, some companies may buckle under the confusion (and perhaps political pressure), and simply initiate the project without any real analysis, noting that "we really didn't have a choice here...this was a technical necessity." It's difficult to say exactly how to prepare a business case in this particular situation, but it's safe to say that the kind of thought process just described will not serve the company well as a long-term behavior.

Meets Operational Objectives

As the name suggests, this is the operations corollary to *Meets Business Objectives*. As a generic example, consider a company that manufactures one-time-use cameras. In particular, consider the cycle time to produce these cameras—that is, the total elapsed time from the moment raw materials enter the factory to the moment when packaged units are shipped to distributors.

It is quite likely that a company like this would have a long-standing operational goal to minimize the overall cycle time of that entire operation. Any number of projects might be considered justifiable because they fall within the realm of projects that meet operational objectives—in this case, to minimize cycle time.

This example offers the opportunity to describe another interesting phenomenon that can make the project justification process a bit tricky. I'm referring specifically to the phenomenon of *shared benefits*—or as some call them, *competing benefits*. These terms describe situations in which more than one project claims the same benefit. In this case, I would be willing to bet that a company like this could very well identify 10 projects, each of which promises to shave a day off the process. Each is given a green light to proceed—after all, every one is aimed at meeting a key operational objective of reducing cycle time.

Regrettably, the projects are not analyzed or financially justified (and maybe not even executed) in a coordinated fashion. The overall result: Although their cumulative effect is expected to be a 10-day cycle time reduction, the company only realizes a 4-day improvement. Why? Because several claimed the *same benefit*. And because no meaningful, coordinated analysis was performed, this fact never surfaced. Some companies are left scratching their heads and wondering why.

Research and Development

R&D is one of the trickiest strategic models to get a firm grasp on, due to the fact that a significant amount of R&D projects (particularly those involved in pure research) are frequently not tied directly or conclusively—or in a cause-and-effect manner—to specific benefit streams.

Many other R&D projects, though, exist in support of some of the other strategic models identified earlier. For example, let's go back to the manufacturer of ultra small cellular phones. A very likely candidate for a justifiable R&D project in this company would be one that includes experimentation, bench testing, and trade trials that promise to result in "a breakthrough in the company's ability to further miniaturize cell phones."

Will it happen? Who knows?

This offers the opportunity to point out yet another distinct phenomenon that occurs in many companies. Because it's largely unknown exactly what will result from this body of work, no attempt is made to analyze the situation. In my view, this is an unfortunate oversight. Because even if the numbers are very, very fuzzy, I contend that inherent benefit exists in the process of speculating possible outcomes, possible benefits, and possible costs. If nothing else, it gives company managers at least some insight regarding what they're about to get into.

In these situations, applying the value analysis process, however imperfect, can be an important move in the right direction.

Using the "Must-Do" Framework to Identify Prioritization Attributes

I have a confession: The whole concept of the "must-do" project really bugs me! But I frequently hear the following argument: "This is a project that we must do...we don't have a choice."

This is incorrect. A company always has two possible options: Do the project or don't do the project.

Although, in most cases, I will admit that the performing analysis may not change the final outcome, I once again contend the inherent value exists in performing an analysis. If nothing else, it helps the company understand what is at stake and what is the specific and quantified effect of inaction, and it can be quite enlightening with regard to risks and risk management.

With that in mind, let's take a look at some of the traditional "must-do" models for project attribute scoring.

Operational Necessity

The operational necessity model centers on the notion that, if no action is taken, the result will be some sort of failure or catastrophic event. For example, let's say a company owns a critical piece of equipment that is deemed to have an exceptionally high probability of imminent failure or breakdown. It's likely that an argument will surface that sounds like, "If we don't replace this equipment soon, this entire operation will come to a screeching halt!"

In these types of situations, it's easy to fall into a trap of complacency. Very often, the programmed response to the situation is that replacing the equipment is something that the company must do.

In reality, this kind of situation offers an opportunity for some creative thinking and some deep analysis. Questions such as: "Do we need to do this process?," "Is the system even worth saving?," and "Is there a better way to do this?" should come to the surface at this point.

Legal Mandate

An excellent example of projects related to legal mandates would be all of the provisions that companies are expected to make that satisfy laws relating to the Americans with Disabilities Act (ADA). While it is certainly true that providing accommodations for disabled persons is the right thing to do, it's also fair to say that one of the driving forces in complying with ADA laws is the legal implications (i.e., stiff penalties) associated with a company's noncompliance.

Regulatory Compliance

Many projects that fall within this justification model relate to compliance with government regulations, and in many ways these are similar to legal mandates. Complying with government regulations can take any number of forms. One common example of regulatory compliance is that a substantial amount of projects are initiated for the purpose of complying with the substantial volume of rules, regulations, and guidelines associated with pollution control and emissions permitting.

Pet Project

Perhaps the most insidious of all "must-do" projects is the *pet project*. Pet projects often are suggested by powerful organizational figures and generally lie outside of the typical processes of project identification, such as strategic or operational planning. Although these projects may be exceedingly weak from a business-justification standpoint, they are frequently difficult to kill, due to the political implications. Very few people in the organization are anxious to stand up and declare the project created by a senior manager is in fact lacking a solid business foundation. Very often, these types of projects will continue until the person who initiated them eventually recognizes that the project has little or no real merit.

AN OVERVIEW OF THE ATTRIBUTE SCORING METHODOLOGY

To me, the application of attribute scoring methods really represents the best of both worlds (financial and nonfinancial). First, it can be configured to ensure that project selection is heavily influenced by financial considerations, which is very good business. But it also allows for the fact that frailties exist in financial calculations, and therefore allows for other factors to play into the decision-making process. Further, it allows for the so-called intangibles, or soft benefits to be included in the analysis. And finally, whenever managers recognize discrepancies in their subjective evaluation of projects, the ensuing discussions can enhance everyone's understanding of projects and situations; this is quite healthy for the company.

So...What Attributes Could Be Considered?

Before considering the actual mechanics of attribute scoring, we first must consider what we will use as inputs to the process. The choice of specific attributes will be purely situational, depending on the type of projects under consideration.

Three important points about attribute scoring must be made, however:

1. Each portfolio category will have its own set of attributes.
2. To reduce later arguments, widespread consensus should exist on what represents appropriate attributes.
3. All projects within a given portfolio category must be evaluated using the same model.

Figure 6.7 lists some of the attributes that may be used in attribute scoring models. Note that several of the attributes shown are somewhat vague (e.g., impact on existing products, safety considerations, confidentiality issues). When applied in an actual scoring model, these terms must be clarified to meet specific project circumstances.

So...What Attributes Should Be Considered?

Figure 6.7 lists dozens of attributes. But which ones make sense? Which ones will provide the best chance for making good decisions regarding priority? Which ones will everyone be likely to agree on?

These are all difficult questions to answer. One approach that can be quite effective for identifying which attributes should be used is affably referred to as the *Poor Man's Hierarchy* by its creator, J. Davidson Frame. The Poor Man's Hierarchy is an adaptation of a decision-making approach called the Analytical Hierarchy Process (AHP), which was developed in the 1970s by Thomas Saaty, and described in his 1982 book, *Decision Making for Leaders*. The approach attracted widespread attention and popularity because it does an excellent job

Financial

Net present value

Internal rate of return

Payback period

Profitability index

Cash requirement

Maximum exposure

Sales & Marketing

Market size

Market share

Strategic potential

Impact on existing products

Consumer acceptance

Estimated market life

Impact on customer safety

Ongoing service requirement

Personnel/HR

Availability of labor resources

Employee acceptance

Employee satisfaction

Training requirements

Intergroup communication needs

Ability to support project internally

Change in size of workforce

Operations

Production costs

Facilities requirements

Availability of raw material

Energy requirements

Impact on existing operations

Compatibility with other processes

Safety considerations

Ability to support with existing people

Ability to support with existing technology

Required development time

Disruption to operations

Equipment/machine downtime

Required installation time

Miscellaneous

Compatibility with IT systems

Requirement for new IT support services

Vulnerability to single source supplier

Strategic alignment

Shareholder satisfaction

Compliance with government standards

Need for consulting support

Confidentiality issues

Legal considerations

Geographic considerations

FIGURE 6.7

Common attributes used in attribute scoring models.

of organizing and structuring something that is inherently riddled with subjectivity and confusion—gaining consensus from a group in expressing relative preferences.

Unfortunately, the full application of AHP can be somewhat complicated and mathematically intensive. Frame developed the Poor Man's Hierarchy as a way to introduce AHP concepts to managers in a simplified fashion. It can be used quite effectively for our purposes to identify a useful set of attributes that can be used to construct attribute scoring models. Figure 6.8 illustrates one example of how the Poor Man's Hierarchy can be applied in identifying appropriate attributes for a project in the product expansion portfolio category.

	Market size	Market share	R &D investment	After market service requirement	Cannibalization to existing products	Additional resource requirement	Payback period	Net Present Value	Patentability	Strategic alignment	Facilities requirement	Effect on company image	TOTAL SCORE
Market size	●	1	1	1	1	1	1	0	1	1	1	1	10
Market share	0	●	1	1	1	1	1	0	1	0	1	1	8
R &D investment	0	0	●	1	0	0	0	0	1	0	0	1	3
After market service requirement	0	0	0	●	0	0	0	0	0	0	0	0	0
Cannibalization to existing products	0	0	1	1	●	0	0	0	1	0	1	1	5
Additional resource requirement	0	0	1	1	1	●	0	0	1	0	1	1	6
Payback period	0	0	1	1	1	1	●	0	1	0	1	1	7
Net Present Value	1	1	1	1	1	1	1	●	1	1	1	1	11
Patentability	0	0	0	1	0	0	0	0	●	0	0	0	1
Strategic alignment	0	1	1	1	1	1	1	0	1	●	1	1	9
Facilities requirement	0	0	1	1	0	0	0	0	1	0	●	1	4
Effect on company image	0	0	0	1	0	0	0	0	1	0	0	●	2

FIGURE 6.8

Using Poor Man's Hierarchy to select attributes for evaluation of new product portfolio projects.

PUTTING IT ALL TOGETHER: THE WEIGHTED FACTOR SCORING MATRIX

One of the best methods I've found for attribute scoring is called the weighted factor scoring matrix. It can be an extremely effective of tool for project evaluation and prioritization. This is particularly true if at least one of the attributes is a reflection of the project's economic strength (personally, I prefer NPV), and if that financially based attribute is allowed to play a strong role in establishing relative priority.

Although we will revisit this tool later in the book, let's take a quick walk-through of the example shown in Figure 6.9.

In this case, we are trying to establish which project is "the best." To enable this decision, five attributes have been identified (NPV, image impact, etc.). Next, the model addresses the reality that different attrib-

Project Title	Attributes (Relative Weight)					TOTAL SCORE
	Net Present Value (0.60)	Image Impact (0.15)	# of Users Affected (0.10)	Safety Impact (0.10)	Space Required (0.05)	
Project Alpha	4 / 2.40	3 / 0.45	2 / 0.20	3 / 0.30	4 / 0.20	3.55
Project Beta	2 / 1.20	5 / 0.75	4 / 0.40	5 / 0.50	4 / 0.20	3.05
Project Omega	3 / 1.80	3 / 0.45	4 / 0.40	4 / 0.40	4 / 0.20	3.25
Project Theta	3 / 1.80	3 / 0.45	4 / 0.40	5 / 0.50	3 / 0.15	3.30

FIGURE 6.9

Example of a weighted factor scoring model.

utes really do have different levels of importance or value to accompany. Note in the matrix shown in Figure 6.9 that each attribute is assigned a "weight" with respect to other attributes.

In my experience, the model works best if the number of attributes is limited to a relatively small number, say a maximum of five or six, even though many other attributes exist. Note that in this example, the sum of all attributes totals one. This is necessary for the model to work properly. Management decision-makers should play the leading role in determining not only the attributes themselves, but the relative weights of the attributes as well.

Finally, each project is evaluated with regard to its ability to satisfy each attribute (this is the number in the upper left-hand corner of each cell). Involving key stakeholders in this process is also quite valuable.

Once the weights and the scores have been established, the rest is simple arithmetic. The weight × scores (shown in the lower right-hand corner of each cell) are added across, and voila! The "best" project emerges—the one with the largest total score.

The Advantages and Disadvantages of Attribute Scoring Models

As with any tool, the use of scoring models has advantages and disadvantages. Although we've mentioned a few of each along the way, it might be useful to compile them and list them together.

- **Advantages of using attribute scoring models:**
  - They allow for the use of multiple criteria in the decision-making process, including financial criteria.
  - They are easy to construct and to interpret.
  - They allow for management input, and are therefore a direct reflection of management's perspective.
  - They lend themselves well to "what-if" studies and sensitivity analysis. The effects of performing trade-offs between criteria is easy to model.
- **Disadvantages of using attribute scoring models:**
  - The results obtained are only a measure of the relative attractiveness among projects. There is no absolute verification that any of the alternatives identified in the model are a justifiable investment from a financial perspective.
  - The process relies almost entirely on subjective measures, thus opening it up to issues such as bias, halo effects, and reliance on opinion or judgment.
  - All attributes are assumed to be independent. No allowance is made for interdependencies between or among factors.

We will revisit this method later, as we discuss how it can be applied to the process of constructing the final project portfolio.

CHAPTER 7

Project Portfolio Management, Phase III: Selecting, Launching, and Coordinating Projects

By this stage in the process, many project ideas have been identified, investigated, and evaluated (refer to Figure 5.2). Projects have been prioritized and ranked within portfolios. Getting these projects off the ground (in a portfolio management context) will require four additional steps: (1) identify those projects that are worth pursuing; (2) determine how many of those projects can be supported with resources; (3) launch the supportable projects successfully (efficiently and at the right time); and (4) coordinate the launching of those projects in the context of a collective group, or portfolio (hence the term).

Once that has been accomplished, our focus shifts to more long-term considerations, including the need to conduct project audits as a way to continuously improve portfolio management practices.

In this chapter, we certainly address all these issues. However, we will devote the majority of our attention to methodologies and steps that are integral to the practice of project selection (steps 1 and 2). A much stronger tie exists between the world of business and the practice of project selection than between the world of business and either project launch or project coordination. Launching and coordinating projects tend to be focused more on issues of logistics. (You can find these topics covered very well in many conventional project management books and articles.)

THE PROJECT LISTING PROCESS: A REVIEW

Figure 7.1 presents a pictorial view of the key steps required to generate the initial prioritized project listing, several of which we already

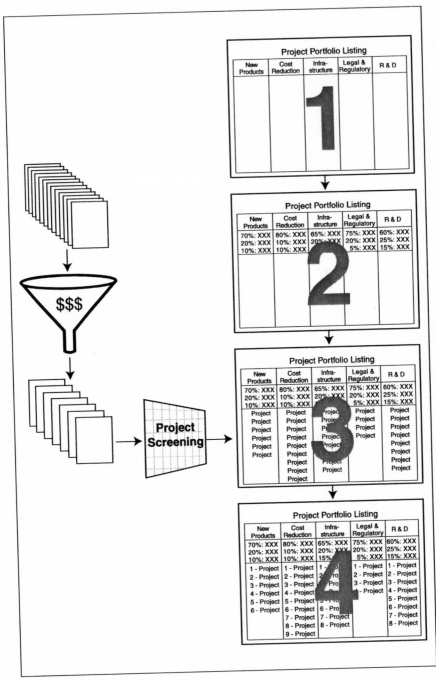

FIGURE 7.1

Basic portfolio construction is a four-step process.

discussed. One of its most notable features is the existence of *two paths*. The path on the left represents the project identification process, while the path on the right represents the process relating to the design of the portfolio structure and development of the project evaluation criteria. They are displayed separately to reinforce the notion that they should be developed separately—a point we'll discuss in this chapter. And, in fact, I believe that the design configuration of the portfolio should really be done in advance of project identification.

We already discussed the process for identifying and analyzing projects at great length in Chapter 5, so I haven't shown much detail of that part of the process in Figure 7.1. However, it's important to note that many companies still have a long way to go in using sound, rational, data-driven approaches for project identification and analysis. Even worse (and in far too many cases), project proposals are hastily assembled.

Perhaps the most severe example of this phenomenon that I've observed occurred recently, while I was delivering a project management training program at a major U.S. corporation (which shall remain nameless!).

On the first day of the program, we discussed the topic of capital budgeting and project identification. On the third and final day of the program, a senior project manager within the company's IT organization pulled me aside during lunch.

He said "Hey Gary, come over here…I want to show you something I think you'll get a charge out of!"

What he showed me was an e-mail he had just received from the company's Chief Information Officer (CIO). The e-mail indicated that $2.5 million had been freed up for IT-related projects in the forthcoming calendar year. On the surface, this seemed like good news.

However, the note went on to task this senior project manager (more or less single-handedly) with identifying a list of projects that would "use up" (the CIO's exact words) the $2.5 million that had been allocated to his group. From a business standpoint, this is *not* good news.

However, the news got worse. The project manager had 48 hours in which to fulfill this request, although the actual expenditure of the funds wouldn't happen for at least 7 months (our training class was in May). As most of us are aware, 7 months in the world of information technology can seem like an eternity, given the constant churn of technology.

Believe it or not, this situation grew even more grave. Because as our conversation continued, the project manager informed me that the cost and schedule estimates for the projects he was about to identify (which, of course, he had no time to investigate, analyze, or plan in any meaningful way) would be the estimates he would be expected to live up to later!

Admittedly, this is an extreme example. But it is a real-life example of how the capital budgeting process still plays out in some companies.

Returning to our study of sound portfolio development, focus your attention on one particular process step that appears in Figure 7.1. It's a step that we'll be discussing in just a bit, and it pertains to the process of selecting the final set of candidates for project prioritization. Symbolized by a funnel with dollar signs, this step is positioned to accomplish a very specific and critically important purpose—to ensure that the only projects permitted to enter the portfolio prioritization stage are those which are financially justified. Financial justification is a key term and concept that we'll examine shortly. The project screening step serves a similar purpose (we'll also be discussing project screening a bit later in the chapter).

The document shown at the bottom of Figure 7.1 is the key deliverable for this phase of the portfolio construction process—a list of projects that have been categorized and prioritized. As Figure 7.1 points out, this document is developed through a four-step process:

1. Identify a logical set of project groupings or portfolio categories
2. Identify the criteria that will be used to prioritize the projects within each portfolio category
3. Place all financially justified projects into the appropriate portfolio categories
4. Prioritize the projects within each portfolio category

Many of the basic methodologies that are integral to accomplishing these four steps were covered in Chapters 5 and 6. As we seek to finalize the portfolio, a few more subtle factors will help us solidify our understanding of project portfolio construction.

SELECTING THE BEST PROJECTS AND CONSTRUCTING THE FINAL PORTFOLIO LISTING

OK...so we've entered the final phase in the creation of one of the most important single documents in the entire portfolio management process—the final (or "official") portfolio listing. For companies that follow an annual planning cycle (which most companies do), this document is recreated every year (or per any other planning cycle). The document that I'm referring to, which will presumably be published and distributed across the company upon its completion, is a structured, organized, and approved list of projects. More to the point, it is a list that contains the specific set of projects to be pursued in the forthcoming year with a reasonable chance of obtaining the necessary resources. Although it may seem superfluous, the qualifying remark about "obtaining the necessary resources" is important.

It is not unusual for companies to identify many more projects than they are capable of effectively pursuing—from the standpoint of human resources as well as from a budgetary perspective. Many companies, in their eagerness to accomplish as much as they possibly can, tend to ignore (or just not fully appreciate) this point. In reality, both these potential constraints should be viewed as important considerations when considering which projects to place on the final portfolio list. Companies must strive to ensure that every project placed on the "official" project list will have the necessary cash and human resources available when the time comes. This helps avoid subsequent confusion and inefficiency. Experience has demonstrated time and time again that pursuing too many projects at a time often has the effect of slowing down all projects. Thus, allowing the practice of allowing so-called "rogue projects" can be inherently unhealthy to a company's otherwise well-oiled project and portfolio management machines. This topic is covered in more detail when we get to the concept of project authorization.

UNDERSTANDING THE DIFFERENCE BETWEEN JUSTIFICATION, SELECTION, AND AUTHORIZATION

As we discuss how final decisions are made with regard to developing the portfolio and deploying the projects in it, we should take the time to clarify some commonly used terms that frequently come into play during this stage.

Justification (or Financial Justification)

In most project management circles, the term *justification* is really short for *financial justification*. As you may recall, Chapter 6 covered several models for evaluating and prioritizing projects. It's crucial to note that only one category of models—the financial models—can truly lay claim to formally and literally justifying management's formal approval of a project from an economic standpoint. All other models can certainly assist management decision-makers in making comparisons between projects, but none can answer the question of whether it makes good business sense to pursue any of them.

Financial justification is relatively straightforward in nature. Any project whose net present value (NPV) is greater than zero, whose internal rate of return (IRR) is greater than the weighted average cost of capital (WACC), or whose profitability index is greater than 1 are all considered to be prudent investments from a purely financial standpoint. Notwithstanding the concerns over potential inaccuracies in the estimating process, this point is absolute and indisputable. It also represents the formal meaning of the term "justified project," or as many say, "financially justified project."

Selection (or Selection Criteria)

Not surprisingly, *selection* refers to a set of methodologies directed at choosing which specific projects are to be pursued within a given time frame. The methods and criteria for making these choices can vary. However, any method used to select projects—other than financial justification—must be recognized as not only comparative, but also inherently subjective in nature. These approaches are designed to represent decision-makers' preferences—they do not determine whether a given project is financially justified. This is a key point, because one of the more difficult portions of the project selection process consists of identifying the criteria by which projects are selected. If the selection process is not rooted in the principle of financial justification, the result may be the perpetual selection of projects that, over time, fall short in facilitating a company's quest to achieve its business objectives.

It's very important to understand the relationship between justification and selection—and to understand their implication at this stage in the process. So at the risk of being repetitive, please allow me to take a shot at doing that now:

The concept of project justification is financially based and is absolute. The process of project selection is not necessarily this way. More to the point, they are not equivalent terms. For example, it is quite possible that some projects could be financially justified, yet not selected. This occurs most often when a company is able to identify an extensive list of very strong projects. Many projects are justifiable, but an insufficient quantity of cash or human resources (or both) exists to support them all. In a way, this is a good thing.

Conversely (and unfortunately, in the case of far too many companies), some projects may be selected that are not justified. This occurs most often in companies that do not believe in—or do not wish to expend the effort to perform—rigorous financial analyses. I suspect that nearly anyone would recognize that this is a bad situation from a business standpoint, but I must say that I have found this phenomenon alarmingly prevalent. Other forms of selection criteria, such as scoring models, are based on preference and are not absolute.

Judgments are made based on factors other than financial considerations, are reflective of decision-makers' opinions, and adhere to the notion that acceptable projects must meet some sort of minimum pass criteria (presumably determined in advance). It is quite possible that some projects could be selected, yet not financially justified.

One company, for example, was pursuing more than 50 projects at the time they called me in to work with them. For the most part, the company had chosen to "select" these projects because all seemed like very good ideas. They had, in fact, not taken the time to substantiate whether these projects were financially justified. To me, this represented an enormous red flag. Over a period of about 3 weeks, I worked alongside their project teams to perform a financial analysis of every one of the projects. Admittedly, these analyses were not overly rigorous, but they were certainly sufficient to provide us with directional information and valuable insight.

When the dust finally cleared, more than half (27 to be exact) did not have positive NPVs! Needless to say, these findings were an eye-opener for this company; what they soon came to realize was that they had actually been paying out money for the privilege of pursuing these 27 projects.

Authorization (or Approval)

In many ways, selection and authorization are similar concepts. However, two critical distinctions must be made regarding the specific act of project authorization.

The first is recognizing the integral relationship that exists between the project authorization process and specific steps of project funding and project initiation. Even though a given project may have been selected and listed in the portfolio of projects, technically speaking, it has not yet been authorized to begin. In fact, many projects that are selected as part of the portfolio building process may have to wait several weeks (or months) until funds are released to support project initiation. Companies often stagger the launch of projects as a way to control the flow of cash and to help regulate the allocation of human resources. They develop what may best be referred to as a *project launch sequence* or *project launch plan*, which not only identifies which projects have been selected, but exactly when those projects are authorized to begin. We revisit this topic a bit later in the chapter.

The second critical distinction of project authorization does not relate so much to a specific project process, but to the notion of controlling (and in effect, limiting) which projects people are formally permitted to work on. Especially important in companies in which resource management is a critical issue, the identification of "formally authorized" projects has another meaning beyond funding approval. It implies that employees should not be working on any unauthorized projects.

Which brings us back to the subject of *rogue projects* (I love that term!).

Companies that must confront the issue of resource shortages may actually be well-advised to elevate this interpretation of formal authorization to a policy-level issue. The company should make it well known that working on a project that is not on the authorized list of projects is unacceptable. Although this might appear dictatorial and overcontrolling, its logic is based in good business sense.

For example, consider the case of one company that I had the pleasure of working with a short while ago. With the help of some coaching and other support, they performed quite admirably in identifying an official, formally funded project list. They did all the right things: They calculated NPVs, ranked their projects using both financial and nonfinancial criteria, and prepared rough-order-of-magnitude estimates to identify resource needs. Ultimately, they were able to identify the most valuable project efforts, including only those projects for which they had funding and resources. All was right with the world until...

The company president issued a statement suggesting that any employees who had "extra time" were free to pursue any other efforts (a.k.a., small projects) that they thought would add value. Unfortunately, this had the effect of opening the floodgates for rogue projects. Soon, people began not showing up for team meetings on projects that were in the official project listing. Formally authorized projects began to slow down considerably. Chaos ensued.

The company didn't really know where its money was being spent, and a number of more valuable things (i.e., financially justified projects) were not getting done. But what bothered me the most, however, was that the process of identifying the most critical projects—an important, rational, data-driven methodology that had taken time, effort, and money—had been severely compromised. This is not good project management, and it certainly is not good business.

The lesson to be learned is obvious: When constructing your final list of projects, make sure it is clearly understood that no other project work should be pursued besides that which has been carefully analyzed and authorized—the "official" project listing. If left unchecked, the phenomenon of rogue projects can easily become widespread enough to have a serious negative impact on the company's ability to successfully execute its carefully chosen portfolio of projects.

AVOIDING THE "SELECTED, BUT NOT JUSTIFIED" SYNDROME

Earlier, we discussed how the methods some companies use for portfolio construction can allow for the selection of projects that are not financially strong. Some companies are actually paying to do projects. It may sound far-fetched, but it can happen. In fact, it happens far too often.

How can this situation be avoided? Actually, the most effective approach for avoiding this possibility—and winding up with a project ranking you can be proud of—is really quite simple and is used effectively in many companies. It consists of three basic elements:

- **Allow only financially justified projects into the final project portfolio ranking process.** Very simply, don't waste everyone's time and energy investigating, evaluating, and prioritizing projects that should not see the light of day in the first place. To ensure that this is an effective screening measure, however, companies must develop the capability to perform sound financial analyses on proposed projects. The value of these financial analyses depends highly on a company's ability to properly model cash flows, being careful to identify and estimate all direct and indirect financial impacts related to a project.

    It is absolutely vital that project teams participate fully in the cash flow modeling process. It is also necessary that you correctly perform the financial calculations. In this regard, you are well advised to the get members of your company's finance department intimately involved in this aspect of the process, if they are not already.

- **Use a weighted factor scoring matrix to help establish final rankings.** This process allows for the introduction and consideration of nonfinancial criteria as part of the ranking process. Make sure that the factors used in the scoring matrix are chosen using a rational process that includes the significant participation (and buy-in) of a cross-sectional group within the company, and that these factors are agreed upon in advance by management decision-makers (this important point is discussed in detail next).

- **Favor financial criteria when establishing relative weighting.** You should give financial criteria (such as NPV) a relatively large amount of weight—somewhere around 60 to 80% is probably a good idea. This is an excellent way of ensuring that the project selection process is strongly influenced by financial considerations, but it allows sufficient room for the appropriate nonfinancial criteria to serve a useful role as "mitigating factors."

APPLYING PROJECT SCREENING TECHNIQUES

The act of eliminating projects that are not financially justified is really just one manifestation of a larger process called *project screening*. In fact, some companies take the screening process well beyond the financial justification restriction. At times, company managers want the projects in their portfolio to possess certain positive characteristics or not possess certain negative characteristics.

To be certain this happens, project screening techniques are utilized. Figure 7.1 suggests the most logical place for project screening within the overall portfolio construction process. By positioning the screening step there, a significant amount of time and effort is saved by ensuring that undesirable projects are eliminated from the process before the project prioritization process begins. Two popular variations of project screening techniques are described in the next sections.

Imposing Specific Constraints

Using this approach, the addition of any given project to the final portfolio listing is contingent upon the satisfaction of certain conditions. In most cases, these conditions are specific constraints that the company imposes on all projects. For example, a company may develop a mandate that states "No project will be authorized if its implementation could result in a potential degradation of product quality, as perceived by the end user."

Perhaps a bit wordy, but hopefully you get the point.

Constraints may be imposed for a variety of reasons. Most often, they are imposed to satisfy a given set of operating conditions (such as limited internal resources), to preclude the possibility of undesirable trade-offs (such as the "degradation of quality" mandate above), or simply because a company wants its project portfolio to possess certain characteristics that are perceived as desirable (such as the ability to market any new product internationally).

Specific examples of project constraints might include:

- Must have an NPV in excess of $_____
- Must have an internal rate of return in excess of ____%
- Must have a payback period of less than ____ years
- Must not require more than ____% outsourced labor
- Must have a long-term potential of achieving a minimum ____% market share
- Must be able to utilize existing distribution channels
- Must not result in significant cannibalization of existing products
- Must not require the use of patents other than our own

- Must not be perceived as being detrimental to the local community
- Must not precipitate significant legal exposure or risk

Some caution may have to be exercised to ensure that the imposition of constraints is not used to promote relatively isolated opinions or to advance the political agenda of a relatively small group within the company. If done properly, imposing constraints on projects can be an appropriate, meaningful, and useful method of project screening.

The Murder Board Approach

As we observed, all claims, assertions, predictions, and even estimates should be subject to scrutiny by the group participating in the project evaluation and scoring process. The Murder Board approach is really an extension of this philosophy.

The approach consists of assembling a panel of reviewers. This panel should have representation from all relevant departments within the company, and it should be a group different from the group that ultimately prioritizes and ranks projects. Essentially, this group plays a role very similar to that of an investigative reporter. Their mission is to put project proposals and their associated business cases through extremely rigorous scrutiny (obviously, this is to be done in a constructive and nonthreatening manner).

The objective is to ensure the project proposals and business cases have been tightened up; that is, to verify claims, substantiate the validity of estimates, and test all logical arguments upon which project proposals are based. This can be a very effective method for screening weak business cases, and in particular, projects that may have surfaced for the wrong reasons.

GUIDELINES FOR ADMINISTERING AN EFFECTIVE PROJECT PRIORITIZATION PROCESS

We have discussed some of the specific tools, models, and methods for evaluating and prioritizing projects. But what can be done to ensure that the overall process goes smoothly? Here are some general guidelines, which may help you work through the project ranking and selection process as rationally and logically as possible—particularly if it's your company's first time:

- **Design the selection process (including selection criteria)** *before* **specific projects are identified.** Once the portfolio configuration has been determined, projects can be placed into those portfolios, and the process of evaluating the relative attractiveness of projects within each portfolio can begin. However, it may prove valuable to develop the scoring system (the methods and criteria for determining relative attractiveness of projects within each portfolio category) before any specific projects have been identified. This may reduce the possibility of introducing manipulation or political influencing into the process. To be blunt, be aware that those with favorite projects may be tempted to adjust the scoring system in a way that ensures that their project "wins."

- **Be certain all decision-makers fully understand the procedure.** A very unfortunate situation can result—and a considerable amount time can be wasted—when it is discovered that the results of the project scoring process are of little or no value because participants didn't properly follow guidelines or didn't really understand the definitions, ground rules, or the overall process itself.
- **Seek consensus in the validity of the process and the selection criteria.** It is imperative that a reasonable level of cross-functional consensus is established with respect to the validity of the approach used for project selection and ranking. If a substantial proportion of the decision-making group does not have faith in the value or reliability of the process, it is very likely they might abandon the process altogether and simply begin "flying by the seat of their pants," should difficulties arise. In addition, any individual decision-makers who have not truly bought into the scoring approach are more prone to "fudge the numbers" during the scoring process.
- **Be certain decision-makers are knowledgeable about the projects.** I once observed what I thought was a well-designed project evaluation and selection process that utilized a well-structured, well-designed decision-making model. A series of weighted-factor decision matrices were used as scoring sheets and were distributed to management decision-makers. The group proceeded to independently score each project against the developed criteria. One of the outcomes was dramatically different scores across the group on a few of the projects. After some open discussion, it was quite apparent that a significant variation existed in the decision-makers knowledge and understanding of what these projects were all about. From that moment on, formal project briefings became an integral part of the overall process for making final project portfolio selections.
- **Follow the prescribed process unfailingly.** It can be quite tempting for some participants to vary from the process and

launch into tangents in the middle of the scoring process, while discussions are taking place about potential projects. This is not the time to start rethinking prior work or generating new ideas. Another interesting challenge you may face is ensuring that powerful organizational figures also follow procedures unfailingly—which, at times, may be a difficult and sensitive task.

- **Provide for an open review of the scoring.** Remember, some criteria used for project scoring will be subjective in nature and subject to issues such as perceptions and feelings. One of the greatest opportunities for a learning, open dialog, and a healthy exchange of ideas comes when management decision-makers have the opportunity to openly compare their scores on projects.

- **Establish a climate in which claims can be challenged.** All claims, assertions, predictions, estimates, and even data should be considered to be open to scrutiny by the group participating in the project evaluation and scoring process. In my experience, it is quite common for estimates to be understated and benefits to be overstated at this juncture. Remember that this may be a company-wide process, with project proposals coming from several different departments. It is not uncommon for distortions to occur in a project's assumption base. It's not uncommon, in fact, for claims to be "amplified" in proportion to how avidly presenters feel about seeing their project survive.

- **Make sure those involved in selecting projects are the "real" decision-makers.** If you fail to get the right people involved in the process the first time around, don't be surprised if you must perform radical surgery on your project list, or worse, must do the process a second time using the right participants. If the process is set up in such a way that the outputs from one group must be sanctioned by a second, higher group, this is an indication that you are not dealing with the real decision-makers. This situation should be avoided whenever possible.

KNOWING WHERE TO DRAW THE LINE: IT'S ALL ABOUT LIMITATIONS

Figure 7.2 is a simplified representation of what a basic portfolio listing might look like. The dotted line portrays the final step in the basic portfolio construction process. As the figure points out, a "cutoff line" must be identified within each portfolio group. Projects above the line are authorized; the projects below the line are not. Not all projects will be selected. The reason for this is tied to limitations—most notably, limitations in cash and limitation in human resources.

Project Portfolio Listing

New Products	Cost Reduction	Infra-structure	Legal and Regulatory	R&D
70%: XXX	80%: XXX	65%: XXX	75%: XXX	60%: XXX
20%: XXX	10%: XXX	20%: XXX	20%: XXX	25%: XXX
10%: XXX	10%: XXX	15%: XXX	5%: XXX	15%: XXX
1 - Project	1 - Project	1 - Project	1 - Project	1 - Project
2 - Project	2 - Project	2 - Project	2 - Project	2 - Project
3 - Project	3 - Project	3 - Project	3 - Project	3 - Project
4 - Project	4 - Project	4 - Project	4 - Project	4 - Project
5 - Project	5 - Project	5 - Project		5 - Project
6 - Project	6 - Project	6 - Project		6 - Project
	7 - Project	7 - Project		7 - Project
	8 - Project	8 - Project		8 - Project
	9 - Project			

[dashed box] = Total organizational allocation

FIGURE 7.2

Drawing the line: recognizing limitations.

Financial Limitations

Very early in this chapter, we discussed the practice of capital rationing. Simply stated, this is the practice by which companies limit the amount of funds they are willing to invest in projects. Therefore, one way to determine where the line should be drawn very simply comes down to the question of at what point the company runs out of money. Typically, companies will allocate a certain percentage of the overall available financing to each portfolio category. This allocation should be reflective of the company's strategic objectives. For example, the company whose primary competitive strategy is product leadership (remember Treacy and Wiersema?) is likely to allocate a significant amount of funds to a category such as new product development. Conversely, the company whose primary competitive strategy is operational excellence is likely to allocate a large portion of its overall funds to the cost-reduction portfolio.

Resource Limitations

This form of limitation is coming to the forefront as a critical factor in more and more companies. As the quest to be "lean and mean" intensifies, having a sufficient quantity of people to execute projects is a legitimate concern. Consequently, it is unusual for some companies to draw the line in their project listing at the place at which they run out of resources—specifically, people. If the company wishes to pursue more projects that the size of the existing resource base will allow, it must consider options to develop specific plans around the prospect of outsourcing some of their project work.

Unfortunately, far too many companies either ignore or are oblivious to the issue of resource limitations. This type of behavior often results in a pattern of chronic project delays and late deliveries, because the resources assigned to all of the projects simply cannot keep up.

CONDUCTING A FINAL PORTFOLIO REVIEW

The process of identifying the specific set of projects that will be included in the forthcoming year's portfolio is just about done. It's worth noting that these project proposals may have arrived at this point from any number of different directions. For the most part, we have been examining projects as relatively independent entities. Since the overall project portfolio has only recently "come together," we must recognize that we have not spent a tremendous amount of time considering the portfolio as a whole.

With that in mind, this represents an excellent time to review the portfolio. A final portfolio review may encompass many aspects and might be examined from a number of different angles. However, two of the most important issues that must definitely be considered are *interproject dependencies* and *overall portfolio balance*.

Make Sure You Consider Project Dependencies

When making final portfolio selections, the nature of the dependencies that exist between projects must be considered. Relationships between projects can assume any of these four basic forms:

- **Independent projects.** In this situation, the choice of any one project has no direct effect on the selection of any other project. This is the most common circumstance in project portfolio construction and typically is not cause for alarm.
- **Contingent projects.** In this situation, the choice of one project dictates that one or more other projects also must be selected, if

some set of overall objectives is to be satisfied. When this situation occurs, contingent projects should be combined into a program that can be managed in a coordinated, logistically sound way. More important, though, is that this program must be financially justified and authorized. The projects that comprise the program also should be visibly grouped and identified as a program within the project portfolio listing. From time to time, this approach is subject to abuse through the practice of *piggybacking*. Here, a weak project (that would probably otherwise not have been selected) is inappropriately attached to a very strong project. Obviously, this practice should be discouraged.

- **Counteracting projects.** In this situation, the choice of one project may be counterproductive to another project within the portfolio. This particular phenomenon is one of the most important reasons to review the total portfolio prior to its formal release. This situation also may exist within a given project. It is quite possible to encounter a situation in which one particular segment of the company (a department or work flow process, for example) may be adversely affected by the implementation of a project. Unfortunately, though, the adverse effects have been ignored (either unintentionally or intentionally) during project analysis. This phenomenon can be prevalent in large companies, particularly within companies that have adopted a system of localized, independent methods for measuring and rewarding departmental performance.
- **Mutually exclusive projects.** In this situation, the choice must be made between two or more projects that are often characterized as *competing* projects. In this case, the projects are vying to satisfy the same business objective. Although this is an unlikely situation in project portfolio construction, it can occur. When it does occur, a side-by-side evaluation should be performed. The most attractive project should be selected, while the others should be eliminated from the portfolio.

Make Sure You Consider Portfolio Balance

In Chapter 6, we discussed that one of the key attributes of a strong project portfolio is to achieve some sort of relative balance across the entire portfolio. Referring to Figure 6.2, you may recall that we identified the following dimensions of balance:

- Strategic balance
- Product balance
- Market balance

- Business unit balance
- Geographic balance
- Technology balance
- Risk balance (severity)
- Risk balance (type)
- Resource balance
- Investment balance (size)
- Investment balance (type)

The concept of balance in the project portfolio simply means that the overall portfolio should reflect some level of *proportionality* across these dimensions of balance. Further, the proportionality should reflect how the company is operated. For example, a company pursuing a product leader strategy would seek a higher proportion of high-risk projects and high-technology projects. Conversely, the company pursuing a strategy of operational excellence might have the opposite proportion in these particular portfolio dimensions.

It's important to note that the term balance is not intended to convey the notion of equality. Take the dimension of project size, for example. The concept of maintaining balance in project size does not mean that an equal number of small, medium, or large projects must exist. Similarly, in the area of risk, the term relative balance does not necessarily mean that an equal number of low- and high-risk projects is the goal.

DEVELOPING A PROJECT LAUNCH SEQUENCE

We've finally come to the point where we have a final project portfolio listing! We have identified, analyzed, evaluated, and ultimately selected the specific set of projects that we intend to tackle "next year." And we're anxious to get started.

This sentiment often leads to the phenomenon of *front-end loading*. This refers to the situation in which everyone intends to begin working on their projects on January 1 (if their planning cycle follows the calendar year). In most cases, this happens because a number of the projects in the portfolio are driven by several different departments across the company, and each department is anxious to get its projects initiated as soon as possible in the calendar year.

A noble intention, but one very big problem exists with this situation.

Although it's true that these departments (and their projects) are largely independent on an organization chart, they are ordinarily required to share the same pool of resources—which includes cash as well as human resources.

On the cash side, the issue is primarily one of balanced spending. Generally, companies try to maintain their spending rate at a reasonably consistent rate. Obviously, if a mad dash occurs to execute all projects immediately after the ball drops in Times Square, a disproportionately large amount of spending takes place in the early part of the year. For many companies, this is not desirable.

As far as human resources are concerned, the dilemma is obvious. When project personnel are spread too thin (in this case, by virtue of working on too many projects), all active projects tend to slow down, and inefficiencies begin to creep in. This, of course, is an equally undesirable situation.

This dilemma can be resolved through the preparation of a *project launch sequence*, which is the intentional staggering of project start dates throughout the calendar year. The primary objective of this practice is to smooth out the expenditure of funds and the utilization of resources as much as possible. Since each individual department is anxious to get its projects started, the development (and perhaps the enforcement) of the project launch sequence must be administered by a different group. If your company has a project management office, this is a logical function for that group.

CONSIDERATIONS DURING PROJECT INITIATION

The intention of this book is to cover issues related to business, and the interface between projects in the world of business. Accordingly, the purpose of this particular topic is not to address the various methods and approaches for initiating projects. Many project management texts, articles, and other reference materials are available to offer detailed descriptions on the various procedures relating to the project initiation process, such as team-building, enlisting a project sponsor, conducting a kick-off meeting, and so forth.

However, a few items *do* have business implications. These really are just some "good practices" that I suggest you consider as part of your overall project initiation procedure. As you'll see, they may be particularly useful in light of the project launch sequence. Occasionally, a considerable gap can exist between the time the project is listed in the portfolio and the time when the project is actually launched. In my view, these practices may have the potential to impact the effectiveness of your project, thereby adding more value to the company.

Revisit the Project's Financial Justification and Business Case

Undoubtedly, your project's economic analysis (and subsequent financial justification) was not based on perfect information. It was based on estimates, the opinions of various subject matter experts, and many, many assumptions. As part of your project initiation procedure—and well before significant resources are committed to the project—consider reviewing and validating the entire assumption based upon which the project was initially justified. This applies to the project's business case as well, assuming one had been prepared.

Revalidate Project Objectives with Customer

Although this is a subset of the assumption base just discussed, I believe that this step is worthy of special mention. In addition to having the value of revalidating assumptions relating to customer objectives, the step can have a useful secondary value. It can provide the kind of "jump start" in the process of building your knowledge of the project's customer and their business.

Verify Resource Availability

Ordinarily, your company pursues several projects at once. Many of these projects will move faster or slower than originally planned. Some projects may be added or removed from the portfolio. Some may be on hold. Meanwhile, the launch of others may be delayed.

All these possibilities point to the same conclusion: Although resource availability may have been considered at the time your project was selected, that certainly does not guarantee that these resources will be available in the right quantities for the project you are about to launch. So, as people come onto the project team, I strongly urge you to verify that each one of them will have the necessary time to devote to your project effort. One of the largest errors of omission that occurs during project initiation is bypassing this step, assuming that, just because resources have been assigned to work on the project, they are able to devote the appropriate amount of time.

Make Sure Team Members Are Knowledgeable of the Customer and Their Business

A project manager who possesses a deep knowledge and understanding of the project's customer and his business has tremendous value in ensuring that the project is properly guided. In many cases, the same can be said regarding project team members.

Earlier, we discussed how customers are beginning to rely on project teams to address their long-term business problems. Project managers are well advised to enlist the support of the entire project team in carrying out this mission. To do this will require a significant amount of customer knowledge across the entire project team.

Consider Identifying a Few Business-Based Project Metrics

For years, companies that "did project management well" set up metrics to help them gain a higher level of understanding with regard to their ability to meet cost and schedule targets. As we discussed in Chapter 1, the world is changing. "Doing project management well" now goes beyond excellent cost and schedule performance. Future measures of project success will begin focusing more and more on the measurement of business results—metrics that are more closely tied to the bottom-line than project cost and schedule results.

With this in mind, you should begin the process of identifying those metrics that do not simply measure cost and schedule performance. Consider identifying and tracking metrics that are tied to business impact. In many cases, these kinds of metrics can be identified by examining the project's business case, where claims of positive business results are most likely to reside.

Coordinating the Overall Project Portfolio

It is not unusual for companies to execute projects at any given time. Managing the overall portfolio—which simply consists of providing coordination across the individual projects in the portfolio—is an activity that is well worth the time invested. For some companies, the challenge is in trying to figure out who will actually be doing what. This is an ideal activity for the project management office.

Issues such as addressing resource conflicts, managing interdependencies between projects (functional- or deliverable-oriented), and redirecting individual projects as needed to maintain portfolio balance, are all efforts that can lead to a higher level of overall portfolio effectiveness.

In the long run, however, portfolio coordination is largely an issue of logistics. A significant amount of reference materials is available if you would like to understand more about the topic of portfolio coordination.

CONDUCT POST-PROJECT (AND PORTFOLIO) AUDITS

Despite what Figure 5.2 portrays, the overall portfolio management process is not really done until *after* the individual projects in the portfolio have been completed! It is widely recognized that the full spectrum of excellence in project management includes post-project audits: the practice of examining the actual results of projects after completion, searching for ways to improve the overall project process. Companies deeply involved in project portfolio management recognize that the same principle holds true for *project portfolio audits*. The practice of conducting project portfolio audits is in its infancy.

A significant amount of reference material is available to describe in detail how to conduct in-process as well as post-project audits on individual projects. But, once again, although much of the material addresses the individual project audit process, the intent is to make you think about the implications of that process on the way the company manages its overall project portfolio.

The Basic Components of the Auditing Process

Before we get too specific about the auditing process, let's go up 50,000 feet and take a look at the auditing process. At the highest level, we recognize just two basic components to auditing: (1) *comparing* predictions against actual results; and (2) *explaining the differences* between predictions and actual results.

Comparing Predictions against Actual Results

When we examine how to perform a financial analysis on a project (Chapters 8 and 9), we will observe that decisions regarding those projects that should be selected and exactly what is expected from those projects are based largely upon predictions. Once a given project has transitioned into the project outcome life cycle (remember our discussions from Chapters 1 and 2?), a very logical question becomes, "Just how accurate were those predictions?"

The answer to this question should be examined in the context of two very different—but equally valid—dimensions:

Accuracy Dimension #1: Performance Results. This metric really addresses the question of the functional impact (presumably positive) that a given project is expected to have on a company or organization. The specific elements found within the dimension are ordinarily the drivers behind benefits claims. Examples of some typical predictions of performance results may include:

- An increase in sales
- An increase in operating effectiveness (i.e., higher yields)
- A simplified process
- A reduction in material usage or waste
- An increase in work output

As part of the financial justification process, these predictions then are translated and expressed in terms of financial results. This leads us to the second accuracy dimension.

Accuracy Dimension #2: Financial Impact. All the examples of performance results identified above certainly seem desirable. Taken by themselves, however, questions abound: How desirable are these performance improvements? Exactly how do they benefit the company? How can we effectively compare one set of performance results with another set of performance results?

Many of these questions can be answered effectively if we translate performance results into financial results. This is the essence of Chapter 9, where we examine the process of performing a financial analysis on an actual project.

A dilemma exists, however. One of the key factors that renders the financial analysis a somewhat controversial subject is tied directly to concerns over the validity of the input numbers used in the analysis. As is the case with just about any analytical process, higher-quality input values produce a higher-quality result.

This is precisely why companies must commit themselves to excellence when it comes to this accuracy dimension. As a metric of auditing, this dimension helps us understand how accurately we are able to translate the stated claims of functional improvements into dollars and cents. Few would argue that this is a very difficult thing to do, which leads us right back to the controversy discussed at the beginning of Chapter 9. For our purposes in this chapter, it can be extremely useful to make this kind of evaluation an integral component of our auditing process.

Explaining the Differences between Predictions and Actual Results

This is, of course, the logical extension of the process of comparing predictions and results. If you are familiar with the practice of conducting "lessons-learned" on projects, you undoubtedly recognize and appreciate the value in being able to explain why differences exist between predictions and actual results. Gaining an understanding of exactly why these differences have occurred is a necessary element in any continuous improvement process.

Unfortunately, however, gaining that understanding can be extremely challenging (and, at times, perhaps even impossible!). This may become more apparent when we discuss problems and issues related to auditing a bit later.

The Benefits of Auditing

Once again, if you are someone who has participated in conducting lessons-learned at the individual project level, you are very familiar with the inherent benefits of that process, which is really just post-project auditing. In many ways, the benefits of auditing at the project portfolio level are similar to those of the individual project auditing process. Here are a few of the more notable benefits:

Improves Forecasting Techniques

Auditing improves forecasting techniques. It enhances the benefits side of cash flow modeling and assists those people whose job it is to estimate the anticipated benefits stream of proposed projects. Comparing actual benefits received to projected benefits (several years into the project outcome life cycle) can be very insightful for those who must generate forecasts. It is particularly valuable when the same group is responsible for estimating the benefits of a particular type(s) of project over a long period.

For example, I worked with one company that had amassed a significant string of disappointing projects. All were related to new-product development projects. Eventually, the company realized that their marketing department (which was responsible for generating the company's new-product sales forecasts) had chronically over-stated the appeal of these products. No one outside the marketing department was really looking at the evidence. However, if an open, systematic, and objective auditing process had existed, one that included comparisons of predicted sales forecasts to actual sales forecasts, there is little doubt that this situation would have been uncovered much, much earlier. This would have averted what nearly became a legitimate financial crisis.

Improves Estimating Techniques

Many companies adhere to the practice of estimating project costs as part of cash flow modeling. Unfortunately, far too many companies have a project process in which those people who prepare project cost estimates have little or nothing to do with project execution. This can be a big problem at times, particularly if the estimators do not have a significant amount of project experience or won't have responsibility for project execution.

If this custom creates problems, it can be revealed not by simply comparing variances between estimated costs and actual costs, but by also reconciling them (i.e., trying to explain them away). This is not always done as well as it could be, due to one peculiar phenomenon: When projects exceed their budget, a tendency often exists to "direct attention" (a euphemistic term for blame) to the project team's performance and not to the accuracy of the original estimate. In many cases, the reality is that the original estimates were flawed, especially if they were produced under duress.

In cases in which the estimating process is to blame, systematic auditing and objective reconciliation allows for valuable information to feed back into the company, thus improving the quality of estimating procedures over time. This can yield large economic benefits for companies and organizations.

Improve Assumption Methods and Approaches

This benefit of auditing is pretty obvious. Project proposals are built largely on assumptions. And in many respects, the practice of generating assumptions is an art and science unto itself. Companies that routinely compare the accuracy of their baseline assumptions put themselves in an excellent position to improve the quality of their assumptions over time. Although the term assumption is often thought of as an issue that exists at the project level, it can also pertain to portfolio management, encompassing those assumptions made about reasonable portfolio size, level of interaction between projects, quantity and severity of intraproject resource conflicts, and many other issues.

Strengthen Decision-Making Models

A methodology (either formal or informal) usually exists in the way that decisions are made by a company or an organization. Unfortunately, it can be difficult to measure the validity of the decision-making approach itself. However, when any specific (poor) decision is made, an objective analysis of "why did we decide to do that?" often can have great value. In many cases, this analysis consists of examining those elements that comprise the decision-making process and that led to the poor decision, such as:

- The types of risk factors considered (or not considered)
- How those risk factors played into the decision
- The reliability of certain mathematical models, if any were used
- The use of objective (versus subjective) input data
- Who was allowed to participate in the decision-making process
- The speed at which the decision was made

Improved Operations

This may strike you as a curious benefit. Admittedly, it is a bit theoretical in nature, but let me try to explain the theory behind it: Generally speaking, projects are approved because they benefit the company. These benefits usually assume the form of improvements in operating performance. Whenever the improved performance is based even partially on forecasts and predictions made by people who work in a company, these people often feel they have put their reputation on the line. Knowing that the validity of their predictions will be measured can create—for some—a strong incentive to live up to what they've promised.

Identify New Opportunities

This may also strike you as an unusual benefit, but it really just reinforces an activity that all companies should be pursuing. Many projects represent a particular direction that the company is taking, or an initiative that the company is pursuing. This could refer to the implementation of a new process, the application of a new methodology, or even a forecasted volume of product sales.

Sometimes, though, it's quite possible to reach a point where an initiative just isn't working anymore. However, if no one is paying attention to whether the initiative is delivering on its promises, positive change may not happen rapidly enough. The result may be a significant waste of time, resources, or even money.

One of the many benefits of a comprehensive auditing process occurs in those situations when a project's stated benefits simply aren't being achieved. Through auditing, the systematic evaluation of long-term benefit streams may create an awareness that a given project initiative should be terminated, redirected, or modified from its original long-term path.

The Logistics of Auditing

Assuming that I've convinced you that a project portfolio audit represents a worthwhile activity, the next logical step is to discuss the logistics of how an audit is actually conducted. We'll address this issue using three elements—when, how, and what.

When to Audit

Actually, the decision regarding what represents "good timing" for portfolio auditing and analysis is situational. Audit frequency can depend on organizational issues, such as the quantity of resources available to conduct the audits. It also depends on the inherent characteristics of the portfolio itself, such as the quantity of projects that comprise the overall portfolio in any given calendar year. Because a large part of portfolio analysis is actually derived through the analysis of individual project audits, project characteristics also can affect the timing of portfolio audits as well, such as the amount of change anticipated throughout the project outcome life cycle. A project whose benefits stream is rock-solid and not expected to change may not require as much scrutiny as one with a potentially volatile or questionable benefits stream.

An approach that works pretty well (for companies that conduct audits) consists of performing audits at a minimum of four points: at project completion, 1 year after completion, 3 years after completion, and 5 years after completion.

How to Audit

The process of portfolio auditing is very similar to conducting a lessons-learned at the project level. It ordinarily requires a team of people who are qualified to discuss what went well, what didn't go well, and what conclusions can be drawn from the answers to those questions. Although the focus here is on portfolio-level auditing, it certainly makes sense to ensure that at least part of the auditing team is comprised of a representative sample of the actual project teams. The audit team also should include representatives of several other functional departments within the company, such as marketing and sales, operations, human resources, and finance.

What to Audit

What specifically should be measured and evaluated? This is largely at the discretion of the company or organization performing the audits. One obvious practice that facilitates the information-gathering process consists of simply pulling out the original cash flow diagram and evaluating actual results against predicted results in terms of cash flows. Other logical metrics can be used as well.

Here are some examples of typical questions that would be posed as part of the auditing process:

- Were project results achieved (tests quality of the project management function)?
- Were benefits achieved (tests quality of forecasting and assumption methods)?
- What were actual cash outflows (improves project estimating procedures)?
- What were actual cash inflows (improves ability to forecast and express as dollars)?
- Were there excessive interproject resource conflicts (tests staggering practices)?
- Do we have the information needed to evaluate portfolio management (tests quality of information systems or record-keeping)?

Problems and Issues Related to Auditing

No process is free from problem areas. I've listed a number of difficulties that can plague the project portfolio auditing process. Although most are somewhat self-explanatory, I have included qualifying remarks, for added clarity:

- **Difficulties related to measurement and analysis**
  - Ability to substantiate cause-and-effect (i.e., link specific projects to specific benefits)
  - Ability to know "what would have been" (if a given project had not been done)
  - Skewing from external effects (effects on project/post-project that no one could have anticipated)
  - Potential for punishment of those supplying data or performing analyses (can skew the process)
- **Difficulties related to staffing and funding**
  - Finding the people to do it (and funding the actual auditing efforts)
  - Requires investment to develop tracking capabilities (information systems, etc.)
  - Requires long-term resolve (auditing has a long-term time horizon)
  - Tendency to only audit "troubled projects" (especially when resources are short)
- **The threat of dead-end results**
  - Effects of conflict of interest (especially when people auditing are affected by results)
  - People responsible for forecasting have moved on (impact of change is diminished)
  - Auditing must yield new info (or it will risk extinguishment)

Chapters 5, 6, and 7 have provided us with a thorough examination of the portfolio management process. Let's now shift our attention to the business of analyzing individual projects, exclusively from a financial standpoint. This will be our focus in Chapters 8, 9, and 10: Project Economics, Parts I–III.

PART 3

APPLYING SOUND BUSINESS PRACTICES AT THE PROJECT LEVEL

CHAPTER 8

Project Economics, Part I: Foundational Principles

One of the most important concepts stressed throughout this entire book is tied to the recognition that projects are financial investments. As is the case with just about any financial investment, a common set of fundamental, interrelated questions arise, such as: "Will I make money on this investment?" and "Exactly how much money will I make?," and "Could I lose money on this investment?"

When applied to the world of projects, a specific approach exists that will answer these kinds of questions. As we will see in upcoming chapters, the approach focuses considerable attention on the calculation of any project's net present value (NPV)—a term we have already defined and referenced a few times. In Chapter 9, Project Economics, Part II: Preparing for the Financial Analysis, we examine the role that a project's NPV plays in the project evaluation and prioritization process. In this chapter, we focus on establishing a solid understanding of the many foundational principles on which the NPV methodology is based.

Before proceeding any further, though, I'd like to take a moment to establish perspective on the bigger picture. The process for calculating project financial metrics (such as NPV) is actually a subset of a much larger process called *cost versus benefit analysis*. However, cost versus benefit analysis should not be viewed merely as a narrowly focused, analytical technique composed of a series of process steps and arithmetic calculations. I would strongly urge you to adopt cost versus benefit as a fundamental mindset. To truly be considered a business-savvy project manager, cost versus benefit should become one of your most important frameworks for analysis and decision-making, and a key component of your overall management style.

Incorporating a cost versus benefit orientation within your day-to-day decision-making regimen is one of the most valuable steps you can take in your quest to effectively merge good business practice with good project management.

With that perspective in place, let's return to the focus of the next three chapters—how to perform a financial analysis on any project. Most cost versus benefit approaches (including the calculation of a project's NPV) are built on a general methodology called *discounted cash flow*. In turn, the discounted cash flow methodology is based on the principle of the *time value of money*. So, this is where we'll begin.

THE TIME VALUE OF MONEY

Just as cost is one of the most important business terms you'll learn, the time value of money is undoubtedly one of the most important business concepts you'll learn. The time value of money concept is strongly tied to financial decision making, which in turn, has its roots in the concept of cost versus benefit.

Consistent with the cost versus benefit perspective, financial decision-making is concerned with determining how the overall value of a project is affected by the specific outcomes (financial returns) associated with various alternatives. Very often, these financial returns will be realized at one or more points in the future. Here, decision-making is virtually impossible without applying the time value of money concept. For example, imagine that I offered you a choice between two investment alternatives: The first returns $4,000 after 5 years or $6,000 after 8 years. Assuming they had identical up-front costs, which investment alternative would you choose? To answer this question, you must evaluate which alternative has the greater value to you, that is, which one is "worth more" to you?

And that question cannot be answered without knowing (or in many cases, assuming) how the value of money will change over time. All other things being equal, a dollar received soon is worth more than a dollar expected to be received in the distant future. This is true for two different, yet related reasons: First, the sooner you get the dollar back, the sooner you can reinvest it and earn a positive return; second, due to the forces of economic inflation, the dollar we receive in the distant future will have proportionately less buying power than it does today. The concept that relates to how the dollar's worth can change is called the time value of money. The principles of time value analysis have many applications, ranging from setting up schedules for paying off loans to decisions about whether to acquire new equipment. In project management, the time value of money concept is a foundational element to performing a financial analysis on a project, as we soon discover. For now, we will limit our exploration to the foundational elements of the time value of money concept: future value, present value, and the process of compounding.

FUTURE VALUE AND COMPOUNDING

The future value concept is most often connected with savings invest-ment situations. Specifically, *future value* is the calculated value of an investment based on an assumed rate of interest paid at the con-clusion of an assumed period of time. The most basic form of future value, called *simple future value*, is calculated only on the beginning principal. Before showing this calculation, let's clarify some of the basic mathematical terms we will be using:

FV = future value
PV = present value
r = interest rate, or rate of return
n = number of time periods involved in the analysis

Using these terms, we calculate simple future value using the fol-lowing mathematical formula:

$$FV = PV + PV(r)$$

Here then, is how we would calculate the future value of $1,000 for 1 year (or one time period) at an interest rate of 10%:

$$FV = \$1,000 + \$1,000(.10)$$

$$FV = \$1,100$$

If the simple interest spanned several time periods, the formula would be:

$$FV_n + PV + PVrn$$

So, for 8 years, the future value of $1,000 and an interest rate of 10% would be:

$$FV_n = \$1,000 + \$1,000(.10)(8)$$

$$FV_n = \$1,800$$

Although simple interest is an important foundational concept, most investments are not calculated using this approach. Most finan-

PV = $1,000 r = 10% Periods ▶	0	1	2	3	4	5	6	7	8
Value from simple interest (no compounding)	$1,000	$1,100	$1,200	$1,300	$1,400	$1,500	$1,600	$1,700	$1,800
Value when interest is compounded	$1,000	$1,100	$1,210	$1,331	$1,464	$1,611	$1,772	$1,949	$2,144

FIGURE 8.1

The effect of compounding.

cial arrangements assume that future values are periodically recalculated. This recalculation process is referred to as compounding. With
compounding, future value is calculated not only on the original
investment amount, but also on any earned interest accumulated
along the way. In other words, with compounding, the investor earns
interest on interest. Interest may be recalculated annually, monthly,
weekly, or even daily. As the frequency of compounding increases, so
does the future value of the investment.

With compounding, the investor's value grows at a more rapid
rate that it would with simple interest, as Figure 8.1 reveals. This chart
was developed using the following formula for future compound value:

$$FV = PV(1+r)^n$$

Assuming the values shown in Figure 8.1 for input variables, the
formula for calculating the future compound value at the end of the
eighth year would be:

$$FV = \$1,000(1+.10)^8$$

$$FV = \$1,000(2.1436)$$

$$FV = \$2,143.60 \text{ (or } \$2,144 \text{ if rounded)}$$

PRESENT VALUE AND DISCOUNTING

As you may have suspected already, the *present value* concept takes
the opposite view of the time value of money discussed above. The
present value concept suggests that the value of $1,000 5 years from
now must be some amount that is less than $1,000 today. Although
future value and present value look at the situation from opposite
directions, the underlying principle is the same: A dollar today is
worth more than a dollar in the future, because today's dollar could
be invested to start earning interest immediately.

The present value of any delayed (future) payoff can be calculated by multiplying the future payoff by a *discount factor*. In a way, discount factor is conceptually similar to interest working in reverse.

But how is the discount factor established? Let's say, for example, someone agrees to return $1,000 to you 5 years from now, if you give them some amount of money today. How much would you feel comfortable giving them? A more insightful question would be: Exactly how much money would you give them today, such that the return of $1,000 in 5 years represents a break-even situation to you?

This question—and the concept of discounting—is best answered by looking at the situation in terms of *opportunity cost*. When we give this person our money, we are forgoing the opportunity to earn interest on that money over the next 5 years. So, what is the cost of this missed opportunity?

To answer this question, we first must make a basic assumption regarding how "safe" our money will be with this person—we need to assess the risk associated with the whole arrangement. If we trust the person, we would consider this to be a relatively safe (low-risk) investment. We now must consider how much interest we could expect to receive on an investment having that same amount of risk. That is the return we are forgoing by giving the person our money.

This entire train of thought—and the associated mathematical calculations—is crucial to the business of investing. Here's why: If you were somehow able to give the person in our story less than the break-even amount—and get back the same $1,000 in 5 years—in essence, you would have earned money on that arrangement, given the amount of risk you assumed by doing it.

Now that we've discussed the concept, let's talk about the calculations. The mathematical formulas for calculating present value are:

$$PV = FV / (1 + r)^n$$

or,

$$PV = FV(1 + r)^{-n}$$

Let's take the previous scenario as our example. If someone offers to give you a future payoff of $1,000 5 years from now, what amount would you give them today to consider this a break-even situation? We are about to calculate:

The estimated value right now (PV), of $1,000 we expect to receive later (FV), discounted over a 5-year period (n = 5), using a discount factor associated with a low risk investment.

So, if we believed that we would have no problem getting a 6% return on a similarly safe investment (placing it in a savings account), the actual calculation would look like this:

$$PV = \$1,000 / (1 + .06)^5$$

$$PV = \$1,000(1 + .06)^{-5}$$

$$PV = \$1,000(.7473)$$

$$PV = \$747.30$$

So what does all of this mean to the concept of investments? Well, it allows us to appreciate scenarios such as this: Given this set of assumptions, if you entered into an arrangement where you were to give someone less than $747.30 today, and were to receive $1,000 from them 5 years from now, you have just made a wise investment, compared to placing your money in the savings account.

THREE METHODS FOR CALCULATING
THE TIME VALUE OF MONEY

So far, we've used the same approach for making our time value of money calculations, by posing and then solving algebraic equations. However, this is only one of three possible methods you can use to calculate future value and present value.

The Numerical (or Basic Calculator) Approach

This is the approach we used in all the examples above. It involves the process of formulating and solving algebraic formulas. The good news is that this approach can be used with little more than a basic calculator at your disposal. The bad news is that, generally speaking, it is the most difficult approach. This is particularly true for situations involving multiple future returns, uneven cash flows (different amounts each year), and other potential complexities that we will soon be examining.

The Tabular Approach

As with the numerical approach, the tabular approach also requires the construction of some basic arithmetic formulas. However, instead of using a calculator to solve the equation, you can combine some of the terms to create *factors*. Those factors can then be looked up on tables that are readily available in most books having anything to do with finance and accounting.

Determining Future Value Using the Tabular Approach

Using the examples above, let's take a closer look at these things called factors. Earlier, we calculated future value using this formula:

$$FV = \$1,000(1+.10)^8$$

In this equation, the value $1,000 refers to the initial amount of money invested (or PV, the present value). And the value .10 is simply the decimal equivalent of a 10% interest rate (or r, the rate of return). Finally, the number 8 refers to the number of times that the interest will be recalculated (or n, the number of time periods). It's worth noting that, for this example, the term *time period* is defined as 1 year. In other compounding situations, the time period could be some other length of time.

Using these values, we could rewrite the term $(1+.10)^8$ and express it as $(FVIF_{10\%,8})$. The above formula now becomes:

$$FV = \$1,000(FVIF_{10\%,8})$$

The full name for the term $(FVIF_{10\%,8})$ is "future value interest factor for 10% through eight periods." This factor can be found in commonly published financial tables. Not surprisingly, the title of this table will be either *Future Value Factors* or *Future Value Interest Factors*, depending on what reference book you use. A copy of this and other time value of money factor tables appear in the Appendix.

Figure 8.2 shows a section of a Future Value Interest Factors table. Notice that all the values in this table are greater than one. This is a simple reflection of our earlier contention: A dollar is worth more in the future than a dollar is worth today. To find the value for $(FVIF_{10\%,8})$, you need only find the intersection of the 10% column and the row corresponding to eight time periods. At this intersection, you will find the value 2.1436. As you'll recall, this matches the calculated value for $(1+.10)^8$ that we computed previously.

Determining Present Value Using the Tabular Approach

Now that you see how the future value interest factor approach works, I doubt you'll be very surprised with how present value is calculated using factors.

Future Value Factors Table

Periods	9%	10%	11%
...	...	...	...
6	1.6771	1.7716	1.8704
7	1.8280	1.9487	2.0762
8	1.9926	2.1436	2.3045
9	2.1719	2.3579	2.5580
10	2.3674	2.5937	2.8394
...	...	...	...

FIGURE 8.2

FVIF—10% through eight periods.

Once again, let's start with a previous example. In a situation in which we gave away a certain amount of money in return for receiving a $1,000 payoff in 5 years, here is the equation we used:

$$PV = \$1,000(1 + .06)^{-5}$$

In this equation, the $1,000 refers to the expected payoff (or FV, the future value). The value .06 refers to the *discount rate* of 6% (or r), which was the opportunity cost associated with passing on the chance to put this money toward some other investment possessing an equivalent amount of risk. Finally, the value 5 refers to the number of time periods (or n). As with the previous example, a time period is defined as 1 year.

Using these values, we can rewrite the term $(1+.06)^{-5}$ and express it as $(PVIF_{6\%,5})$. The above formula now becomes:

$$FV = \$1,000(PVIF_{6\%,5})$$

The formal name for the term $(PVIF_{6\%,5})$ is "present value interest factor for 6% through 5 periods." Similar to future value factors, present value factors can also be found in a table. In this case, this

Present Value Factors Table

Periods	5%	6%	7%
...	...	...	...
3	.8638	.8396	.8163
4	.8227	.7921	.7629
5	.7835	.7473	.7130
6	.7462	.7050	.6663
7	.7107	.6651	.6228
...	...	...	...

FIGURE 8.3

FVIF—6% through five periods.

table will be called either *Present Value Factors* or *Present Value Interest Factors*, depending the reference you're using. A copy of this and other time value of money factor tables appear in the Appendix.

Figure 8.3 shows a section of a Present Value Interest Factors table. Notice that all the values in this table are less than one. Once again, this supports our earlier contention: One dollar today is worth more than one dollar in the future. To find the value for $(PVIF_{6\%,5})$, you need only find the intersection of the 6% column and the row corresponding to five time periods. At this intersection, you will find the value .7473. Once again, this is identical to the result we got when we calculated $(1 + .06)^{-5}$ using the numerical approach.

The Financial Calculator Approach

Here's where the fun begins—at least for those who enjoy using calculators (I know you're out there!). Actually, a financial calculator can be a tremendous aid in making time value of money calculations. Many common financial equations have been programmed into most financial calculators on the market today. (**Note:** Although many of the most popular financial calculators function in a similar manner,

PV	present value	I/YR	interest rate per year
FV	future value	N	number of periods
NPV	net present value	CFj	cash flow entry

FIGURE 8.4

Common financial calculator functions.

the one I'll be using to demonstrate the application and use of financial calculators will be the Hewlett-Packard Model 10BII).

First, some basic orientation to the use of financial calculators. Most involve the manipulation of several different keys that represent various financial terms. Figure 8.4 illustrates some of the more commonly used keys used in performing time value of money calculations.

Determining Future Value Using the Financial Calculator Approach

In demonstrating how to use the financial calculator, there's really no substitute for going through an example step-by-step. So, to practice making future value calculations using the financial calculator approach, let's return to our original future value example, which was:

$$FV = \$1,000(1+.10)^8$$

Figure 8.5 describes the steps required and the corresponding buttons relating to the financial calculator solution of this equation. As you work your way through this process, it's important to keep three things in mind:

- Before nearly every calculation you make, you'll need to clear the calculator; the appropriate buttons for performing this operation are shown in Figure 8.5.
- The "Gold Key" is the button used to access the secondary-level functions that appear on the sides of the keys (this is similar to the way many calculators work).
- As the calculator is clearing, you'll notice something that looks like 1 P_Yr appear on your display for just a second. This indicates that the calculator currently assumes that a time period equals 1 year (you will probably have to adjust this setting the first time you use the calculator, because the default position on the HP10BII is 12 periods per year).

Steps You Perform	Numbers You Input and Buttons You Push	What You See in the Display
1. Clear the calculator.	GOLD C ALL	1 P_Yr
		0.00
2. Make initial value negative (*outflow*).	1000 +/−	−1,000
3. Input this amount as the present value.	PV	−1,000.00
4. Input the annual interest rate.	10 I/YR	10.00
5. Input the number of time periods.	8 N	8.00
6. Request the unknown (*future value*).	FV	2,143.59
7. **Answer: $2,143.59**		

FIGURE 8.5

Calculating future value.

The use of financial calculators—and the way in which we enter some of the input variables—can actually help to improve our understanding regarding the nature of these kinds of investment transactions. For example, you undoubtedly observed that we pressed the "+/−" key in Step 2, thus making the present value ($1,000) a negative amount. Can you guess why?

It's because making this value negative simulates how we gave away $1,000 to initiate this investment (in financial terms, this is referred to as the *initial cash outflow*). Notice that calling this a cash outflow—and making it a negative amount—suggests that we structured this investment transaction from our perspective—the investor. Financial transactions are almost always viewed from the investor's perspective.

Determining Present Value Using the
Financial Calculator Approach

The process for making present value calculations with the financial calculator is very similar to the previous process. Again, using the previous present value problem, the equation was:

Steps You Perform	Numbers You Input and Buttons You Push	What You See in the Display
1. Clear the calculator.	GOLD C ALL	1 P_Yr 0.00
2. Input the payoff amount.	1000 FV	1,000.00
3. Input the annual interest rate.	6 I/YR	6.00
4. Input the number of time periods.	5 N	5.00
5. Request the unknown (*future value*).	PV	−747.26
6. **Answer: $−747.26**		

FIGURE 8.6

Calculating present value.

$$PV = \$1,000(1 + .06)^{-5}$$

Figure 8.6 describes the steps required and the corresponding buttons relating to the financial calculator solution of this equation for calculating present value.

In this situation, you'll notice that the answer provided by the calculator is a negative number. As you may have guessed based on our previous discussion, the negative value here simulates how we would literally hand over that amount today, in anticipation of receiving $1,000 5 years from now.

RATE OF RETURN: THE BASICS

In all our previous time value of money calculations, we were concerned with these four variables:

- FV = future value
- PV = present value
- r = interest rate, or rate of return
- n = number of time periods involved in the analysis

In each case, we knew three of these variables. In one case we knew *PV*, *r*, and *n*. In the other case, we knew *FV*, *r*, and *n*.

Now suppose that we knew what the present value and the future value were, and we wished to understand what was happening to the investment between those points in time? Assuming we knew the overall length of the time period involved, we could, for example, calculate the *rate of return of the investment*. The rate of return of an investment represents the speed at which the value of an investment is either growing (the interest rate, if we're thinking ahead to a future value), or is being reduced in value (the discount rate, if we're thinking backward, toward a present value). The rate of return can be calculated by using the same three approaches we just used: the numerical approach, the tabular approach, and the financial calculator approach. Let's examine how that's done.

Determining Rate of Return Using the Numerical Approach

Imagine an investment that is expected to return $100,000 5 years from now. If the initial cash outlay for this investment was $50,000, what rate of return would this investor be receiving?

Let's begin our calculation by looking at the basic formula that ties present value and future value together:

$$FV = PV(1+r)^n$$

Now let's think about what we know about this situation. We have been given three of the four values in the equation. We know:

PV, the initial investment, or cash outflow, which is $50,000; *FV*, our expected payoff, or cash inflow, which is $100,000; and *n*, the period of time between these two points, which is 5 years.

If we further assume that we are compounding annually, we're now ready to "plug and chug," as the saying goes. So, the formula now looks like this:

$$\$100,000 = \$50,000(1+r)^5$$

Now some bad news: No really easy or direct method exists for calculating *r* when using the numerical approach. If all you have at your disposal is a basic calculator, I'm afraid you will have to use a trial-and-error approach until you solve the equation. Given that reality, let's move forward and use an easier method for making this calculation.

Determining Rate of Return Using the Tabular Approach

Unfortunately, this is not a direct method either, but it is considerably easier than the numerical approach. The most challenging thing we must do is interpolate between two numbers, once we've located them on the factor tables. Let's start our analysis where we left off in the numerical approach. We have plugged in the values provided in the problem statement and have created this formula:

$$\$100{,}000 = \$50{,}000(1+r)^5$$

Now let's consider one element of this equation, namely:

$$(1+r)^5$$

What exactly is this element? Well, whatever it is, we know that its value must be 2 to make the equation correct, don't we?

Recalling our previous discussion on the tabular approach, you may have recognized this element as a *future value interest factor* (feel free to pat yourself on the back if you knew that!). More specifically, though, it's a future value interest factor that is able to propel this investment from a present value of $50,000 to a future value of $100,000 in a 5-year period at some unknown interest rate. Putting that statement into a factor form, we're looking for:

$$(FVIF_{r\%,5}) = 2.0$$

Determining what this factor is will allow us to determine r, which is the interest rate that makes a future value of $100,000 in 5 years and a present value of $50,000 equivalent sums of money.

Now, give yourself another pat on the back if you recognized that we also could have said that we're looking for this value:

$$(PVIF_{r\%,5}) = 0.5$$

This, of course, is the factor that takes us from a future value of $100,000 back to the present value of $50,000 through a 5-year period at an unknown discount rate. So, take your choice and refer to whichever factor table you'd prefer. To follow along in finding the solution to this problem, look at Figure 8.7, where we contrast and compare methods for finding the value of r using both tables.

Notice that we came up with exactly the same answer, 14.9%, on both factor tables, by doing some simple interpolation. I told you that determining the rate of return using the tabular method was a lot easier than the numerical approach, didn't I?

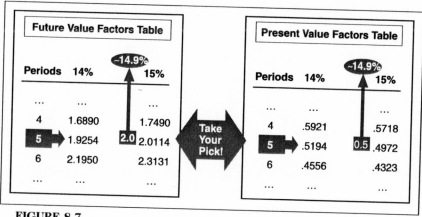

FIGURE 8.7

Interpolating $(FVIF_{r\%,5}) = 2$ and $(PVIFr_{\%,5}) = 0.5$ to find "r."

Determining Rate of Return Using the Financial Calculator Approach

By now, I'm sure you understand the rate of return concept, so let's move directly into solving the problem. Once again, here's the original equation:

$$\$100,000 = \$50,000(1+r)^5$$

And here are the input variables that we know:

- FV = $100,000
- PV = $50,000
- n = 5

All that's left now is the button-pushing. Figure 8.8 illustrates the steps, the corresponding buttons, and the various displays you will see as you calculate the rate of return on your financial calculator.

By now, you may have picked up on a recurring theme relating to the use of the financial calculator approach. Generally, the routine boils down to simply inputting the variables that you *do* know, then concluding the process by pushing the button related to the variable that you *don't* know. You've probably also observed that the financial calculator (with much greater ease than other methods, I must say) often yields a more precise value.

If you're anything like me, going through calculations such as this leads you to feel like you never want to let your financial calculator out of your sight again!

Steps You Perform	Numbers You Input and Buttons You Push	What You See in the Display
1. Clear the calculator.	GOLD C ALL	1 P_Yr 0.00
2. Make initial value negative (*outflow*).	50000 +/–	–50,000
3. Input this amount as the present value.	PV	–50,000.00
4. Input the future value.	100000 FV	100,000
5. Input the number of time periods.	5 N	5.00
6. Request the unknown (*rate of return*).	I/YR	14.87
7. **Answer: 14.87%**		

FIGURE 8.8

Calculating rate of return.

DISCOUNTED CASH FLOW METHODOLOGY

As we will discover in Chapter 9, performing an economic analysis on a project is based on an approach called the *discounted cash flow methodology*. So, what does the term discounted cash flow methodology mean?

Let's begin by considering the term that we're already familiar with—discounted. Earlier in this chapter, we discussed the concept of time value of money. Our discussion on the time value of money led us directly to the concept of discounting: the recognition that a future payoff amount is worth something less than that amount today.

All the previous situations we examined (and the associated calculations we made) consisted of *a single transaction now and a single transaction in the future*. But how would we deal with a situation in which, instead of dealing with a single future payoff, we were dealing with a series of future payoffs? This situation describes a new and important term: *cash flow*.

The existence of cash flows is very common in the world of projects. By definition, an initial outlay of cash (called a *cash outflow*) marks the beginning of a project effort. At some later time—normally on or about project completion—financial benefit will begin to accrue to the company (called a *cash inflow*). Typically, these financial benefits will accrue on a continual basis, over a long period of time, often for several years. When considered individually on a year-by-year basis, these financial benefits are called *future cash flows*. When considered as a group, over some period of time, these financial benefits are referred to as a *stream of cash inflows* or a *benefits stream*.

The graphical tool (and technique) commonly used to map out cash inflows and cash outflows is *cash flow diagramming*.

Cash Flow Diagramming

Cash flow diagramming is a common way of visualizing any combination of cash inflows and cash outflows. As a graphical tool, the cash flow diagram is very simple, yet eloquent and powerful. Let's begin our study of cash flow diagramming by looking at the anatomy of a cash flow diagram, as illustrated in Figure 8.9.

Most cash flow diagrams use the same notations that we used earlier in this chapter, including:

- FV = future value
- PV = present value
- r = discount rate *or* interest rate (depending on whether you're looking forward or backward in time)
- n = number of time periods involved in the analysis

In addition, cash flow diagrams typically employ the following conventions:

- Time flows from left to right across the diagram. The horizontal line is time scaled, showing time intervals, or periods. Although

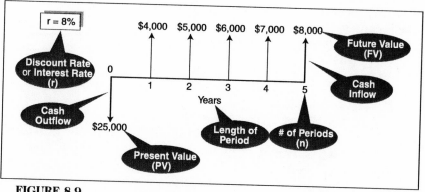

FIGURE 8.9

Anatomy of a cash flow diagram.

a period can be any length of time, in projects, it is for periods to be expressed as years.

- The first year of the investment is considered "Year 0" (zero). This convention is tied to the way interest and discounting calculations are made. It recognizes that no change in the original cash flow takes place in the same year that the investment is initiated.
- Cash flows normally are viewed as a one-time event occurring at the end of a period. Referring to Figure 8.9 for example, the cash inflow of $7,000 is viewed as occurring at the end of Year 4.

The direction of the arrows signifies a type of cash flow, and this direction must be based on a specific perspective. For example, assuming that the cash flow diagram in Figure 8.9 is interpreted from the standpoint of the investor (or lender), a downward pointing arrow indicates a cash outflow (negative cash flow, payout, or investment), while an upward pointing arrow indicates a cash inflow (positive cash flow, receipt, or return). If the cash flow diagram in Figure 8.9 was viewed from the perspective of the borrower, the direction of all arrows would be reversed.

Cash Flow Diagramming: A Few Examples

As a way to become more familiar with cash flow diagramming, let's take a few of the situations we discussed earlier and convert them into cash flow diagrams. When we first discussed future value and compounding, we examined a situation in which we started with an investment of $1,000 and watched it grow in value over eight periods and interest rate of 10% per period. As displayed in chart form in Figure 8.10, the potential result of compounding would have yielded a payoff of $2,144.

The cash flow diagram that portrays this situation would look like Figure 8.10.

You may have noticed that we have introduced a new graphical feature in this cash flow diagram. The hash lines in the diagram are there for the sole purpose of indicating the passage of time and are not associated with any cash flows. This is a common convention in cash flow diagramming.

Figure 8.10 offers us the opportunity to introduce two more key terms that we will rely on quite heavily when we get to Chapter 9, Project Economics, Part II: Preparing for a Project Financial Analysis.

The first term is called *economic equivalence*. This term (and concept) is quite common in the world of investment analysis. When we examine how to perform a financial analysis on a project, the concept of economic equivalence becomes the basis by which NPV is calculated, an

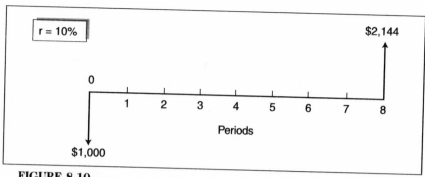

FIGURE 8.10

Cash flow diagram for the compounding situation.

important metric in measuring the financial attractiveness of a project. Economic equivalence is said to occur when an investor is indifferent to whether they receive some present sum of money or a future payoff (or series of payoffs). In other words, the sum of all cash inflows and the sum of all cash outflows are equal, assuming that the effects of compounding or discounting have been appropriately applied to all values.

Referring to Figure 8.10, the $1,000 present value investment and the $2,144 future payoff are viewed as being economically equivalent. This, of course, is based on the notion that the investor views a 10% return as satisfactory, if not expected.

The second term is *net cash flow*. Net cash flow is defined as the difference between the total of all cash inflows and the total of all cash outflows within a given period. As you've probably guessed, this concept also is applied to the calculation of a project's NPV.

These two terms play off one another rather handily. Specifically, we can state that economic equivalence occurs at the exact point at which the total net cash flow equals zero. For example, referring back to the situation above (and assuming that the investor's anticipated return is 10%), the net cash flow calculated by comparing a future payoff of $2,144 (in 8 years) to an initial investment of $1,000 is zero. This describes a situation of economic equivalence.

To illustrate the concept of net cash flow, let's look at a slight variation of this situation. Imagine for a moment that you invested $1,000 today, and that your expected return was 10%. Now imagine that someone has offered to pay you $3,000 at the end of eight periods. You would be quite wise to grab that investment opportunity, because it would result in a favorable (positive) net cash flow of about $400 in current-day dollars. Why? Because a future payoff of $3,000 in eight periods, assuming a 10% discount rate, would be worth about $1,400 in current-day dollars. Being the wise investor that you are, however, you only paid $1,000 to initiate this investment. You therefore realize a $400 positive net cash flow. (Note that it is customary to express everything in terms of current-day dollars when analyzing net cash flows). One caveat, though: It's important to understand that you would not actually realize the positive net cash flow until 8 years had passed.

Now, let's consider another example. Earlier in this chapter, when we addressed the topic of present value and discounting, we posed this hypothetical situation: "Someone has offered you a future payoff of $1,000 5 years from now. What amount would you give them today to consider this a break-even situation?"

As you may recall, we believed that we would have little difficulty in getting a 6% annual return on a similarly safe investment (placing it in a savings account), so we identified 6% as your expected return. It therefore became the discount factor used in our calculation of present value.

The cash flow diagram that illustrates this set of circumstances would look like Figure 8.11.

Note that, in Figure 8.11, we have displayed an unknown value (represented by the ???), which is intended to signify an initial cash outflow (your investment). In this hypothetical situation, you are asked to identify what this value would have to be for you to consider this a break-even situation. Rephrasing this question using our new terminology, you are really being asked to provide a value for the initial cash outlay in which—in your view, at least—economic equivalence would be established. If your memory is better than mine, you may recall that we calculated this amount to be $747.30.

So, how could we introduce the concept of net cash flow in this situation?

We actually have to work the numbers from the opposite direction, as compared to the previous example. Let's imagine that you

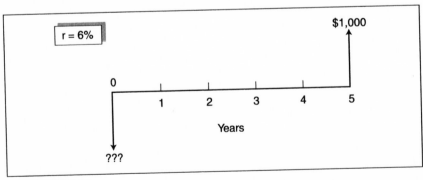

FIGURE 8.11

Cash flow diagram for the discounting situation.

actually pay out just $700, and receive the same $1,000 as a future payback 5 years from now. In this case, it can be said that you realize a favorable (positive) net cash flow amounting to $47.30. Once again, this is precipitated by the notion that you have actually paid out $47.30 less than expected (in present-day dollars) to receive that future payback of $1,000. Remember that the concept of equivalence is all about expectations. As with the last example, it's important to understand that you would not actually realize the positive net cash flow until 8 years had passed.

Calculating the Value of a Stream of Cash Flows

It is normal for projects to result in the realization of regular, periodic cash inflows, commonly referred to as a benefits stream. It is also quite normal for these cash inflows to vary in size from year to year. The situation is referred to as uneven cash flows—or *uneven cash inflows*, to be precise.

In situations such as this, the application of cash flow diagramming techniques really begins to add value.

To illustrate this, recall Figure 8.9, where we displayed the anatomy of a cash flow diagram. Figure 8.12 displays that diagram without the descriptive balloons. In this example, the sum of all cash inflows is $30,000, while the original cash outlay is just $25,000.

Would this be a good investment for you?

The reality is that we can't really answer this question without applying discounted cash flow methodology. So, let's do that.

To add some intrigue, let's begin our analysis by working backward. Referring to the cash flow diagram in Figure 8.12, you notice that we expect to realize a $8,000 return (or payoff) at the end of the fifth year. If we isolate this part of the problem, considering only the

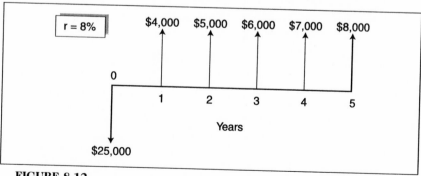

FIGURE 8.12

An example of uneven cash flows.

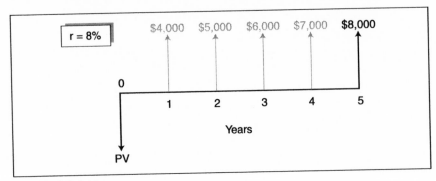

FIGURE 8.13

Isolating the present value (PV) of the Year 5 return.

actual present-day value of that $8,000, Year 5 cash inflow, the result is the cash flow diagram shown in Figure 8.13.

Applying the time value of money concept, we immediately recognize that this estimated future payoff of $8,000 will have less value to you when stated in terms of current-day dollars.

What exactly is its value to you today? The answer to that question comes in the form of a simple calculation of present value using the discounting technique.

So, if we wanted to use the numerical (or basic calculator) approach, the equation that we would use to get the answer would look like this:

$$PV = \$8,000 \, / \, (1 + .08)^5$$

Note that this equation only addresses the *Year 5 return*. That's why we've used 5 as the exponent in this equation.

So, our isolated question really is this: "What is the present value of an $8,000 cash flow, received 5 years from now, assuming a discount rate of 8%?"

Continuing to solve:

$$PV = \$8,000(1 + .08)^{-5}$$

$$PV = \$8,000(.6806)$$

$$PV = \$5,444.80$$

Thus, the Year 5 financial return (payoff), which we estimate to be $8,000, will actually have a present day "buying power" of $5,444.80 by the time it is ultimately received.

Figure 8.14 provides a graphical representation of the above calculation.

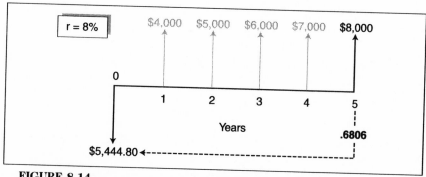

FIGURE 8.14

Calculating the Year 5 return by discounting.

One of the main reasons I chose to isolate one specific future cash flow and analyze it individually is because it actually reflects the fact that the total value of a stream of cash flows is actually calculated through a series of steps such as this.

The method for calculating the present value of an ongoing, regular stream of uneven future cash flows actually consists of discounting each cash flow individually, then adding them together.

The sum of all discounted cash flows then is compared to the current year's cash flow (in this case a $25,000 cash outflow) to determine

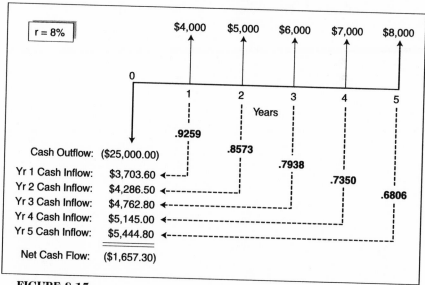

FIGURE 8.15

Calculating the NPV of an uneven stream of cash flows.

the net cash flow for that investment. Figure 8.15 illustrates the entire analysis, which reveals whether this would be a good investment.

Note the common convention of indicating negative values by placing them in parentheses. In this situation, a negative value implies an unfavorable net cash flow (remember, the cash flow diagram was constructed from your perspective). So, if you had accepted this arrangement, you would have paid $1,657.30 more than the future (uneven) cash flows were worth.

Following the analysis we have just performed, you are well on your way to being able to calculate the NPV of any project. And that's exactly what we explore in the next chapter.

CHAPTER 9

Project Economics, Part II: Preparing for a Project Financial Analysis

Armed with a firm understanding of the foundational principles related to project economics, we are now in a position to make the preparations needed to apply those principles in the actual process of performing a financial analysis on a specific project.

When we get to Chapter 10, we will be working our way through the actual financial analysis process in detail, from beginning to end. The main focus of this chapter is to understand the project-specific preparations required prior to performing that financial analysis. As with so many other kinds of work, preparation is the most critical step. In an actual project situation, it is no exaggeration to make this claim: If this part of the process is done well, "cranking the numbers" is a snap.

To better understand the direction we are going, and the data we must gather to get there, let's begin with a brief lesson on anatomy—the anatomy of a project's cash flow.

THE ANATOMY OF PROJECT CASH FLOW

Before covering the details on how to model the cash flow on a specific project, it may be helpful to take a look at the big picture first. Figure 9.1 provides that high-level view by displaying the *cash flow profile* assumed by most project investments. Several important elements that comprise a project's overall cash flow are highlighted in this illustration.

At the highest level, project cash flow curves can be viewed as subdividing into two basic phases, as indicated in Figure 9.1. The first

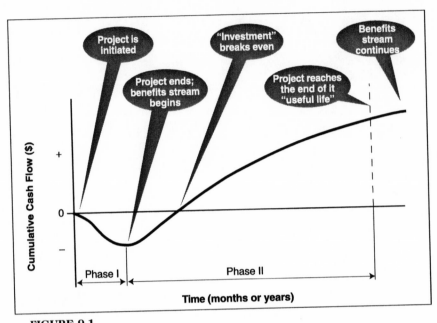

FIGURE 9.1

Anatomy of the overall cash flow of a project.

phase charts the cumulative effects of *project spending* and is comprised almost exclusively of cash outflows. The second phase, which
typically extends several years into the future, is that portion of the
overall project life cycle that was referred to as the *project outcome
life cycle* in Chapter 2. This phase of the overall life cycle may be
composed of a combination of cash inflows (incremental benefits)
and cash outflows (incremental costs).

Figure 9.1 introduces us to a new term—*useful life*. The meaning of this term seems obvious, but can actually be a bit misleading.
On the surface, we might be tempted to interpret useful life as that
point in time at which product sales have died out, a piece of production machinery has entirely broken down, or the project and its deliverables are no longer viable. Although certainly a loose connection
exists between these scenarios and the term useful life, it's important
to note that useful life is actually an accounting term. Very simply, the
useful life of a project investment is the window of time within which
the financial analysis is performed. The process of defining a project's
useful life is ordinarily guided by your company's finance and
accounting department. Also worth noting (and as Figure 9.1 reveals),
it is very possible for the benefits stream to extend well beyond the
useful life of the investment.

THE FOUNDATION OF ANY FINANCIAL ANALYSIS: THE CASH FLOW CHART

You may be wondering how the curve shown in Figure 9.1 is generated. This is because—in a sense—we jumped ahead. The reality is that we must construct a *cash flow chart* before we can intelligently model a project's *cash flow curve* like that shown in Figure 9.1. Figure 9.2 illustrates the relationship that exists between these two critical forms of project documentation.

Developing an accurate and realistic cash flow chart is the natural starting point in any financial analysis. Just like cash flow curves, cash flow charts are developed by combining project expenditures and increases in operational spending (incremental costs), along with added revenues and other financial returns, and reductions in operating costs (incremental benefits). In the cash flow chart, combining each period's incremental costs and benefits yields an *incremental*

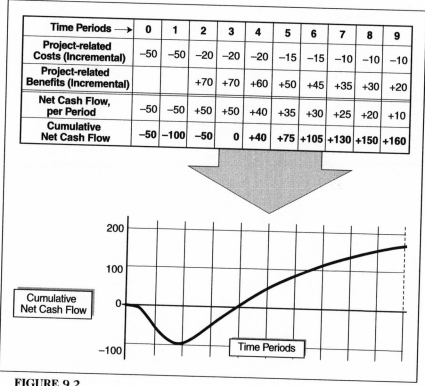

Time Periods →	0	1	2	3	4	5	6	7	8	9
Project-related Costs (Incremental)	–50	–50	–20	–20	–20	–15	–15	–10	–10	–10
Project-related Benefits (Incremental)			+70	+70	+60	+50	+45	+35	+30	+20
Net Cash Flow, per Period	–50	–50	+50	+50	+40	+35	+30	+25	+20	+10
Cumulative Net Cash Flow	–50	–100	–50	0	+40	+75	+105	+130	+150	+160

FIGURE 9.2

A project's cash flow curve is actually a graphical representation of the project's cash flow chart.

net cash flow. The combined effects of these periodic net cash flows are called the *cumulative net cash flow.* The cumulative net cash flow value (running total, if you will) forms the profile of the actual cash flow curve.

THE PROCESS OF IDENTIFYING AND MODELING THE CASH FLOWS OF A PROJECT

Identifying and modeling cash flows is the most important, yet the most difficult, step in the entire financial analysis process. Often, many different variables are involved, and many individuals and departments should participate in the process of identifying and modeling cash flows.

For example, the cash outflows associated with the launch of a new product should be obtained with the support of the product development group, along with the engineering and marketing departments. Identifying and estimating the inevitable changes in production and operating costs are likely to require the help of production department experts, purchasing managers, engineers, quality managers, human resource specialists, and cost accountants. Finally, determining the costs and benefits associated with supporting the ongoing product sales and support phase logically requires input from individuals connected to warehousing, distribution, and shipping, as well as those in sales and support departments.

Within each of these areas, more challenges exist. An additional set of variables must frequently be considered as part of the process of accurately modeling cash inflows and cash outflows. In the new product development situation, for example, the marketing department must generate forecasts around annual sales and unit pricing. To do this, they must consider factors such as price elasticity, product demand, advertising cost versus impact, competitor reactions, trends in consumer taste, and the general state of the economy, just to name a few. We now begin to see how difficult it can be to properly model cash flows.

Given this fact, we can certainly use all of the help we can get. From a process standpoint, that means ensuring that the following four elements are in place, to aid in optimizing the validity and accuracy of any analysis based on cash flow models:

- Input data (specifically, cash inflow and cash outflow data) should be supplied with the help of every department having any significant connection to the project.
- Everyone supplying input data must have a reasonably sound understanding of the project and its anticipated effects.

- Everyone supplying input data must use a consistent set of assumptions regarding the project and its anticipated effects.
- Input data must be free of bias.

In some situations, or in some companies, ensuring that data are free of bias can be a very big challenge indeed, as any number of organizational-level forces may be at work.

Bias sometimes can be introduced by managers (at any level) who are emotionally attached to a project or who have a stake in its outcome. More specifically, it may include the very difficult situation that arises when a senior manager identifies a pet project that may be of questionable merit and proceeds to initiate an "analysis" of whether the project should be approved. I have personally observed this particular situation far too many times.

Typically, no one associated with performing the analysis wants to be viewed as the person who "shot down" the project, thus dashing the dreams of the senior manager. So, inevitably, the result is often a financial analysis riddled with bias. I'm sure you can figure out the rest of this story.

GUIDELINES FOR MODELING CASH FLOWS

Three fundamental considerations exist when it comes to properly modeling the cash inflows and cash outflows on any project. The first consideration is how to properly estimate the magnitude of each individual cash flow item. This can be tricky. Often, forecasts must be developed for a variety of factors, for example, when the marketing department was tasked with generating forecasts of annual sales and unit pricing. In addition, an ever-present risk exists that bias will be introduced into the estimating process.

We will not address either of these estimating issues (forecasting and bias) to any great degree in this book. Quite honestly, I'm not sure I have a tremendous amount of sage advice on exactly how to deal with either of these situations, because both are highly situational and highly political in nature—and not really the focus of this book. However, I can offer some general advice for addressing estimating issues:

- Adopt a comprehensive, thorough, data-driven approach.
- Involve as many subject-matter experts as needed to address all functional aspects of the project.
- Provide the opportunity for "second opinions" on estimates and forecasts whenever possible.
- Specifically urge all involved to remain as objective and impartial as possible when generating estimates.

- Do not forget to include the post-project life cycle in your cash flow estimates.

The second consideration in properly modeling cash flows (often more important than estimating the accuracy of cash flows) is ensuring that you have identified all relevant cash flows. In the process of cash flow modeling, relevance is a critical term (and concept). It refers to the practice of identifying those cash flows—and only those cash flows—that are appropriate to a given project. This topic is covered a bit later in this chapter, as we discuss three basic classifications of projects and the relevant cash flows associated with each.

A third consideration is ensuring that you fully understand all the basic ground rules or guidelines associated with proper cash flow modeling, no matter what type of project you may be considering. Let's take a look at some of these guidelines, and how to deal with them.

All Cash Flows Must Be Expressed as Incremental Amounts

The concept of incremental cash flow revolves around one simple question: What affect will a given project have on each of the company's existing cash flows?

Let's consider an example: If a company was to execute a new-product development project, several different cash flow streams within the company undoubtedly would be affected. If product sales were robust, an incremental increase in the company's existing revenue stream would result. Only that incremental improvement would be claimed as a cash inflow, or benefit, associated with the project.

To further analyze this new product development project, let's also assume that new production equipment had to be designed, built, and installed on the production floor for the purpose of manufacturing the new product. Presumably, this equipment would have to be regularly serviced by the company's maintenance department (e.g., routine maintenance, equipment refurbishment, and trouble calls). Obviously, this is a chunk of work that had not previously existed. More to the point, this particular work exists only as a result of the existence of this new product development project.

The increase in sales revenue (benefit) and the increase in maintenance expense (cost) are classic examples of incremental cash flows.

Probabilistic Estimating of Cash Flows Is OK (If Not Desirable)

Nothing in this world is absolute. This is especially true when it comes to modeling project cash flows. One of the more difficult problems we face when modeling cash flows occurs in situations in which some question arises of whether the cash flow actually will be realized.

For example, imagine a situation in which our company is contemplating the development and eventual introduction of a new product. This product has the potential to generate a huge amount of revenue for our company. Unfortunately, it is also similar to an existing product currently sold by one of our competitors, and concerns have been raised with respect to patent infringement. It's no big surprise that our legal department has advised us that we might be open to legal action if we were to release this product.

As we set out to perform a comprehensive financial analysis on this potential project investment, the patent situation must be considered somehow. But how do we deal with a scenario in which our competitor may or may not take legal action against us?

The answer is *probabilistic estimating*. As the name suggests, probabilistic estimating not only considers the magnitude of a cash flow, but *also the likelihood* that it will actually come to pass. Once you become comfortable with this concept, the mechanics are really quite simple. In this situation, for example, let's assume that—if it were to happen—the cost of the potential litigation is estimated to be $12 million. Further, our legal experts have informed us that they believe a 25% chance exists that we would be sued for patent infringement by our competitor. These circumstances would result in the identification of a cash outflow of $3 million somewhere on our cash flow chart (probably the year of product introduction). An explanation of the derivation would be provided as well.

If you are uncomfortable with the accuracy or precision of the actual amount of this cash outflow ($3 million), I cannot argue. However, accuracy and precision is not necessarily the sole objective here. Instead, I would urge you to focus on how this approach simply seeks to offer a thorough model of the future. Its specific intent is to provide a balanced and insightful representation of all possible future outcomes. And if we do that well, we have put our management decision-makers in the best possible position to make a decision with their eyes wide open. For example, if we were to ignore and exclude this possible outcome from our analysis, simply because it is "not for sure," we not only expose our company to a possible future surprise, we portray an unrealistically favorable view of this project to management decision-makers. Conversely, if we include the entire $12 million in our financial analysis simply because "it might be out there somewhere," we would be offering an equally distorted and unrealistically pessimistic view of the project to management decision-makers.

Although this approach is highly subjective, it really does represent the most reasonable method for modeling the uncertainty that lies before us, as we evaluate whether this proposed project investment should be approved.

Be Sure to Consider All Externalities

Quite often, projects that are proposed by one department or organization can have any number of effects on one or more other organizations within the company. These effects are referred to as *externalities*. The previous example of proposed automation illustrated one variation of the effects of externalities. However, the externality described in that situation was pretty straightforward, as employees displaced by automated machinery projects were immediately and directly deployed to other departments within the company.

Other types of externalities can be considerably more difficult to recognize, understand, or estimate. One method that I find quite useful in uncovering externalities can be accomplished through *value chain analysis*. Figure 9.3 (which you may recognize from Chapter 4) graphically illustrates this point.

Does this mean there cannot be other effects on other organizations within the company beyond the value chain? Of course not: But, I have always found this to be an excellent starting point. A discussion regarding the effects that a project may have on the value chain often can trigger the recognition of additional externalities.

Remember: Internal Labor Is a Project Cost!

Most projects involve the acquisition or creation of fixed assets. Assets that are acquired (purchased) from outside companies are an obvious *cash outflow* and should be included as a project cost.

But what happens on projects in which a company utilizes its own internal resources to create assets? Should they be counted?

And what happens, for example, in the case of a small company where a piece of equipment is purchased from an external supplier, but the small company's own people are used to install and get the equipment running properly?

Or what happens in a large company that may have sufficient internal resources to design, develop, build, and install a piece of equipment?

These important questions can sometimes represent a significant source of confusion. I can recall a conversation I once had with the CEO of a relatively small company about this very topic. The conversation came after I had noticed a significant discrepancy between

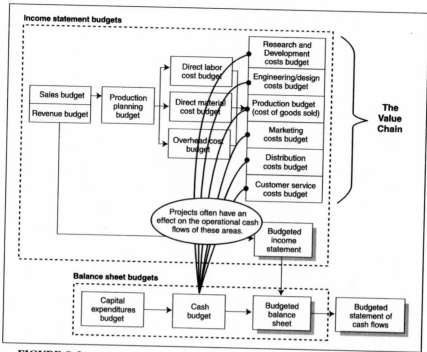

FIGURE 9.3

The search to uncover externalities.

the scope of several of their projects and the projects' respective cost estimates. After just a few minutes of discussion, we arrived at the heart of the matter, which revolved around the application of the company's internal resources to those projects.

The CEO's argument was simple. He contended that the people he had working on projects were already on the company's payroll and that he was already paying their salary. On this basis, he argued that these people represented "free resources."

Although this appears to be a logical argument, it is inconsistent with the ground rules related to the world of standard accounting and finance practices. Also, resources are normally viewed as being employed by a firm for the purpose of conducting ongoing business operations. As I pointed out to the CEO, assigning people to work on projects represented a conscious decision that he had made—a decision which diverted the energies of his employees from conducting day-to-day operations to the process of creating fixed assets for the company.

And finally, the federal government expects companies to appropriately and accurately attach a fair and reasonable acquisition cost to all their fixed assets (called asset valuation) for purposes such as the payment of income tax and declaration of depreciation expense. They also interpret the use of internal resources as a practice that adds value to a company's fixed assets.

Cash Flows Must Be Viewed from an Overall Company Perspective

Many projects—particularly internal improvement projects—are pursued because they benefit a particular organization within the company. A common cash flow modeling pitfall in these types of project circumstances occurs when the department performing the financial analysis adopts a parochial perspective to the concept of cash flows. This can be problematic, because a true cash flow is relevant only when viewed from the perspective of the overall company.

Take, for example, the case of one of the largest manufacturing companies in the United States (which shall remain nameless). During the 1970s and 1980s, this company pursued many projects that consisted of automating manufacturing or production operations that were very labor-intensive. One of the more significant sources of positive cash flow (and a primary justification for many of these projects) came in recognizing that automating a manufacturing process would enable a reduction in headcount—that is, a reduction in the quantity of labor resources utilized within that particular manufacturing department.

Unfortunately, the financial analyses performed on many of these projects were significantly flawed. More often than not, the employees whose jobs had been eliminated as a result of these projects were simply transferred to another department within the company. As a result, no actual net effect occurred on the company's overall cash flow. The company had paid money out, but had received nothing in return.

Only in two sets of circumstances could the cash flows generated through the reduction of labor in these departments been legitimately counted. The first, of course, would have occurred if the employees affected by the project actually left the company. Another, more subtle, circumstance would have occurred in situations in which employees were transferred to departments that would have hired new people from the outside, if the redeployed employees had not come along. This situation is a good example of how subtle and intricate cash flow modeling can sometimes be.

All Benefits Must Be Realistic and Attainable

One of the more common areas in which bias can enter the process of modeling cash flows comes in the form of "claims" that are made with regard to the achievement of benefits. People who are anxious to see a project approved may be inclined to inflate, or overstate, potential project benefits. Others may claim benefits that do not actually exist or are not realistically attainable. Obviously, the situations serve to distort the financial analysis in favor of project approval.

In fact, the only benefits that should be included in a financial analysis are those considered to be realistic, reasonable, and attainable. The following are three very different examples of when and how "bogus benefits" may be included in a financial analysis.

The first example is the situation we just discussed, in which automated equipment was installed. In that case, a benefits claim was made regarding the resultant reduction in workforce. Once again, however, no real benefit accrued to the company, because the relocated workers were still employed by the company after the project had been completed.

Another common benefit pitfall relates to the phenomenon of *shared claims*. From time to time, two (or more) projects may exist within a company's project listing, each laying claim to the same set of benefits. Obviously, any given benefit can only be "cashed" once. However, it would not be out of the realm of possibility to see that benefit show up in the financial analysis of more than one project.

Yet another all-too-common pitfall occurs when a benefit is claimed that actually includes a significant amount of excess capacity, excess capability, or excess functionality. Projects such as this often are sold on the promise of a potential benefit. The potential benefit is then included in the financial analysis. In reality, it is extremely unlikely that this excess benefit will ever be realized. Be careful though, because a pitfall within a pitfall exists here.

In some cases, having excess capacity, capability, or functionality may serve to facilitate future expansion—often a wise decision from a business standpoint. The pitfall that I'm referring to is specifically targeted at the situation in which a relatively high probability exists that the benefit will never be realized.

Proper Timing of Cash Flows

Inevitably, the question arises regarding exactly when cash flows should be recorded. Because the time value of money is viewed as a continuum, it follows (in theory, at least) that cash flows should be recorded at the exact moment they occur. Obviously, this approach is excessively complex from the standpoint of modeling cash flow diagrams. Also, it may not appreciably improve the accuracy of the financial analysis, given the fact that cash flow projections represent approximations anyway.

So, considering the complexity and cost of real-time cash flow recording, the customary approach used by most analysts simply is to assume that all cash flows occur at the end of each reporting period. For most, this translates into the practice of recording cash flows at the end of each calendar year.

PROPER TREATMENT OF SPECIAL CASH FLOW TYPES

Many types of cash flows are pretty straightforward. That is, they relate to relatively obvious cost expenditures and relatively obvious savings (albeit difficult to estimate). Many other types of cash flows aren't quite so straightforward. Here are a few of the more common ones.

Cost Protection

One special type of cash flow that is not always well understood or appropriately applied is called *cost protection*. The difficulty encountered with the cost protection category is that it may appear to some as a kind of "shady deal," because it allows for a considerable amount of subjective judgment.

Let's say, for example, our company owns a particular piece of production equipment that is vital to a manufacturing operation. This equipment has worked hard for many years, but is definitely beginning to show its age. It is so old, in fact, that the consensus among subject-matter experts (SMEs) is that this equipment is living on borrowed time—catastrophic failure is definitely in the future for this piece of equipment.

Should catastrophic failure take us by surprise, the results would be traumatic and exceedingly expensive. In addition to being incapable of making product for some amount of time, the SMEs are afraid that other equipment could be damaged by the impending failure.

By replacing this doomed piece of equipment now, we are able to protect ourselves against the potential future costs that would be associated with the catastrophic failure of this equipment, including loss of sales and equipment damage. The value of these items should be recorded as a cash inflow under a line item called cost protection.

The concept of cost protection also is used quite frequently on projects related to *product development*. In these situations, we may pursue a particular project effort now as protection from potential erosion in our market share. In this case, the value of the eroding sales should be listed as a cash inflow in the financial analysis.

Skeptics of the cost protection concept point out that this category is prone to fabrication. Those wishing to see a given project approved will simply make up stories of impending doom as a way to generate support for their project. Although I'm sure this behavior does exist, my response to the skeptics has always been the same: If a company thinks it has employees who will behave this way, they really have behavior and conduct issues that transcend the topics and tools we're addressing in this book. Unfortunately, though, I have observed companies that have disallowed the use of cost protection as a project cash flow to assuage their suspicions. However, instituting such policies does nothing to effectively address the underlying behavior and conduct issues. It also discounts a legitimate business practice. Bottom line: The fact that cost protection could be abused doesn't nullify it as a proper and legitimate element of sound, business-based decision-making.

Cost Avoidance

The concept of *cost avoidance* is similar to the concept of cost protection. In both cases, we are protecting ourselves from an unfavorable negative future financial impact. Cost protection applies to scenarios in which an element *inside the company* is in a state of decline, and a large, unfavorable financial impact is imminent. In contrast, cost avoidance more frequently relates to situations in which the financial threat comes from *outside the company*. One classic example of cost avoidance arises when the government mandates some kind of corporate reform—for example, a new set of safety requirements. As we all know, noncompliance would likely result in government-levied penalties or fines. Another classic example would be situations in which actions that we take (or not take) may result in litigation (law suits, damage claims, etc.).

In both examples, we are able to avoid the imposition of unfavorable, externally driven costs by taking action now (i.e., pursuing a project). These avoided costs should be listed as cash inflows in the financial analysis.

Unfortunately, cost avoidance can fall victim to the same suspicions as cost protection.

Cannibalization

In one of the cost protection examples, we took action aimed at protecting our company from the erosion of market share in a particular product arena. But what if we did something to *cause* that erosion? That phenomenon is referred to as *cannibalization*.

Companies that are in the practice of continually introducing new products or variations of existing products are at greatest risk of encountering this phenomenon. It is a type of project cash flow that frequently exists, yet sometimes goes undetected (or unacknowl-edged) by those performing the financial analysis.

Cannibalization occurs in situations in which the introduction of a new product into the marketplace precipitates a decline in the sales of that company's existing product(s). Let's say, for example, our company manufactures food products, and our line of potato chips is a big seller. We are seriously considering the introduction of the new type of potato chip, one that assumes an entirely new shape. This is a significant project: We would have to retrofit at least one of our pro-duction lines to accommodate this totally new chip. Naturally, the focus of this project's economic analysis will be the forecasted sales volume for this product. The reality is that it would be unreasonable to expect that the demand for this new chip would come entirely from "new" sales (sales in addition to existing potato chip sales). In fact, some consumers would purchase these new chips instead of our exist-ing chips, thus triggering a decline in the demand of our existing chips. This adverse effect on existing sales should be listed as a cash outflow in the financial analysis.

Proper Treatment of Sunk Costs

A *sunk cost* is an outlay of funds that already has been spent or irrev-ocably committed. Whenever you are performing a financial analysis on a project (or in any other decision-making circumstance), it's important to recognize that the decision you are making can only affect the future. As the saying goes, you can't change the past. Therefore, any past expenditures that cannot be recovered should *not* be included in your analysis.

For example, one company I worked with was contemplating a new and exciting venture. They were cautious, though, and an exten-sive analysis was commissioned. The analysis included marketing research and a variety of technical studies. It took them a while, but they eventually decided to take the plunge and pursue the new venture.

When it came time to prepare the program's financial analysis, they included the costs associated with the original study. At this stage in the financial analysis, however, that money was long gone, and could never be recovered. Irrespective of whether the project venture was approved, that fact would not change. It was therefore identified as a sunk cost, and was not relevant to the current analysis.

Proper Treatment of Opportunity Costs

Opportunity costs are another unusual, but important type of cash flow; these costs are defined as cash flows that could be generated from assets the company already owns, provided they are not used for the project in question.

For example, I once worked with a company that was in the business of retail sales. One day, a parcel of land came up for sale in a very desirable location. The senior management of the firm became enamored with this property, viewing it as an excellent location for potential expansion, and decided to purchase it.

A couple of years later, a project was identified that consisted of building a retail store on that property. In this case, the company wanted to exclude the original purchase cost of the land, identifying it as a sunk cost. However, a key attribute of sunk costs relates to the fact that it represents a past expenditure that cannot be recovered.

That is not the case here. If the project under consideration was not approved, the land could be resold at market value. Therefore, that same market value should be identified as a cash outflow (project cost), under the classification of opportunity cost.

Proper Treatment of Interest Expense

As discussed in Chapter 2, the money used to finance projects comes from a combination of debt financing and equity financing. Because of this, you may be tempted to identify the interest paid on these borrowed funds (the weighted average cost of capital) as a cash flow associated with execution of the project.

As we will soon see, however, the discounting process (which we reviewed in Chapter 8) will be applied to all the project's future cash flows. This process of discounting is actually how the interest expense is dealt with. In other words, if we were to deduct interest expense in our project cash flow diagrams, then discount the resulting cash flows, we would be *double counting* the cost of debt. Bottom line: *Do not subtract interest expenses* when calculating a project's cash flows.

Proper Treatment of Depreciation

Depreciation revolves around the notion that fixed assets are continually being "used up" throughout their operating life. It is not actually (or literally) a cash flow, because no money changes hands, so to speak. But depreciation ultimately *does* have an effect on cash flows: Its effects are somewhat indirect, but nonetheless real.

Depreciation is essentially an accounting concept. Companies are permitted to use depreciation as a kind of tax write-off. In essence, they capitalize on the notion that they are "using up" any given asset to operate their business. From the standpoint of accounting practice, depreciation deductions allow companies to reduce their *apparent income*, thus providing a limited amount of sheltering from their income tax burden. The result is an actual reduction in income tax (which *is* a cash flow). This becomes much clearer later in the chapter, as we illustrate the specific procedure for dealing with depreciation as part of cash flow modeling.

The determination of the rate at which various assets are "used up" was standardized by the United States government in 1986. As part of the Tax Reform Act of 1986, Congress established guidelines through the Modified Accelerated Cost Recovery System (MACRS).

MACRS offers two alternatives for computing depreciation deductions. The most commonly used approach is called the *General Depreciation System* (GDS); the other system is called the *Alternative Depreciation System* (ADS). Most companies use GDS, because it accelerates the depreciation process, yielding greater deductions sooner. Under MACRS, tangible depreciable property (which is typically created by projects) is categorized into asset classes. The property in each class is then assigned a class life (categories of items with similar "durability"). Figure 9.4 offers a sampling of asset classes and their corresponding recovery periods. It also provides specific information on the actual allocation of depreciation across years (called the *depreciation schedule*).

It's critical to note that MACRS applies only to tangible assets placed in service after 1986. Other more familiar depreciation approaches, such as the straight-line method, the declining balance method, the sum-of-the-years-digits method, and the units-of-production method are still alive and well. However, they apply only to assets placed in the service prior to 1987, as well as those assets that do not qualify under MACRS, such as intangible assets. In addition, the more often traditional methods are specified by the tax laws and regulations of state and municipal governments within the United States, the more often they are used for depreciation purposes in other countries.

THREE BASIC PROJECT CASH FLOW MODELS

As we are all aware, a virtually limitless variety of projects is possible. This, of course, further implies that an even more limitless variety of project cash flow types exist (is it possible for something to be *even more limitless*?)

So, to provide some structure to this situation, it may be useful to consider most projects as falling into one of these three basic project models:

- Product development, marketing, and sales projects
- Contract, service, and consulting projects
- Internal company projects

Asset Classification	Class Life	Recovery Period (GDS)	Recovery Period (ADS)
Special manufacturing tools	3	5	5
Automobiles	3	5	5
Light duty trucks	4	5	5
Information systems, including computers	6	5	6
Manufacture of electronic systems	6	5	6
Office furniture and equipment	10	7	10
Fabricated metal products	12	7	12
Telecommunications equipment	18	10	18
Commercial and industrial buildings	39	20	39

	No. of years of asset utilization										
	1	2	3	4	5	6	7	8	9	10	11
5-year recovery period (% per yr)	−20	−32	−19	−11.5	−11.5	−6					
7-year recovery period (% per yr)	−14	−24.5	−17.5	−12.5	−9	−9	−9	−4.5			
10-year recovery period (% per yr)	−10	−18	−14.5	−11.5	−9	−7.5	−6.5	−6.5	−6.5	−6.5	−3.5

FIGURE 9.4

MACRS guidelines for establishing depreciation.

It's useful to identify different project models because each one has a somewhat different set of cash flows. Within each, however, you will find a substantial amount of consistency with respect to the types of cash flows that you will encounter when performing a financial analysis on that particular type of project. It's important to recognize that these models do not necessarily equate to a type of company. Although any one of these project types may represent the majority of a company's project portfolio, it is possible—if not likely—for any combination of these project types to exist within any given company.

The three models are examined in some detail here. In each case, I will begin by describing key characteristics of that model. Then, to help you understand how you might go about performing your own financial analysis, I've provided a partial listing of some of the more common types of cash outflows and cash inflows associated with each model.

The Product Development, Marketing, and Sales Model

This project type focuses on the creation of a new product or service. The new products or services typically are sold to customers, clients, consumers, or other users who are external to the company. Most people have little difficulty connecting concepts such as cash flow and net present value (NPV) with product development projects, because sources of cash flow are reasonably common and intuitively obvious. Typically, a company must ramp up to produce new products by building new machinery and equipment (the typical cash outflows). New products are then manufactured and sold to the consuming public (the typical cash inflows).

But don't be fooled by the existence of the typical, obvious cash flows: The story definitely doesn't end there. To properly assess the economic attractiveness of new product projects, several other costs, such as marketing and sales costs, really need to be included in the overall financial analysis. A variety of other cash flow types must be considered as well.

Typical Cash Outflows from Product Development, Marketing, and Sales Projects

Predictably, most of the costs associated with this project type are focused on what it takes to develop a product configuration, prepare for production, and sell the product. The following cash outflows are typical:

- Research costs
- Product design costs
- Development and testing costs
- Acquisition costs (facilities, equipment, etc.)
- Rental or lease costs (facilities, equipment, etc.)
- Capital project (startup) costs
- Overhead (project) expense
- Purchase costs (production support materials)
- Cost of goods sold (unit manufacturing cost × volume)
- Increased operating costs (operators, maintenance staff, etc.)
- Marketing and distribution costs
- Sales support

Typical Cash Inflows from Product Development, Marketing, and Sales Projects

Once again, no real surprises here. Typical and cash inflows associated with this project type focus on the increase in revenue that comes from selling a product that is new to the company. Typical cash inflows include the following:

- Increased sales revenue
- Increased service revenue
- Lower production cost
- Increased operating efficiency
- Material savings

It's worth noting that the cash flow types identified here are not exclusive to the development of new products alone. Slight variations exist within this type of project, such as product enhancements and product line extensions.

The Contract, Service, and Consulting Model

These types of projects certainly can include efforts in which ongoing support, rather than specific deliverables or results, is the focus. From a business standpoint, however, I would prefer to focus more on those project types in which the focus is a contractual agreement tied to specified deliverables or outcomes.

In their book *The Project Manager's MBA*, Dennis J. Cohen and Robert J. Graham very eloquently describe the changing business environment that surrounds these types of projects, which they refer to as *client engagement projects*. Cohen and Graham express it this way:

> These projects are conducted for an external client or customer. They are the type of project traditionally evaluated in terms of outcome, budget, and schedule constraints. These measures have been used because such projects are carried out under a contract that specifies them, and because it has traditionally been of little concern to the project manager what the customer does with the project outcome once the project is completed.
>
> However, customers now expect total solutions for their problems and thus expect contracting organizations to work with them to help them market or otherwise employ the project outcomes. In such a market-driven business systems approach, the project manager will be much more aware of the customer situation, and thus much more likely to create successful solutions. So even for this type of project, the old days of measuring success strictly by outcome, cost, and schedule are gone. Those measures are being supplemented by measures of increased economic value for both the project organization and the client organization.

This sentiment—although applied to outsourcing projects—is quite consistent with our discussion in Chapter 1, where we described the importance of adopting a total asset life cycle perspective, and redefined the project investment to include the period of time that extends long after the original deliverables have been created. As Cohen and Graham point out, adopting this same perspective has the potential to create a significant competitive advantage for companies that are in the business of executing contract-driven projects.

Typical Cash Outflows from Contract, Service, and Consulting Projects

As with product development projects, many people are able to connect concepts such as cash flow and NPV to these project types with relative ease. Among the more common types of cash outflows are:

- Product/service design
- Product/service development
- Technical support
- Warranty work
- Ongoing maintenance
- Material costs
- Administrative support
- Travel expenses

Typical Cash Inflows from Contract, Service, and Consulting Projects

This is a relatively short list. Most cash inflows resulting from this project type come from "payment for services rendered." So the more common cash inflows here include:

- Contract payoff
- Ongoing service revenue
- Ongoing consulting revenue
- Revenue from follow-up maintenance work

Any costs or revenues encountered during the post-project life cycle may or may not be written into the terms of the original contract. Either way, these types of cash inflows and cash outflows really should be included in the initial financial analysis.

The Internal Company Project Model

Internal company projects often are associated with the notion of increases in efficiency, process improvements, and reengineering efforts. They normally do not generate new revenue streams for the company. Instead, the terms most commonly associated with these types of projects are *cost savings* or *cost reduction*. Because most forms of cost savings do not include "hard dollars" flowing in or out of the company, internal projects are often met with the highest level of skepticism. As you may recall, we began this chapter with a discussion on this particular topic. To aggravate this situation, internal projects also may include efforts related to employee satisfaction, or benefits may be extremely difficult to accurately estimate in terms of dollars and cents. It also may include so-called mandatory projects such as *legal* or *regulatory compliance*, in which the estimation of benefits is difficult *and* the need to perform any type of financial analysis is questioned under the pretense "there's no need to analyze it...we *have* to do it." The response is simple: Although legal and regulatory compliance may certainly be the prudent action, significant value still can be associated with understanding what's at stake on any of these types of projects from an economic standpoint.

Typical Cash Outflows from Internal Company Projects

Although many different types of internal company projects are possible, they share significant commonality with regard to cash outflow types. Typical cash outflows on internal company projects include:

- Research costs
- Design costs
- Development and testing costs
- Capital project (startup) costs
- Internal labor costs
- Material purchase costs (project)
- Equipment purchases
- Rental or lease costs (facilities, equipment, etc.)
- Overhead (project) expense
- Purchase costs (production support materials)
- Increased operating costs (operators, maintenance staff, etc.)
- Shipping and distribution costs (internal or external)
- Legal costs
- Remediation costs

Typical Cash Inflows from Internal Company Projects

Consistent with our earlier discussion, cash inflows that come from internal company projects often are precipitated by efforts and activities related to increases in efficiency and process improvements. Some of the more common cash inflows seen on the internal projects include:

- Labor savings
- Increased work output or efficiency

- Increased utilization of assets
- Reduced inventory
- Reduced rental/lease expenses
- Reduced waste
- Material savings
- Reduced operating cost

It's worth noting that this list barely scratches the surface when considering the wide variety of cash inflows that can be encountered in internal company projects.

A thorough identification and accurate estimation of all the various cash flow types described in this chapter is the hardest part of the entire financial analysis process. If you take the time and trouble to do this well, you will be virtually guaranteed of achieving a high-quality assessment of your project's financial strength. The only thing left to be done is to work through the math. This is our focus in Chapter 10.

CHAPTER 10

Project Economics, Part III: Performing a Project Financial Analysis

In Chapters 8 and 9, we established a firm understanding of the many principles and preparations that must be properly positioned before performing a financial analysis. Now, we're ready to examine (in detail, I might add!) how to apply those principles to the process of performing a financial analysis on a specific project. Before getting underway, though, let's take a moment to really understand our motivation—why are we doing all of this in the first place?

SEPARATING FACT FROM FICTION IN THE PROJECT FINANCIAL ANALYSIS PROCESS

At the core of the various financial analysis methods we'll examine lies the procedure for determining the net present value (NPV) of a project. The NPV expresses the amount of wealth generated through the execution of a project investment. And, although we will examine other methods for expressing financial strength, the NPV method—which has been around for quite a while—continues to serve as a useful, reliable, and insightful measurement of project attractiveness for many of the companies that perform financial analyses. It is logically and directly tied to the very reason companies are in business: to generate wealth.

Not everyone within the community of project management practitioners shares this view, however. Recently, the NPV method has come under fire. Some have referred to it as "unreliable," while other, even stronger opponents of the method, have gone so far as to refer to it as "irrelevant."

Not too long ago, for example, I read an article in a prominent project management periodical. The article suggested that information technology (IT) projects should be exempt from any kind of financial analysis. The authors were particularly scornful of the NPV method. Supporting their rationale was the notion that IT projects typically accrue a wide array of soft benefits—euphemistically dubbed the "intangible" benefits. Against this backdrop, the authors of the article argued that performing a financial analysis on such projects was simply a waste of time; they dubbed the process passé.

Occasionally, I hear a similar argument when I am covering the topic of financial analysis as part of my project management training programs. Once again, the contention is that, on some projects, estimating the value of certain financial benefits (cash inflows) to a very high degree of accuracy can be extremely difficult.

I cannot argue this point—a good financial analysis is *very* difficult to do. However, some take this argument a step further and suggest that this is a legitimate excuse to invalidate—and therefore to avoid—the performance of *any* sort of financial analysis on a project.

To this I say...hogwash! I'd like to bring some clarity to this debate.

I have a much different perspective on the application of financial analysis techniques to projects in general, and approaches such as NPV calculations, in particular. This perspective is widely shared by many, especially by my colleagues who live and work deep within the business world. I would encourage you to consider adopting this perspective as well. So, before we get into the details of this chapter, I'd like to take a moment and share this perspective with you.

It is critical, if not essential, that we differentiate between the inherent value of any tool (such as NPV analysis) and the difficulties and challenges associated with applying that tool in an effective manner. What the NPV concept strives to accomplish (expressing the wealth generated by a project initiative) is a vitally important element in a company's ability to make wise, well-informed, business-based decisions related to project prioritization and selection. I urge you and your company not to discount (and therefore discard) a tool such as NPV analysis, simply because it may be challenging to use or because it cannot be executed with 100% accuracy.

What we really need to focus on—and strive for—is the identification and use of techniques and approaches that will optimize the effective application of any tool that we use. In the case of NPV analysis, this equates to two critical elements.

Curiously, the first element consists of acknowledging the argument made by the skeptics. We must recognize the difficulty—but even more so, the vital importance—of developing accurate, thorough models of a project's cash flows. Identifying all cash inflows and cash outflows related to a project—and estimating their value within a reasonable level of accuracy—is the foundation to effectively performing an NPV analysis. To me, this simply means that we must redouble our efforts and strive to do the very best job possible in accurately modeling a project's cash flows.

For many companies, there exists a surprisingly easy method for accomplishing this (perhaps this should be added to the revelations in Chapter 1?). Simply *involve project teams earlier in the life cycle of the project investment*. Often, one of the key contributors to the imprecision that exists in a project's financial analysis can be traced back to the simple fact that those who perform the analysis are not sufficiently knowledgeable of the project's details. Building spreadsheets and solving financial equations are the relatively easy components of an NPV analysis. *Cash flow modeling* is the foundation—and the most challenging component—of the financial analysis process.

The second critical element in properly applying NPV analysis as an effective tool in making sound, business-based decisions comes in acknowledging the presence of risk and uncertainty in any financial analysis. If we recognize that developing accurate estimates for cash flows is a challenging endeavor, this suggests the need to apply enlightened risk-management techniques, such as *sensitivity analysis*. When applied appropriately, sensitivity analysis is an excellent way to acknowledge, reveal, and articulate the inherent level of uncertainty that may exist in our ability to accurately estimate a project's economic attractiveness. (We will address this potential uncertainty when we get to Chapter 11, Project Risk Management, Decision-Making, and Business.)

Now, let's return our focus to this chapter by ensuring that we fully understand what the target outcomes are in performing a financial analysis. What exactly are the key deliverables of the financial analysis process?

For us, the deliverables will be four of the most popular, basic, yet useful financial measures of project attractiveness. The calculation of these four basic financial metrics will form the foundation of your ability to communicate the concept of *financial strength* to your management decision-makers.

THE FOUR BASIC FINANCIAL METRICS

OK, so we've talked about discounting, cash flow types, and how to construct a variety of different cash flow models. Now what?

If you're as impatient as I am, you're probably saying, "So when are we going to learn how to 'crank the numbers' already?"

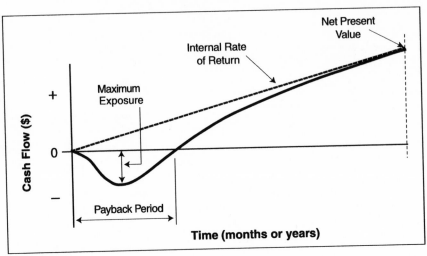

FIGURE 10.1

Visualizing the four basic financial metrics.

The good news is, we're about to walk through a comprehensive example of an entire financial analysis. The bad news is that we have one more step to cover before that. To aid in understanding what we're doing during the analysis, it's important that we understand the end point where we're going with the analysis. The end point is, in fact, the calculation of four basic financial metrics. These four metrics are illustrated in Figure 10.1.

Most management decision-makers who seek to assess the economic viability of projects and make project approval decisions based on the so-called "financials" frequently rely on some combination of these four measures of financial strength.

Net Present Value (NPV)

NPV still remains a very common and useful measure of financial strength. As we saw in Chapter 1, the process of generating wealth for a company begins with high-NPV projects (Fig. 1.5).

Some of the key characteristics of NPV include:

- It answers the question: "How much money will this project make (or save)?"
- It is actually a calculation of the present-day value of all future cash flows.
- It is expressed in terms of dollars.
- It is roughly analogous to the concept of profit.

Internal Rate of Return (IRR)

In the past, IRR was the primary measure of financial strength. Some companies continue to use this as their primary measure today. One drawback of relying solely upon IRR is that it does not identify the amount of wealth being returned to a company. It is very possible to encounter a project with an extremely high IRR, but generating a very small economic benefit.

Some of the key characteristics of IRR include:

- It answers the question: "How rapidly will money be made?"
- It is actually a calculation of the annualized rate at which the project "investment" returns wealth.
- It is expressed as a percent (%).
- It is roughly analogous to the "effective yield" of an investment.

Payback Period

In contrast to NPV and IRR—which are aimed at evaluating the positive contribution made by a project—payback period is aligned more closely with the concept of potential downside risk. Organizational managers, who must exist in a world of high uncertainty, rapidly shifting technology, or the ongoing threat of project termination are particularly interested in this metric.

Some of the key characteristics of payback period include:

- It answers the question, "When will the original investment be recovered?"
- It is actually the point where the cumulative discounted cash flow equals zero.
- It is normally measured in years.
- It is also referred to as the "break-even" point.

Maximum Exposure

As with the payback period metric, maximum exposure adopts a similar downside risk perspective. Most managers literally consider maximum exposure as a measure of how much of the company's money is "at risk."

The key characteristics of maximum exposure are:

- It answers the question, "What is the largest amount of money that the company will have invested at any one point in time?"
- It is actually the point of maximum negative cumulative cash flow.

- It is measured in terms of dollars.
- It is also referred to as "cash hole."

The precise value of each of these metrics can be determined by a properly constructed and executed financial analysis. Let's walk through an example, step-by-step, beginning with the construction of a cash flow chart.

PERFORMING A PROJECT FINANCIAL ANALYSIS: A COMPREHENSIVE EXAMPLE

For our example, I'd like to consider a relatively small and straightforward Internal Company Project. It's important to note that we could just as well be examining a Product Development, Marketing, and Sales Project, or a Contract, Service, and Consulting Project. Although many of the specific cash flow entries would be somewhat different, the basic approach, mathematical calculations, and analytical interpretation of results would be very similar.

So let's consider the case of a departmentally funded capital improvement project, aimed at increasing the efficiency of a portion of that department's manufacturing operations. Including the development phase, project execution is expected to take one year.

The following cost expenditures have been estimated for this project:

- Design and engineering costs are estimated at $70K (all will be spent during the year the project is initiated).
- Capital implementation costs (building and installing equipment) are estimated at $170K (all will be spent the year the project is initiated).
- Annual operating costs are expected to increase by $50K (beginning the year immediately following project completion).

These annual cost savings also are expected to begin immediately after project completion:

- Routine maintenance costs will be reduced by $80K.
- Material usage costs will be reduced by $40K.
- Waste-related costs will be reduced by $30K.

Other important considerations related to this project:

- All the assets being created as a result of this project have a class life of 6 years and a recovery period of 5 years.
- The company's cost of capital is 10%.

The project investigation team has assessed the potential impact of this project on all the elements within the value chain (Fig. 9.3). Obviously, the engineering/design community is affected, because they are supplying the bulk of the upfront resources required to design and develop the necessary modifications to the equipment. The production community also is affected, due to the impacts on equipment maintenance, material costs, and waste expense. But because this is a "local" project (and to simplify our example), no other departments within the value chain are assumed to be impacted as a result of this project.

Building the Basic Cash Flow Chart

Ideally, project teams (or at the very least, a group familiar with both design engineering and operations) should provide all the estimating data listed. Unfortunately, however, it doesn't always happen that way. One of the greatest sources of conflict in organizations—and one of the leading causes of faulty financial analyses—occurs when individuals outside the project team or outside the project or operations community produce cash inflow and cash outflow estimates without the participation (and quite often, even the agreement and buy-in!) of those responsible for executing the project and cashing the post-project benefits.

It's nearly impossible to overstate the importance of thoroughly identifying and properly estimating all sources of cash flows. And it's vitally important to recognize that the mathematical manipulations demonstrated throughout this chapter are the easy part of the overall process: The tough part is coming up with the proverbial "good numbers."

Assuming that the estimates above are "good numbers," we're now in a position to construct the basic cash flow diagram for this project in Figure 10.2.

Note that this chart only extends 6 years into the future (beyond project completion). This reflects the 6-year asset class life mentioned in the setup assumptions.

A few additional items must be considered as part of a proper financial analysis. Some of the more common considerations that would apply in this sort of project are defined in the following sections.

Completing the Cash Flow Chart: Change in Working Capital

The term *working capital* refers to the cash required to purchase the *current assets* needed for startup and subsequent support. Examples of working capital include materials inventory, spare parts, tools, and

Cash Flow Type	Number of Years after Project Initiation						
	0	1	2	3	4	5	6
Cash Outflows:							
Design and Engineering	−70						
Capital Implementation	−170						
Operating Costs		−50	−50	−50	−50	−50	−50
Cash Inflows:							
Routine Maintenance		+80	+80	+80	+80	+80	+80
Material Usage		+40	+40	+60	+60	+80	+80
Waste		+30	+30	+20	+20	+10	+10
Gross Cash Flow/Year	−240	+100	+100	+110	+110	+120	+120

FIGURE 10.2

Basic cash flow chart for internal project example.

personnel training. It's assumed that initial working capital is recovered when the asset is retired. In situations involving sales support, working capital can fluctuate, and the incremental change is charted. It's possible for working capital to be negative (savings), such as when the project actually reduces the amount of working capital that had been required to support an operation.

In this example, funds required to purchase these current assets (estimated at $50,000) are identified as a cash outflow at the point in time when the operation starts up—in this case, the year immediately following project completion. We only include *incremental values* when constructing a cash flow chart. Consequently, we only include the necessary changes in working capital in our cash flow chart. This entry is illustrated in Figure 10.3.

Completing the Cash Flow Chart: Salvage Value

The term *salvage value* refers to the estimated value of an asset when we are done using it and decide to sell it. Also referred to as *market value*, this is the expected selling price of a property when the asset can no longer be used productively by its owner. If you look at the depreciation schedules in Figure 9.4, you will note that the sum of all the annual depreciation percentages for each line item is 100%. This doesn't necessarily mean that an asset has no salvage value. However, the realization of salvage value—that is, the actual sale of the equipment—will probably not take place until well after the study period of 6 years. With that in mind, our example does not include a line item

Cash Flow Type	Number of Years after Project Initiation						
	0	1	2	3	4	5	6
Cash Outflows:							
Design and Engineering	−70						
Capital Implementation	−170						
Operating Costs		−50	−50	−50	−50	−50	−50
Working Capital		−50					
Cash Inflows:							
Routine Maintenance		+80	+80	+80	+80	+80	+80
Material Usage		+40	+40	+60	+60	+80	+80
Waste		+30	+30	+20	+20	+10	+10
Before Tax Cash Flow	−240	+50	+100	+110	+110	+120	+120
Depreciation Deduction		−48	−76	+45	+28	+28	+15
Taxable Cash Flow		+2	+24	+65	+82	+92	+105
Income Tax on Cash Flow		−1	−10	−26	−33	−37	−42
After Tax Cash Flow	−240	+49	+90	+84	+77	+83	+78

FIGURE 10.3

The next step in cash flow chart development.

for salvage value. Had we believed that we would be selling the equipment at the end of 6 years, we would have included its fair market value as a positive cash flow in year 6.

Completing the Cash Flow Chart: Depreciation and Its Effect on Income Tax

Depreciation is the decrease in value of any physical properties (assets) with the passage of time and use. It is an accounting concept that establishes an annual deduction against before-tax income, and it is eventually displayed as a component of a company's financial statements. For our purposes in cash flow charting, depreciation is used primarily as a method for properly estimating the cash flows relating to the income tax that is applied to positive cash flows. This process has two basic elements: (1) identifying the specific and appropriate values for asset depreciation; and (2) calculating the effect of asset depreciation on the income tax burden.

The first major step in dealing with depreciation simply consists of understanding exactly what values to plug into the cash flow chart for depreciation. This information was illustrated (in part) in Figure 9.4, The MACRS Guidelines for Establishing Depreciation. Note that this chart does not provide information on the break-down for all classes of assets. If you are interested in more detail, complete information on MACRS can be found through an Internet search.

The second major step in dealing with depreciation is knowing how to adjust cash flows in a way that properly incorporates their effect on project cash flows. It's important to note that depreciation is not an actual cash flow—it is primarily an accounting practice. The common rationale given to explain the fact that depreciation isn't a cash flow relies on recognizing no money actually "changes hands." However, depreciation does affect the amount of income tax associated with a project's positive cash flow, and income tax *is* an actual cash flow. Perhaps the best way to show the effect of depreciation is by simply continuing our analysis.

All the assets we are placing in service on this project are in the 5-year recovery period category. Let's further assume that the corporate income tax rate is 40%. We already know that the total value of the assets is $240,000.

Figure 10.3 illustrates how the cash flow chart would look after including the effects of working capital and the income tax adjustment due to depreciation. Note that the after tax cash flow (which is essentially the "punch line" here) is calculated by subtracting the income tax burden from the before tax cash flow. The intermediate line items are shaded to enhance this critical point.

That's just about everything for this example; we've covered all the basics. It is quite possible that you will encounter other elements as you begin performing your own financial analyses, but this example provides you with a good idea of the process and components involved in a financial analysis.

However, one very big element of the overall financial analysis is still missing. If you know what it is, you can go to the head of the class.

You guessed it—the time value of money! That will play out in the next step—when we finally do perform the full set of financial calculations.

CALCULATING THE FOUR BASIC FINANCIAL METRICS

This is where everything we've been discussing (i.e., time value of money, discounting, the cost of capital, hurdle rates, and cash flow diagramming) finally comes together! Let's begin by calculating the NPV of this hypothetical project.

Calculating Net Present Value

To calculate NPV, we are essentially replicating the procedure illustrated in Figure 8.15. The first step consists of converting the cash flow chart (Fig. 10.3) into a cash flow diagram. This conversion is illustrated in Figure 10.4.

The second step consists of adding the effects of discounting. In this example, we will assume a hurdle rate of 10% (as you'll recall, this is the company's *cost of capital*). This means that we must discount all future cash flows by 10%, as shown in Figure 10.5. Note that values shown in the figure are rounded to the nearest hundred dollars, to simplify the diagram.

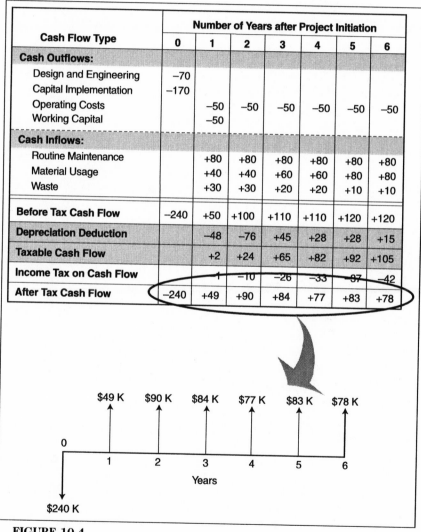

Cash Flow Type	Number of Years after Project Initiation						
	0	1	2	3	4	5	6
Cash Outflows:							
Design and Engineering	−70						
Capital Implementation	−170						
Operating Costs		−50	−50	−50	−50	−50	−50
Working Capital		−50					
Cash Inflows:							
Routine Maintenance		+80	+80	+80	+80	+80	+80
Material Usage		+40	+40	+60	+60	+80	+80
Waste		+30	+30	+20	+20	+10	+10
Before Tax Cash Flow	−240	+50	+100	+110	+110	+120	+120
Depreciation Deduction		−48	−76	+45	+28	+28	+15
Taxable Cash Flow		+2	+24	+65	+82	+92	+105
Income Tax on Cash Flow		−1	−10	−26	−33	−37	−42
After Tax Cash Flow	−240	+49	+90	+84	+77	+83	+78

$49 K $90 K $84 K $77 K $83 K $78 K

Years

$240 K

FIGURE 10.4

Converting the cash flow chart to a cash flow diagram.

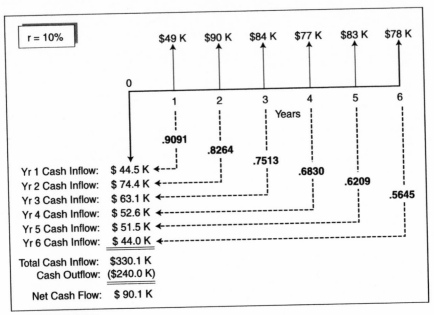

FIGURE 10.5

Calculating the net present value of the example.

Also shown in Figure 10.5 is the third step, which consists of arithmetically combining all cash flows. This leads to the calculation of an NPV of $90,100 for this proposed project.

Does this project represent a good investment? On the surface it would seem so, because the NPV is a positive number—the financial return on this project is large enough to service the debt required to fund it *and* return $90,100 of wealth to the company. Generally speaking, this would seem like a good thing.

However, in the interest of making a more well-informed decision, we should probably look at some of the other financial metrics related to this project investment.

Determining the Payback Period and the Maximum Exposure

Both of these useful financial metrics can be found by examining Figure 10.6, which modifies the previous version of the cash flow chart to add the effects of discounting and to provide "running totals," or *cumulative cash flow values*. You may also note that this cumulative cash flow value approach is yet another way of deriving NPV. The final value in the cumulative discounted cash flow line (lower right-hand corner) is the NPV.

Cash Flow Type	Number of Years after Project Initiation						
	0	1	2	3	4	5	6
Cash Outflows:							
Design and Engineering	−70						
Capital Implementation	−170						
Operating Costs		−50	−50	−50	−50	−50	−50
Working Capital		−50					
Cash Inflows:							
Routine Maintenance		+80	+80	+80	+80	+80	+80
Material Usage		+40	+40	+60	+60	+80	+80
Waste		+30	+30	+20	+20	+10	+10
Before Tax Cash Flow	−240	+50	+100	+110	+110	+120	+120
Depreciation Deduction		−48	−76	+45	+28	+28	+15
Taxable Cash Flow		+2	+24	+65	+82	+92	+105
Income Tax on Cash Flow		−1	−10	−26	−33	−37	−42
After Tax Cash Flow (ATCF)	−240	+49	+90	+84	+77	+83	+78
Discounted ATCF	−240	+44.5	+74.4	+63.1	+52.6	+51.5	+44.0
Cumulative Discounted ATCF	−240	−195.5	−121.1	−58.0	−5.4	+46.1	+90.1

FIGURE 10.6

Adding discounting and cumulative totals to the cash flow chart.

If you visually scan across the cumulative cash flow line, you can determine the payback period and the maximum exposure. In this case, the payback period occurs somewhere very early in Year 5 of the post-project life cycle, where the cumulative cash flow "crosses over" from a negative value to a positive value.

The maximum exposure is just as easily determined. It is the largest negative value of all the cumulative cash flow totals. Its value is $240,000, and occurs at the end of Year 1. This is not a huge surprise, because this was a nominal year-long project, with benefits accruing immediately upon project completion.

Calculating the Internal Rate of Return

Calculating the IRR for a uneven stream of cash flows (which is what most projects are) is similar to the approach we covered in Chapter 9—just a bit more complex. There are two reasonable methods for calculating IRR—the numerical approach and the calculator approach. Let's consider the numerical approach first.

Calculating IRR by formula isn't quite as easy as it sounds. The process involves using the equation for calculating NPV:

$$NPV = \frac{Cash\ Flow_{Year\ 0}}{(1+r)^0} + \frac{Cash\ Flow_{Year\ 1}}{(1+r)^1} + \frac{Cash\ Flow_{Year\ 2}}{(1+r)^2} + ...+ \frac{Cash\ Flow_{Year\ N}}{(1+r)^N}$$

Where:
N = useful life
and
r = the discount rate, cost of capital, or required return

To calculate IRR using this formula, NPV is set to zero, and the equation is solved for "r." Using our example, the equation to be solved would be:

$$0 = \frac{\$ -240\ K}{(1+r)^0} + \frac{\$ 49\ K}{(1+r)^1} + \frac{\$ 90\ K}{(1+r)^2} + \frac{\$ 84\ K}{(1+r)^3} + \frac{\$ 77\ K}{(1+r)^4} + \frac{\$ 83\ K}{(1+r)^5} + \frac{\$ 78\ K}{(1+r)^6}$$

Unfortunately, solving this as an equation is doable, but quite tedious, because it must be done through trial-and-error.

I would much prefer to pick up my trusty financial calculator and use that to calculate IRR. Figure 10.7 illustrates how the process would play out using the financial calculator approach.

Actually, once you get the hang of it, the pattern is reasonably easy and obvious: You simply program each individual year's cash flow into the calculator. After that's been accomplished, a push of the IRR button (I/YR) is all it takes to get the answer—which, in this case, is 10.31%.

An IRR of 10.31% makes sense here. Since the project has a relatively small, but positive NPV, we would expect the project's IRR to beat the 10% cost of capital by a small amount. In practice, you will find that taking a few minutes to do a quick reality check, then reconciling your NPV with your IRR calculations will serve as a useful process step.

PUTTING THE FINANCIAL METRICS TOGETHER: EVALUATING THE INVESTMENT

OK, so we've performed a financial analysis on a proposed project. The result is that we have calculated an estimated value for each of the four basic financial metrics. To recap, here are those values:

- The NPV is $90,100.

Steps You Perform	Numbers You Input and Buttons You Push	What You See in the Display
1. Clear the calculator.	GOLD C ALL	1 P_Yr / 0.00
2. Input the number of payments/year.	1 GOLD P/YR	1.00
3. Input the initial (Year 0) cash flow.	240000 +/− CFj	0 / -240,000.00
4. Input the Year 1 cash flow.	44500 CFj	1 / 44,500.00
5. Input the Year 2 cash flow.	74400 CFj	2 / 74400.00
6. Input the Year 3 cash flow.	63100 CFj	3 / 63,100.00
7. Input the Year 4 cash flow.	52600 CFj	4 / 52,600.00
8. Input the Year 5 cash flow.	51500 CFj	5 / 51,500.00
9. Input the Year 6 cash flow.	44000 CFj	6 / 44,000.00
10. Request the unknown (IRR).	GOLD IRR/YR	10.31
11. **Answer: 10.31%**		

FIGURE 10.7

Calculating the net present value of the example.

- The IRR is 10.31%.
- The payback period is about 4.1 years.
- The maximum exposure is $240,000.

Unfortunately, no hard and fast rules really dictate whether this project should be approved. We can, however, make some insightful observations and useful comparisons using these metrics.

First, the NPV is a positive number. This is inherently a good thing, because any positive value represents a "favorable" investment. However, we really don't know if $90,100 is characteristic of a *relatively strong project*—either within our organization or within the portfolio grouping containing this project. The truth is that we really won't know how relatively attractive any project is until we put all the projects into their appropriate portfolio categories, calculate the NPV of each, and use that as a method for prioritization (see Chapter 7).

How about the payback period? To my way of thinking, this project *seems* to take a long time to return our money. A payback period of more than 4 years is relatively slow. But to truly evaluate the attractiveness of any given payback period, we need to do two things: (1) compare it to the length of time we can reasonably expect the assets being put in place to have useful value, and (2) evaluate the probability that the assets will be rendered unproductive or useless throughout the payback period.

For example, if we could expect the deliverables of this project to have true utility for, say, 15 years or more, reaching the break-even point in 4 years is not a bad deal, even though it has been placed in the 6-year asset class life category (remember, that's primarily a depreciation issue). A 15-year life (or more) is common with so-called "durable assets," such as buildings, office furniture, and many types of manufacturing equipment.

If, on the other hand, the nature of the project deliverables is such that they could wear out, fail, or become obsolete in, say, 4 or 5 years, a payback period of 4 years doesn't look so good. This situation (or worse) can sometimes be the case with assets related to information technology or other assets utilized in the high-tech arena. The key point here is the simple recognition that we remain exposed to a potential loss during the entire payback period.

With respect to this project's maximum exposure, it's difficult for me to know whether $240,000 is inherently good or bad. In an actual company (or organization), you would know, and the answer would likely depend on a combination of critical factors. Some factors are *absolute*—for example, the total amount of cash available for projects, and some factors are comparative, such as the maximum exposure of *other* proposed projects.

Some companies choose to combine the major metrics to create what I often refer to as *second-level metrics*. One popular combination that is used as a tool for comparing projects is the *ratio between the NPV and the total project cost* (noting that total project cost is often equivalent to maximum exposure and cash outlay). Obviously, this ratio serves as a method for simultaneously comparing NPVs. As one method of screening projects (discussed in Chapter 7), a company may decide to establish minimum thresholds for this ratio.

For instance, in the hypothetical project we just analyzed, the numerical value of the ratio is 0.38 ($90,100 divided by $240,000). This ratio could be used as a method for evaluating and/or comparing the relative strength and attractiveness of very dissimilar projects within the portfolio. For example, another project with a completely different cash flow profile, different NPV, and different total cash outlay might have a ratio of 0.75. That would be a more attractive project—from the standpoint of this dimension, at least.

The bottom line is that you can combine the four basic financial metrics in many ways to apply them to project evaluations or comparisons.

FINANCIAL ANALYSIS IN REVERSE: CALCULATING THE MAXIMUM JUSTIFIABLE PROJECT COST

Projects typically solve problems or exploit new opportunities. In the case of problems, we often know what the problem is before we know the solution. In the case of opportunities, we often can define the characteristics of the opportunity itself, but may not know exactly what it's going to take to pull it off.

Let's now take this logic one step farther. If we know what the problem is, we can calculate the value in solving it. If we can describe an opportunity, we often can calculate the value in exploiting it. In either case, we are referring to our ability to calculate the benefits stream before we identify a specific project solution. This is a common situation.

An approach that I refer to as *calculating the maximum justifiable project cost* can have significant value in either situation. It can be used to consider financial feasibility, choose reasonable alternatives to investigate, or even screen proposed projects.

Basically, the approach consists of using the knowledge and methods described earlier—but "in reverse," so to speak.

Let's take the example we just considered—the case of a departmentally funded capital improvement project. This time, though, imagine that we do not yet know what it will take to bring about the desired increase in efficiency in that department's manufacturing operations.

However, we can paint a picture of how this increase in efficiency would likely manifest itself, as a reduction in routine maintenance costs, a decrease in material costs, and a reduction in the amount of waste. Acknowledging that, in many cases, these are relatively crude estimates, we're still able to take a stab at estimating the benefit stream. As a cash flow diagram, it would look like Figure 10.8.

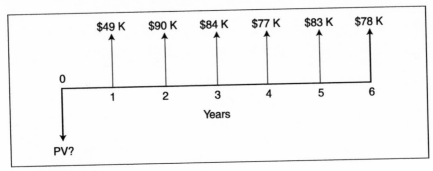

FIGURE 10.8

Calculating the maximum justifiable project cost.

You've probably figured out where we're headed next. If we now calculate the discounted value of this future benefit stream, we have determined the maximum justifiable project cost, because this is the point at which NPV = 0. If we were to spend one dollar more, the result would be an NPV of less than zero. Anything less would yield a positive NPV.

This is definitely not an exact science—in fact it is a relatively crude approach, aimed primarily at establishing a line in the sand. However, it can be a powerful tool in helping us avoid the potentially significant amount of the time and expense involved in conjuring up solutions that ultimately may be unjustifiable.

ENHANCING THE FINANCIAL ANALYSIS PROCESS BY INTRODUCING RISK

And so, we come to the end of the process of calculating the financial attractiveness of a project. To me, this is a cornerstone in the business of appropriately viewing projects as investments and seeking to understand them as such.

But just as we cannot claim that we totally understand a project plan until we have done some risk analysis, the same holds true for a project financial analysis.

Once again, let's consider how most of us address our personal investments, such as stocks and mutual funds. One of the key criteria many of us are likely to use in determining whether we wish to pursue a given financial investment is tied to its *risk rating*. Some investments are riskier than others.

The same can be said of projects—even two projects with identical NPVs. It's inevitable that one of those projects is inherently riskier. Is the difference in financial risk large? What is the nature of the difference in financial risk?

We'll examine projects from this perspective in the next chapter.

CHAPTER 11

Risk Management, Decision-Making, and Business

With regard to the subject of risk management, I have some good news and some bad news.

The good news is that the practice of integrating risk management and project management has truly come into its own over the past several years. Risk management has grown into a skill set that is widely recognized as an indispensable component of the project manager's toolbox. Many of today's project practitioners in many companies do a very good job of assessing and managing *project-level risk*.

The bad news ties directly to my use of the term "project-level risk." This is another way of saying that, unfortunately, the practices of risk analysis and risk management in many companies are more or less limited to dealing with uncertainties and threats that may be encountered on projects *after those projects have been approved*. For the most part, project teams utilize risk management techniques as a means of minimizing the amount of unfavorable variance between the project's final outcome and the targets for cost, schedule, and deliverable performance—targets that were established at the time of project approval.

However, for many companies, there exists a significantly larger potential for improving their overall approach to project management, by simply applying good risk management tools and techniques *before projects are formally approved*. Specifically, these companies can make risk analysis a key component of the project selection process. These improvement opportunities fall within two major areas.

One major area in which companies can reduce risk doesn't even require the application of any specific risk management tools, per se. It comes in the form of simply adopting some of the sound portfolio management techniques that we covered in Chapters 5 through 7. The reality is that many companies today do not *regularly* practice many of the techniques we discussed. They do not recognize (or don't believe in?) the critical importance of developing and adhering to a structured process for developing a balanced, feasible portfolio of projects. Even worse, they don't recognize the legitimate business value gained from using a structured, analytical, data-driven approach to project selection and project coordination. In the absence of sound procedures, inefficient and costly practices abound.

For example, some companies tend to accept (and execute) any and all projects that seem to have merit. They do not put proposed projects through a rigorous process that ensures they are financially justified. They do not actively coordinate the launch and/or execution of projects in order to optimize resource utilization. And they do not consider other critical portfolio management issues, such as portfolio balance, counterproductive project interactions, and competing or conflicting objectives among projects.

Perhaps one of the largest business risks that a company can assume—relating to managing project investments—is the practice of engaging in unregulated and uncontrolled project selection and coordination.

Unfortunately, many companies do not recognize the damage that can accompany this practice, or the potential improvement in business results that can result from the application of sound portfolio management techniques. Hopefully, this will change with time and the growing awareness of the connection between business and project management.

A second, more focused area in which companies may reduce their overall project investment risk comes in the form of applying sound risk analysis techniques as part of the project selection process. Although a given project may appear to be a wise investment, a careful consideration of the results obtained from a thorough risk analysis may lead management decision-makers to a different conclusion. Even if they should decide to move forward with that project, they do so with their eyes wide open—thanks to insights revealed through that same risk assessment. A good risk analysis can help companies avoid choosing projects that aren't right for them.

So, we find ourselves returning to the very beginning of this book, when we presented a number of "revelations." As you may recall, our very first revelation stated: "It doesn't matter how well you execute a project if you're working on the wrong project!" And the simple fact is that companies that do not include risk and uncertainty as basic elements of their project selection criteria run the risk of choosing a set of projects not suited to meet their business goals.

In other cases, a good risk analysis can help companies avoid projects that are not compatible with their orientation toward risk and uncertainty. It's quite possible, for example, that a given project could have a desirable net present value (NPV) when the "most likely" single-point estimates are used to prepare the financial analysis, but it may be judged to be unacceptably volatile, once a comprehensive risk analysis reveals that final results could fall into an extremely wide range of values. Insights such as this are revealed only when risk analysis is part of the project selection methodology.

I suspect that you may be feeling a bit cheated right about now. The material that we covered in the last chapter may have given you the impression that the process for selecting the best projects is pretty straightforward. You may have formed the opinion that simply applying a basic, financially centered procedure to make project selection decisions would put you on Easy Street. More to the point, you may be thinking that all you really need to do is generate unbiased cash flow forecasts, find out what the company's discount rate is, understand how to deal with depreciation and taxes, and crank out NPVs for all the projects under consideration. Unfortunately, the process of ensuring that the best possible set of projects have been selected is a bit more complex than that.

Which leads to even more bad news: Simply following the procedure we've covered in the book so far may not *guarantee* that the highest quality decisions will be made when it comes to project selection. Even companies that have adopted well-defined processes for identifying and selecting projects may remain vulnerable to the prospect of running headlong into significant unfavorable business impacts brought on by those projects. Why? Because they failed to incorporate risk analysis into their project selection process.

So, risk analysis procedures—directed primarily at portfolio management and project selection processes—will be the main focus of this chapter. We examine a number of specific analytical techniques, including sensitivity analysis (several varieties), break-even analysis, and structuring tools. We also direct our attention on when and how risk analysis methods can be applied.

Even if you are familiar with project risk management, I urge you to read on. This chapter provides a slightly different twist on the way risk management techniques are applied. The "classic" project risk management techniques that you are probably familiar with are intended primarily to aid project teams and organizations in avoiding unfavorable circumstances (commonly called *risk events* or *potential problems*) that have the ability to adversely affect the outcome of a given project, once approved.

In this chapter, our focus is slightly different. Although varied in their nature, each of the analytical tools we're about to examine is aimed at the same basic objective—*enabling management decision-makers to consistently make high-quality business decisions in the face of uncertainty*.

THE OBJECTIVES OF RISK MANAGEMENT AND DECISION-MAKING

Whenever you chat with project managers about the subject of risk management, it is a foregone conclusion that one very well-known principle will undoubtedly find its way into the conversation—organizational executives and senior managers *hate* surprises.

The obvious corollary to that principle is the one that states that it is in our best interest to keep organizational managers from being surprised. This kind of thinking has led to the widespread application of the project risk management procedures commonly applied to project efforts today.

But we need to take that logic one more step—backward. We must recognize the fact that these procedures need not be limited to project efforts that have already been authorized. They can (and should) be applied much earlier—to the processes of project selection, project prioritization, and portfolio construction.

With that in mind, I'd like to share another important principle, although one not quite as well understood as those described: Whether they specifically request it or not, most management decision-makers appreciate (and every one of them *should* appreciate!) the opportunity to gather as much knowledge and insight on the *business implications* of projects as they possibly can. And they would really appreciate this knowledge and insight *up front*, before they have made the investment decision.

So, we have put our finger on the crux of the matter and the objective of sound, portfolio-focused risk management: What can be done to help organizational decision-makers avoid the risk of making poor project selection decisions?

First, let's clarify what is meant by the term "poor project selection decisions" by examining a fairly obvious example. Let's consider the decision to authorize and execute a project in which things don't go very well, a project with an unfavorable (and very undesirable) impact on the business.

Now, to be fair, the most obvious problem with this statement is that none of us have a crystal ball—none of us could have *definitively* predicted that kind of an unfavorable future outcome with total certainty. This is true. Regrettably, though, this can be a crippling mindset. Knowing that perfect, totally accurate predictions cannot be developed is the kind of thinking that frequently stalls efforts to perform systematic, rigorous risk assessments on project investments. I have found this perspective to be alarmingly pervasive. In far too many companies, the prevailing attitude is: If we cannot predict the future with absolute certainty, it's simply not worth doing any analysis at all.

This is very unfortunate. Why? Because the fact that none of us can make flawless predictions is really not the driving force behind the application of formal risk analysis methods. Risk assessment is not about predicting the future with unquestionable accuracy or precision—it is about positioning ourselves to make informed, intelligent, eyes-wide-open choices.

To illustrate this point, let's consider Figure 11.1. This graphic provides a pictorial comparison of the inherent variability that exists in the NPV of two projects. In this simple example, let's say circumstances dictate that our management decision-makers must choose to pursue either Project Alpha or Project Beta. Certainly, a comparison of NPVs would enter into this decision.

Before continuing, however, it's worth noting that the curves in Figure 11.1 are representative of the type of graphical outputs that management decision-makers could expect to see from the people performing project risk analyses (we will be examining how these graphs are prepared later in the chapter).

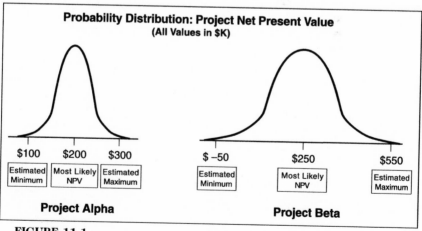

FIGURE 11.1

A risk-based comparison of project NPVs.

With only a brief examination of Figure 11.1, you can probably figure out where I'm going with this example. Although Project Alpha has a smaller NPV, it can readily be characterized as the "safer bet" of the two projects, considering the full range of potential project outcomes for each. In fact, an analysis that considers uncertainty reveals that—under some potential circumstances—Project Beta could actually result in a *negative NPV* (which we now know is a bad thing!).

However, while Project Alpha is clearly less volatile than Project Beta, we cannot categorically state that Project Alpha is the preferred choice for our organization. For example, within organizations that tend to be more *risk aggressive*, a project that holds the promise of achieving an NPV of $500,000 or more may actually be the more appealing choice, despite the recognition that a negative NPV has an equal chance of occurring.

Herein lies one of the beauties of risk analysis. It's true objective is not about the numbers, but in the way it can paint an enlightening picture for management decision-makers that offers them a deeper understanding of the decision they are about to make. In this case, of course, the decision was to select Project Alpha or Project Beta. The picture illustrated in Figure 11.1 would never have been painted if the analysis had been built solely upon *most likely* values—a common approach for organizations that perform financial analyses, but not risk analyses. For them, the clear choice would have been Project Beta—the project with the highest NPV.

But if things had not gone as well as expected on Project Beta (which Figure 11.1 identifies as a possibility), the resulting NPV would have been very small—perhaps even negative. And if that happened, management decision-makers would surely have been—you guessed it—*surprised*!

Another beauty of the risk management methodology is its adaptability. Although NPV is the standard for comparison in Figure 11.1, the same type of analysis of variability could have been supplied to management decision-makers on any number of project attributes that they may be interested in understanding. Analyses such as this are only limited by the needs of decision-makers or, at times, your imagination and common sense.

Perhaps the ultimate beauty relates to the controversy over the accuracy of the input numbers—the unfortunate reason behind the underutilization of the risk management methodology in project-based business analyses. The reality is this: If the input values are *reasonably* valid, it doesn't really matter if either or both of the cash flow projections for Projects Alpha and Beta are 100% accurate. The decision-making value comes from our ability to draw comparisons between these projects and from our newly acquired knowledge of the wide range of potential outcomes associated with both projects.

DEALING WITH RISK AND UNCERTAINTY IN BUSINESS DECISIONS

Nearly everyone who is familiar with life on projects grows to recognize that they are often riddled with risk and uncertainty. At the project level, this often translates into the recognition that potential problems are continually lurking just around the corner—problems that affect our ability to deliver projects on time, on schedule, and at the desired level of performance.

But risk and uncertainty also lurks in a higher level within and across the entire portfolio of projects. A wide variety of critical decisions must be made that will affect the business impact of each individual project, as well as the overall project portfolio itself. These decisions include:

- Which projects should be pursued and which should not
- When each project can (and should) be launched
- Whether projects can be adequately resourced
- The amount of interaction between projects
- Whether we will realize the return on investment we expect

The presence of risk and uncertainty can significantly impact these issues as well as many others in the organization. Before we get too deeply involved in a discussion on how to deal with risk and uncertainty, let's make sure we know what were dealing with.

RISK AND UNCERTAINTY: A QUICK REFRESHER

If you have read up on risk management, you've probably encountered a variety of definitions for the terms *risk* and *uncertainty*. Rather than getting hung up on strict definitions, I'd like to simply take a moment to share what I believe are underlying concepts behind these terms.

Uncertainty stems from the fact that we all suffer from *a lack of perfect information*—particularly with regard to the future. In the case of a new product introduction initiative, for example, we don't know exactly how many units of a product we're going to sell. And because we're dealing with a new manufacturing process, we don't know exactly how much of a profit we will make on each unit. We can't say for sure what impact this new product will have on our existing sales. And we cannot state with total certainty what our competitor's response will be. And so on—you get the point.

So, whether we like to admit it or not, we "make up" numbers—they're called estimates. If we're smart, we openly recognize the fact that we do not have perfect information; consequently, we place ranges on our estimates. And, even if we cannot establish an exact value for something, we can take comfort knowing that the value is likely to fall within some range of values. Normally, the size of this range reflects the amount of uncertainty that exists.

Risk is something we must take on because *we do not have perfect information*. While uncertainly deals primarily with inputs, risk has more to do with outputs—in this case, the decision to choose between Project Alpha and Project Beta. Because we don't have perfect knowledge or information, we are unable to determine the exact identity of the best decision. However, we are obligated to make a decision under uncertainty. When we make that decision, we assume a certain amount of risk. For optimists, the risk is that the decision we make will prove to be less than optimal. For pessimists, the risk is that we will actually make the wrong decision. In reality, both are actually on the same continuum: Risk is essentially a question of degree.

For example, if we were to choose Project Beta, and the actual NPV eventually turned out to be $100K, it's quite possible that this was not the optimal decision (speculating, of course, that Project Alpha would have yielded a higher NPV). However, if we were to choose Project Beta, and the actual NPV turned out to be a negative amount, it would be appropriate to say that this was the wrong decision. Not an overly critical point, but one worth making.

SOURCES OF BUSINESS AND FINANCIAL UNCERTAINTY IN PROJECT INVESTMENT DECISIONS

A tremendous amount of uncertainty exists in nearly any project. Risk and uncertainty are immutably tied together. In nearly every project circumstance, the uncertainty (or risk) will come from a variety of sources and assume a variety of forms, such as technical risk, cost and schedule risk, risk of commercial success, and risk of achieving the predicted profitability. The sources of the uncertainty and risk will be unique to each individual project. They are likely to be embedded within the input variables that you used to predict any given project outcome. The process for identifying which input variables may be appropriate for a risk assessment will be discussed a bit later, when we address the topic of performing a sensitivity analysis.

In some cases, however, sources of uncertainty may exist within the assessment process itself. Let's consider, for example, the process of performing a financial analysis on a project—which typically leads to the full set of *investment decisions* (i.e., project justification, project approval, and project selection). In my opinion (and in keeping with the philosophy of this book), these are certainly among the most important and most valuable risk assessments that you will perform. A particular set of financially oriented uncertainties is likely to exist, specific to each individual project. (We discuss how to uncover them shortly.)

But an equally important—almost universal—set of uncertainties is likely to exist in *any* risk assessment related to the investment decision.

Your knowledge of these process-based sources of uncertainty will form the foundation for your ability (and your organization's ability) to develop a valid and consistent approach to performing risk assessments on investment decisions. Some of the more common process-based sources of uncertainty that exist within nearly every investment decision analysis are described in the next sections.

Uncertainty Source #1: The Reliability and Validity of the Analytical Inputs

Perfect information is rarely available when we are building project plans and making predictions regarding project outcomes. In the absence of perfect information, we develop estimates for these *input variables*.

The essence of risk management comes in recognizing that, sometimes, these estimates are good and sometimes they're bad. Or, to put it in the common vernacular, sometimes they're "sharp," and sometimes they're "fuzzy." This is a reality of life within the world of estimating.

Uncertainty Source #2: The Level of Precision and Accuracy of the Analytical Outputs

Although it may sound a bit unscientific—if not unsophisticated—it is very important that some level of understanding is reached by all parties involved with respect to *exactly how fuzzy* the resulting predictions, or output variables, may be.

It's equally important to note the corollary of this statement: The responsibility for ensuring that management decision-makers understand the quality of predicted project outcomes rests squarely on the shoulders of those performing the assessment. These outcomes might take the form of cost or schedule estimates, predicted levels of deliverable performance, or anticipated financial results.

Perhaps one of the largest sources of chronic misunderstanding that exists between project teams and upper management occurs when project teams provide estimated values and fail to qualify those values with respect to their quality. In most cases, the unfortunate result—and the source of misunderstanding—occurs when organizational managers believe that project teams have a much greater level of understanding, and therefore have things much more "under control" than they actually do. This is exactly when "surprises" start to happen.

The quality (relative goodness or badness) of estimated values and predictions can be expressed using two dimensions: *accuracy* and *precision*. Figure 11.2 attempts to clarify the difference between these two sometimes confusing terms. Accuracy and precision really just represent two different states of nature with respect to your estimates or predicted outcomes.

It is just as important to communicate these states of nature as it is to communicate the estimates or predictions themselves!

Communicating this kind of information, which really just speaks to the quality of your numbers, doesn't necessarily have to be a rigorous study in statistics; in many cases, it can be a simple expression of what the team believes to be true about the estimates or predictions.

For example, the target shown on the left side of Figure 11.2 could be qualified by saying: "We are very confident that this is the 'correct' value if all the contributing factors turn out as predicted. Unfortunately though, many things could change the input data and throw the overall estimate off. That's why the range is so wide."

The target pictured on the right side of Figure 11.2 might be qualified by saying: "The quality of the input data we have—based on the model we've developed—is very good, and not prone to a lot of

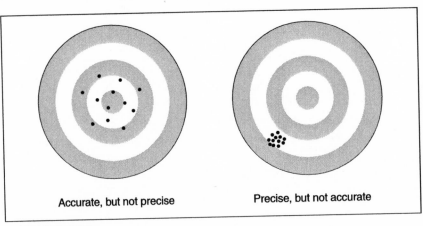

Accurate, but not precise   Precise, but not accurate

FIGURE 11.2

The dimensions of estimates and predictions.

fluctuation. The problem is that we're not sure we've properly captured the whole picture. So, even though the range is pretty small, the bottom-line value itself is somewhat of a guess."

It is certainly not necessary to use these exact words, or anything like them. The key point is that you take the time to communicate these kinds of insights to management decision-makers. A certain amount of risk is always present in any decision they make. You should recognize, though, that the amount of risk assumed in *any* decision is amplified—sometimes by a considerable amount—if decision makers remain unaware of the quality of the estimates and predictions that you put in front of them.

An equally important argument for communicating the quality of your estimates comes in noting that it can often lead to higher quality estimates. How? Because when management decision makers become aware that their decisions may be based on potentially shaky ground, they may choose a course of action aimed at improving estimate quality. Typically, these actions involve giving the estimators the time or resources required to "tighten up" the numbers. Very often, deciding whether it is worth the additional time and expense to improve estimate quality (and presumably the quality of the decision itself) is based on a principle referred to as *the value of information*. (We discuss this concept soon.)

Uncertainty Source #3: The Type of Business that Is Connected to the Project

This source of uncertainty has to do with what line of business the project owner (the one supporting the project) is engaged in. Here, the uncertainty is more germane to organizations (and projects) that are tied to the creation of products and services, and it may manifest itself in any combination of the following ways:

- **The consumer market and its relation to the project's line of business.** Some lines of business tend to enjoy a significant amount of long-term stability, while others are naturally volatile. For example, projects that involve the application of leading-edge technology and concepts that are new to the marketplace tend to be inherently more volatile than those that have been in the market for some time. A company that manufactures a line of household cleaning products is likely to have a significantly smaller level of inherent risk across its project portfolio than a company that prides itself on being a developer and manufacturer of the newest household gadgets. As a result, project investments that are related to more volatile lines of business, new to the market, or that are leading-edge, are likely to have significantly more uncertainty inherent to their estimates, predictions of the future, and therefore financial analyses.

- **The current economy and its effect on consumer spending.** This source of uncertainty is similar to the previous one, except that it is tied more to the general economic environment than to consumer preference. Some lines of business undergo considerable fluctuation depending on the state of the economy. Other lines of business are tied to products and services whose demand will remain relatively stable despite the general economy. In many cases, this phenomenon is tied to the perception of whether a given product is considered a necessity or a luxury. Here, timing is everything. Introducing products or services that are viewed as a luxury in the midst of a strong economy can be wildly successful. Introducing the same products and services during difficult economic times can spell financial disaster for a company. Obviously, projects that are affected by the state of the economy are also the most difficult to predict. To make matters worse, this source of uncertainty is frequently overlooked during the risk analysis phase on a project's financial analysis.
- **The current economy and its effect on corporate spending.** One way that companies react to poor economic times is to restrict the flow of capital to projects. This practice is commonly referred to as *capital rationing*. It can be very interesting to note a company's motivation for doing so. In some cases, a company may have become severely short on cash and is simply reluctant to take on additional debt due to the nature of its business. In most cases, this is an understandable action. Unfortunately, though, I have witnessed other situations involving restricted project spending that is not quite so understandable. I have seen several companies who, in slow economic times, have plenty of cash to spend on projects, but restrict their project activity under a blanket policy of "no unnecessary spending." For some companies, equating projects with unnecessary spending reflects their lack of understanding that financially justified projects actually generate positive cash flows—a good thing during periods of economic hardship. Investing in strong projects is exactly what they should be doing; instead, they do the opposite.

Uncertainty Source #4: The Utility of the Assets Produced by the Project

In some cases, assets created as a result of a project investment are likely to have fairly widespread use. In other cases, assets are created to satisfy a specialized or unique application or function. The value of the asset(s)—and therefore the financial justification of the project investment—depends almost entirely on the demand for its specialized application.

This generally results in a much greater level of inherent risk and uncertainty.

Uncertainty Source #5: The Useful Life of the Project (Length of the Study Period)

As we discovered in Chapter 9, the *useful life* of a project investment is the window of time within which the financial analysis is performed. Generally speaking, the size of this window is determined by a company's financial department. Although the useful life is certainly not an arbitrary value, it is subject to change, based on a variety of factors. It therefore represents a potential source of uncertainty that can have a significant effect on the financial analysis of a project. Projects that are subjected to a shorter useful life must be capable of producing larger, faster financial returns to be considered financially attractive.

REDUCING RISK BY USING HIGHER-QUALITY INFORMATION

Many sources of uncertainty—and therefore risk—can exist in the inputs, outputs, and assumption base used to predict project outcomes, such as the estimated financial attractiveness of a given project investment. For many, the knowledge that major decisions are based on somewhat fuzzy numbers can lead to these kinds of questions:

- Does it make sense to simply accept all the fuzziness embedded in our financial analysis?
- Is there something we can do to reduce the resulting fuzziness in our predictions?
- Would a better decision result from higher quality input values?

These very appropriate—if not insightful—questions should be asked prior to launching into virtually any risk assessment process, and they are directly tied to the principle of *the value of information*. This principle stems from our recognition that, in virtually any financial analysis we perform, decision-makers will be obliged to act upon imperfect information. Accordingly, we cannot always make perfect decisions.

There are two methods for counteracting this situation. We discussed the first method above, which consists of ensuring that management decision-makers are very aware of the amount of imperfection that exists within the output variables, as well as any results or predictions generated via the analytical process. While this is an important step, it is somewhat passive in nature.

A more active approach consists of pursuing actions aimed at increasing the accuracy and/or precision of input values. Any number of actions can be taken to reduce uncertainty and increase the accuracy of the values used in a financial analysis, thus reducing the assumed level of risk:

- Conducting market research studies
- Conducting product trade trials
- Building prototypes or physical modeling
- Conducting bench tests or performance trials
- Developing statistical or numerical models
- Obtaining additional input data
- Conducting additional interviews with subject matter experts (SMEs)

Taking these kinds of actions often improves the quality of a decision. On the surface, it might seem as if we should always pursue these kinds of activities. However, as is so often the case, these types of actions must be analyzed from a cost versus benefits perspective, thus leading to more questions:

- What is the potential cost of a poor decision?
- What is the potential value of a good decision?
- How much will it cost us to obtain better information?

A variety of statistically based methods exist for calculating these costs and values, including an approach that uses decision trees to calculate the expected value of imperfect information. Most of these methods are quite detailed and beyond the scope of this book. However, simply recognizing that this phenomenon exists represents a significant enhancement to your overall business acumen.

REDUCING RISK BY MODIFYING FINANCIAL ANALYSIS PROCESS PARAMETERS

Generally, approaches aimed at using higher-quality information as a way to reduce risk are situational and are typically applied at the individual project level. However, many companies use other methods in an attempt to reduce project risk across the portfolio. These blanket approaches are aimed at reducing the level of risk associated with all project investment decisions or a large group of projects, such as so-called high-risk projects. Many of these approaches simply "raise the bar" on approval criteria, enabling the financial justification (and therefore the approval) of only the strongest projects. Three common approaches may be used in implementing this kind of widespread risk reduction strategy:

- **Adjusting the thresholds for project approval.** In Chapter 9, we identified four methods for expressing the financial strength of any given project: NPV, internal rate of return (IRR), maximum exposure, and payback period (Fig. 9.5). Companies wishing to reduce their overall level of project risk may establish *approval thresholds* for one or more of these measures. These thresholds often appear as specific constraints, and they are used as screening techniques (refer to "Applying Project Screening Techniques," in Chapter 7). Projects will not be allowed to enter the prioritization phase of project-portfolio development if they do not exceed these thresholds.
- **Adjusting the weighted average cost of capital (WACC).** As we discussed in Chapter 2, the WACC is a calculated value, based on the carrying costs associated with debt financing and equity financing. It is also the value identified as the *discount rate* in Chapter 9, and it was used in the calculation of NPV. However, it should be noted that WACC is actually a financial management term and a mathematically derived value. It identifies the minimum rate of return needed to characterize a project as being financially justified. To ensure that only the strongest projects survive—and as a hedge against risk—companies frequently require a rate of return that is some amount higher than the calculated WACC. This higher rate of return is often referred to as the *risk-adjusted rate of return*, the *minimum attractive rate of return*, or simply the *hurdle rate*. This value then is used as the discount rate used to calculate a project's NPV. The result is a reduction in NPVs for all projects.
- **Adjusting the useful life.** Similar to the technique of adjusting the discount rate, some companies may reduce a project's useful life—the study period used to conduct the financial analysis. This is viewed as a way to ensure that only the strongest projects are approved. Projects that are analyzed using a shorter time frame must be able to produce a larger, more rapid return of financial benefits in order to be considered justified.

USING SENSITIVITY ANALYSIS AS PART OF THE FINANCIAL ANALYSIS PROCESS

Every financial analysis that we perform on a project is based on some set of input variables that we use to calculate financial measures such as NPV, IRR, and payback period. To make these calculations, we customarily use *expected values* for each variable, or what we believe to be the most likely estimate (affably referred to as our "best guess"). When we construct our initial cash flow chart and generate our initial calculation of financial metrics such as NPV, we typically use the expected values for every one of the input variables. The outcome of this calculation is commonly referred to as the *base-case scenario*, or in this case, the base-case NPV.

Unfortunately, every one of the input variables we use will undoubtedly have some amount of uncertainty associated with it. Consequently, it's quite possible that each input variable could actually turn out to be some value other than that used in making our base-case calculations. In fact, this will almost certainly be the case for every financial calculation we perform!

Once the reality of this concept sets in, a few logical and thoughtful questions are likely to follow:

- How much could each input variable vary?
- What kind of impact could each variable exert on the financial analysis?
- Which input variables have the greatest effect on the financial analysis?

These questions can be summarized by asking another question: Exactly how sensitive is a given project investment to variations in project parameters that are themselves inherently uncertain?

Hence, the term *sensitivity analysis*.

In a broad sense, sensitivity analysis is an analytical technique that tests the limits of input variables and the resulting effects on output variables. The sensitivity analysis process consists of visualizing our cash flow models as a collection of uncertain input variables, then calculating the consequences of misestimating those variables. In this case, the term "consequences" refers to the recognition that any given project outcome (such as financial strength) may very well be different from that calculated by using all the most likely values.

For example, let's consider a new product introduction project, in which our calculation of NPV was based, in part, on product sales of 1 million units per year over the next 6 years. If we are realistic, we recognize that we will only sell 750,000 units per year over the next 6 years.

What would the NPV be in that case? Would the project still be considered financially justifiable? A good sensitivity analysis will answer these questions.

IDENTIFYING THE APPROPRIATE VARIABLES FOR A SENSITIVITY ANALYSIS

The most critical step in any sensitivity analysis consists of identifying the "right" input variables to examine those variables to which the financial analysis is likely to be *most sensitive*. Often, the individuals who created the cash flow chart are in the best position to make this determination. After all, they are most aware of the factors that went into the generation of the cash flow chart. They also are aware of how accurate or precise the estimated values for each input variable may have been.

The entire field of input variables to be considered ordinarily consists of the line items listed on the cash flow chart, coupled with the variables used to estimate them. For example, in referring to the new product introduction project described here, sales revenue would undoubtedly appear as a line item in the cash flow chart for this project. As you might expect, different assumptions for sales revenue would yield different calculations of NPV.

But where did the estimated values for *sales revenue* actually come from? In this case, they probably were based on a combination of assumptions related to *sales volume* and *profit margin*.

Where did the estimated value for profit margin come from? It was probably based on factors such as *selling price* and *unit manufacturing cost* (cost to produce each individual product unit).

As you can see, the process of identifying all possible input variables can be involved and tricky. However, one tool that can be helpful in mapping out these types of relationships is the *influence diagram*.

Figure 11.3 provides a partial view of the influence diagram for this example if the target metric was NPV. As the diagram suggests, any of the input variables shown in Figure 11.3 will have an impact on the magnitude of the NPV.

The challenge at this point comes in trying to identify those variables that will have the greatest effect on the NPV. Unfortunately, this is not always obvious. In many cases, it requires a detailed analysis that includes the opinions of SMEs and a sizeable number of calculations.

Very often, these calculations are done independently, in the form of one-dimensional sensitivity analyses, then combined into a

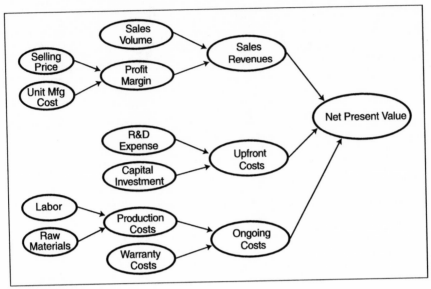

FIGURE 11.3

Partial view of an influence diagram.

multidimensional sensitivity analysis, so that the relative impact of several variables can be examined at a glance. Let's examine how that works.

PERFORMING A ONE-DIMENSIONAL SENSITIVITY ANALYSIS

We know that many of the input variables that determine a project's cash flows are based on some sort of probability distribution rather than being an exact, certain value. We also know that the change in a key input variable—such as the quantity of units sold—will cause the NPV to change.

A *one-dimensional sensitivity analysis* isolates one factor. It is intended to indicate how much a project's NPV will change in response to a change in any given input variable, assuming that all other factors are held constant at their expected value.

To illustrate, let's consider our previous example. Our best guess for the sales of this new product was 1 million units per year. Now let's assume that our base-case NPV (calculated using the expected value for all input variables) is $180,000.

The next step in the process consists of generating estimates of how large and how small we could reasonably expect the sales volume

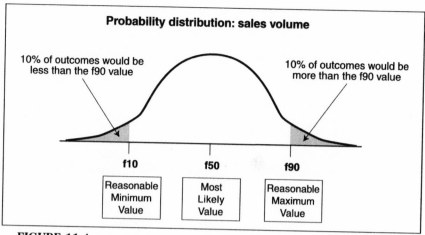

FIGURE 11.4

Establishing the upper and lower limits of a sensitivity analysis.

value to be. Those values will form the basis of our sensitivity analysis. To reveal these reasonable high and low values, we will rely on the statistical concept of f10 and f90 values (Fig. 11.4).

The principle behind the use of f10 and f90 values is based on the recognition that asking extreme questions of SMEs may trigger extreme thinking.

For example, imagine that you were interviewing the SME for product sales, and asked the question, "How big and how small could sales volume possibly be?"

The collective wisdom of interviewing techniques contends that the response you would get for minimums and maximums is likely to represent the most extreme tails of the normal distribution curve for sales volumes, in which only a 1% to 2% chance of actually experiencing a larger or smaller number may be possible. Because of this low probability of actual outcomes, the entire sensitivity analysis could be statistically distorted and somewhat unrealistic.

A better question to ask the SME is, "At approximately what level of sales volumes might there be a 10% chance that the actual volume would be a smaller amount...a larger amount?" These are the so-called f10 and f90 values, respectively (see Fig. 11.4). As unscientific and imprecise as this may sound, this interviewing approach is likely to yield a quite reasonable set of estimated values that can be used in a sensitivity analysis.

Once we have identified the minimum (f10) and maximum (f90) values, the next step consists of making two separate calculations. The first calculates the project's NPV for the scenario in which the actual sales volume is the f10 value; the second calculates the project's NPV for the scenario in which the actual sales volume is the f90 value. Both these calculations are made by reconstructing separate cash flow charts, following the procedure outlined in Chapter 9.

Our example project's base-case NPV was $180,000, based on a sales volume of 1 million units per year. Let's now assume that our calculations reveal that plugging in our f10 value (a sales volume of 750,000 units per year) yields an NPV of $100,000. Let's further assume that the project's NPV is calculated to be $260,000, if we assume the f90 scenario, in which we sell 1,250,000 units per year. Now, we can construct a *sensitivity graph*, such as that shown in Figure 11.5.

A one-dimensional sensitivity analysis often is performed in situations in which it is useful to examine, display, and discuss the impact of a single input variable on a given output variable. It's also used in situations in which it is believed (or known) that the potential variability around the target output variable is dominated by one particular input variable. A more common application of one-dimensional sensitivity analysis is as the starting point for a multidimensional sensitivity analysis.

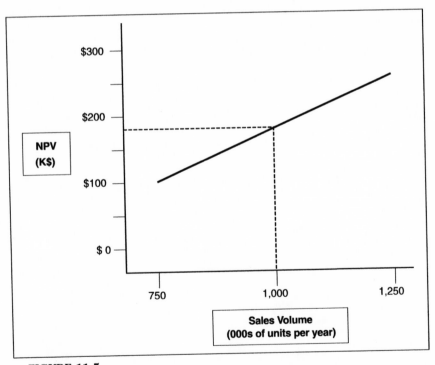

FIGURE 11.5

One-dimensional sensitivity graph.

PERFORMING A MULTIDIMENSIONAL
SENSITIVITY ANALYSIS

A *multidimensional sensitivity analysis* is really just an extension of the one-dimensional sensitivity analysis. The process consists of analyzing and comparing the effects that a number of input variables (ordinarily about four or five) will have on the target output variable. The analysis typically includes the input variables that are able to exert the greatest amount of influence on the output variable under consideration.

To illustrate, let's continue working with our example. Let's assume that the four input variables capable of exerting significant impact on the project's NPV are sales volume, profit margin, capital project cost, and production costs.

To perform our analysis, we must construct eight different cash flow charts and make eight different NPV calculations, because we are actually evaluating eight separate potential scenarios (the maximum and minimum estimates for each of four variables).

Figure 11.6 illustrates a multidimensional sensitivity graph. This type of sensitivity graph is also referred to as a *tornado diagram*, because it assumes that shape when turned on its side.

The tornado diagram packs a tremendous amount of information and insight into a single graphic. To illustrate this point, take a closer

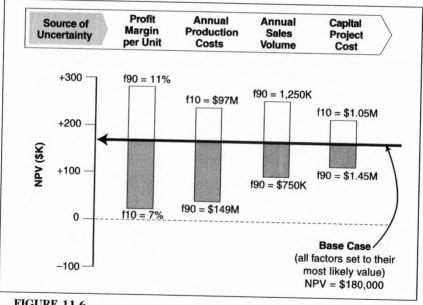

FIGURE 11.6

Multidimensional sensitivity graph (tornado diagram).

look at Figure 11.6. What do you see? When I examine this graph, I'm able to make several interesting and insightful observations:

- The profit margin is the most volatile, most influential factor.
- The capital expenditure cost is the least volatile, least influential factor.
- Annual production costs have significantly higher downside than upside risks.
- While the expected profit margin supports a fairly impressive NPV of $180,000, the lower end of its potential range precipitates a marginal (perhaps unacceptable?) NPV.
- A similar statement can be made regarding annual production costs.
- The capital project cost could vary by as much as 15% from the expected estimate without causing tremendous concern.
- Profit margin uncertainty causes what is probably an unacceptable level of total NPV variability (around $270,000).

In my opinion, the tornado diagram represents the perfect marriage of sound risk management and sound business. It is without doubt one of the most valuable aids to informed decision-making across the entire spectrum of project management documentation.

PERFORMING SENSITIVITY ANALYSIS USING MONTE CARLO SIMULATION

Both sensitivity analysis techniques described here (one-dimensional and multidimensional) are very powerful, given the fact that they can be done manually with relative ease. They do a fine job of examining individual "what-if" scenarios.

And therein lies the rub, because one drawback with both these techniques is that they examine each input variable individually or, one at a time.

The reality is that all various input variables are likely to vary from their expected values by some amount. This creates the possibility for a countless number of possible outcomes. This is where a technique referred to as *Monte Carlo simulation* comes into play. Using Monte Carlo simulation to perform sensitivity analysis is really like playing out hundreds of what-if scenarios by randomly generating values within the specified range of key input variables.

As you can imagine, this would be nearly impossible to do manually, because it would involve hundreds and hundreds of individual calculations. Fortunately, a variety of software tools are available to perform this type of sensitivity analysis with minimal effort.

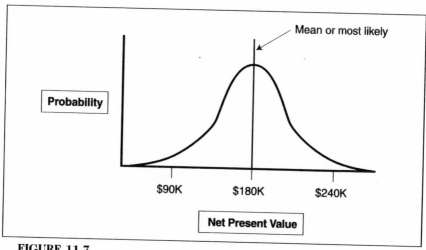

FIGURE 11.7

Sample output from a Monte Carlo simulation.

A detailed description regarding the use of the software tools is beyond the scope of this book. However, we could certainly sneak peek at a sample output of a Monte Carlo simulation (Fig. 11.7).

The simple distribution curve shown in Figure 11.7 really belies the massive amount of computational horsepower that went into its creation. Once again, it is critical to note that this curve was generated through a process that considered *combinations of input variables*, not through an examination of individual variables. In addition to the obvious benefit these tools have as a computational aide, they also add significant value to the overall process, because they force the user to create models for the desired output variables, such as NPV. Finally, it's worth noting that most of these tools also can create the one-dimensional sensitivity graphs and tornado diagrams we discussed earlier.

USING BREAK-EVEN ANALYSIS FOR BUSINESS DECISIONS

When we perform a sensitivity analysis on a project, we ordinarily consider a variety of alternative scenarios that are based on any number of input variables. In effect, we are anticipating—and answering—questions that management decision-makers might ask, such as "How serious would it be if the product sales turned out to be worse than we forecasted?"

Sometimes, management decision-makers prefer to rephrase a question like this and ask it a slightly different way, such as, "How poor would annual product sales have to be for this project to have a negative NPV?" This is actually a very specific "what-if" question. Providing an answer requires a technique called *break-even analysis*.

We examine the break-even analysis technique by applying it to two very different situations. The first is tied to the world of profit and sales. Here, we'll consider an example that will lead to the identification of the so-called *break-even point*—a common business term, frequently related to cost-versus-revenue studies. In the second situation, we'll examine how the break-even analysis approach may be applied to the financial analysis process.

Classic Application of Break-Even Analysis: The Cost-Revenue Function

One of the most common applications of the break-even analysis approach occurs in the situation in which a producer wants to know the minimum quantity of product sales required to begin making a profit. In reality, the producer is actually looking for the break-even point—the volume of sales at which product costs and product revenues are equal.

Let's consider the following set of simple circumstances for one particular producer of a handy household gadget:

- Total fixed cost (infrastructure costs, not dependent on volume) is $1,500,000.
- The unit manufacturing cost (cost to produce a single product) is $3.75.
- Target selling price is $7.50.

Figure 11.8 provides a graphical representation of the break-even analysis for this example.

This analysis reveals that at least 400,000 units would have to be produced and sold before profit could be realized. This is a very common application for break-even analysis. However, break-even analysis can be adapted for use in the financial analysis process as well.

Applying Break-Even Analysis to the Financial Analysis Process

Now let's turn our attention to the question posed by the management decision-maker who asked, "How poor would annual product sales have to be for this project to have a negative NPV?" Break-even analysis can be applied quite effectively to provide the answer to this question.

In this case, we won't go into a tremendous amount of "how-to" detail regarding the development of the solution; my primary objec-

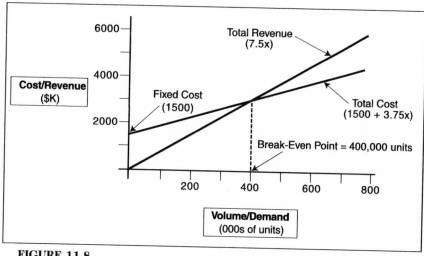

FIGURE 11.8

Break-even analysis for a cost versus revenue example.

tive is to demonstrate the applicability of the break-even analysis approach to project financials and to illustrate some of the business-based tools that can be used to enhance the decision-making process on projects.

That said, let's consider the following set of hypothetical circumstances for a proposed new product introduction project (see Fig. 11.9):

- Product selling price is $6.00.
- The cost to design and build a production facility is $400,000.
- Unit manufacturing cost is $4.00.
- Operational expense includes a combination of fixed ($300K/year) and variable production costs ($4/unit).

To simplify the example, future cash flows have not been discounted. In reality, you would discount all future cash flows.

As is typical with any financial analysis process, the most difficult part of the process comes in gathering accurate estimates for the figures that appear in the table in Figure 11.9. Once this has been done, generating the graph and interpreting the data are relatively easy steps. Obviously, the point at which the cash inflows equals the cash outflows is the point at which the NPV equals zero. In this example, the break-even point occurs around the point at which annual sales equals 183,000 units.

Average Annual Sales	Estimated Annual Revenue, Years 1–6	Project Investment, Year 0 Cost	Operational Expense, Years 1–6	Total Outflow Years 1–6	Total Cash Inflow, Year 1–6
100	600	400	4200	4600	3600
200	1200	400	6600	7000	7200
300	1800	400	9000	9400	10800

(Note: All values are expressed in terms of thousands.)

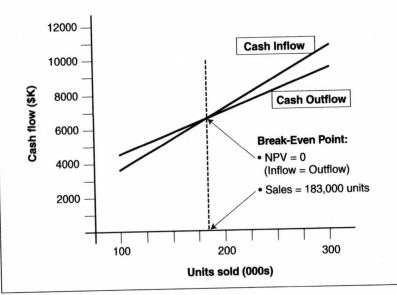

FIGURE 11.9

Break-even analysis for a financial investment situation.

In other words, if the probability of selling more than 183,000 units per year is large enough, this could be looked upon as a favorable project, worthy of additional investigation.

USING DECISION TREES IN FINANCIALLY BASED DECISION-MAKING

Decision trees have widespread application as effective enablers of well-informed decision-making. In fact, they are considered one of the most useful tools within a vast field often referred to as the *deci-*

sion sciences. So, let's take a look at how decision trees—coupled with the basic financial analysis process—can be used to make sense out of an otherwise complex situation.

Let's consider, for example the case of a large property development company that is contemplating the construction of a brand-new complex of luxury condominiums. The company's senior management team is struggling to decide how large to make the complex on the initial build. The situation is complicated by the fact that they are unsure of the demand for luxury condos in this area. The bottom line is that they would like to understand the profitability implications related to building different-sized complexes with respect to different levels of demand or whether the issue is even worth worrying about at all. In a way, this is just another form of a multidimensional sensitivity analysis.

Constructing a simple decision tree can be quite helpful in a situation such as this, when a decision must be made, and the decision hinges on some set of probabilistic, future outcomes.

OK, let's look at the situation in a bit more detail. As a starting point, the property development company is trying to decide whether to build 25, 50, or 75 luxury condos. Not surprisingly, this is referred to as *the decision* in the language of decision tree methodology.

The next consideration that the property development company would like to factor into their analysis is the potential demand for condos like this. In the language of decision trees, this is *an uncertain future event*. The developer wants to keep the analysis simple, and has identified two basic scenarios—one in which the demand would be large and a second in which the demand would be small. In decision tree language, these scenarios are referred to as *the states of nature*. The states of nature must be mutually exclusive (only one could occur) and should be reasonably well defined. In this case, demand would be expressed in terms of a given number of condos sold over a given time period.

Figure 11.10 illustrates the decision tree for this example. Similar to the approach used earlier in creating a tornado diagram, each estimated NPV displayed in Figure 11.10 represents a separate calculation. Using a different set of assumptions to model each potential outcome, six different cash flow charts should be created, leading to six different calculations for NPV.

Armed with the knowledge of how profitable each of the six potential outcomes could be, and coupled with their orientation towards risk (risk-aggressive or risk-averse), the senior management team of this property development company will be better equipped to make an informed decision.

This example also offers an excellent opportunity to illustrate the principle of the value of information. Obviously, a considerable

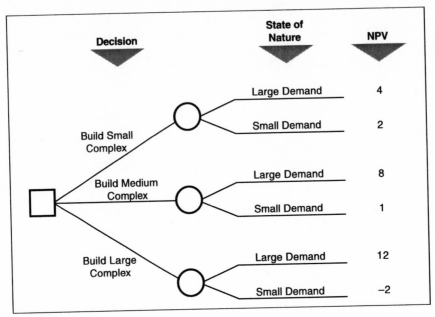

FIGURE 11.10

Decision tree for proposed condominium complex project.

amount of money is at stake, depending on whether these senior managers make a relatively good or relatively poor decision. This suggests that they might be able to justify a significant expenditure to perform an exhaustive marketing research study aimed at trying to gain a high degree of understanding with regard to whether they could expect the demand to be large or small. Gaining insight on consumer demand could prove to be an invaluable enhancement to the decision-making process.

PART 4

PREPARING THE BUSINESS CASE

CHAPTER 12

Business Cases and Business Case Preparation

Throughout the previous eleven chapters, we covered a tremendous amount of material that describes the nature of the interaction between the world of project management and the world of business. We now need to make those worlds collide at the individual project level. This collision (don't worry, it's a *friendly* collision!) is most appropriately accomplished through a document called the *project business case* (or just "business case").

The proper preparation of a project business case is the focus of this chapter. Much of what we've covered in the first eleven chapters will be applied to create this single document. The business case is arguably the single most important document that directly ties project issues to business issues at the project level. More important, the entire business case concept is very much in line with a contention we've held since the beginning of the book—the notion that projects are financial investments.

Unfortunately, formal business cases are not used as often as they should be. However, I suspect a dramatic increase will occur in the application of the formal business case approach over the next several years, as project management moves ever closer to effectively merging with the world of business. In the meantime, though, we must recognize that there's no universal agreement regarding a standard approach or structure related to business case preparation. The reality is that countless varieties of approaches and structures are used among those companies that prepare business cases today.

Against this backdrop, I'd like to offer the same comments I did at the outset of Chapter 5, when we were embarking on our discussion of portfolio management. First, the insights provided throughout this chapter are intended to be for informational purposes only, and not necessarily prescriptive in nature. This is particularly true of the business case structure presented later in the chapter and in the Appendix. Second, I once again contend that, even if you are not an active participant in the process of formal business case preparation (which I certainly hope is not the case), it is imperative that you understand the inputs, the outputs, and the process. This will enable you to be more effective in your role as project manager. With these two points in mind, let's get started.

WHY USE A BUSINESS CASE APPROACH?

Let's take a look at this from a personal perspective:

Question: What do you (or most people, for that matter) ordinarily do before committing to just about any major financial investment?

Answer: A major investigation. After all, your primary interest is to fully understand the financial impact of pursuing an investment before you commit any money to it.

That's really what a business case does for a company, from a project perspective. Generally speaking, a business case is intended to answer the question: What is the business impact associated with this decision? In this question, the term *business impact* focuses primarily on the issue of financial impact, while the term *decision* is often associated with formal management approval to proceed with some kind of project initiative.

More to the point, the reason for developing a project's business case is to justify the application of resources necessary to pursue a proposed initiative. The application of resources is frequently quite sizeable. In the absence of some sort of financially anchored business case approach, companies are left with an environment in which this sizeable investment in resources may be unleashed on the basis of an apparent "good idea," or because a powerful organizational figure offers a suggestion on "something that we should be doing," or even worse, because someone in the organization is an accomplished or aggressive orator. None of these are the hallmark of sound business. Hence, the need for business cases.

WHAT IS A BUSINESS CASE?

This can be a surprisingly difficult question to answer. Why? Because business cases are called upon to fulfill a variety of purposes. As a result, they may assume any number of different shapes and sizes, depending on the needs of the user. Perhaps a good starting point for understanding what a business case is comes in the recognition that they may be *characterized* in many ways. Specifically, it can be said that a well-prepared business case is:

- An analytical tool that supports sound, business-based decision-making

- A comparative form of gap analysis; the current state versus the desired state
- A form of "advice" to decision-makers
- A formally structured, compelling argument for taking some kind of action
- A trigger to obtain funding for a proposed initiative

But this is just one component in the quest to define the business case. The picture becomes clearer when we combine these characteristics of business cases with an understanding of how they can be applied.

GENERAL APPLICATIONS OF BUSINESS CASES

For me, one of the most alluring aspects of the business case concept comes in recognizing that it can be applied effectively in a variety of ways, depending on the needs of the user. Among the more common applications of business cases are:

- To evaluate whether a problem or opportunity warrants a response
- To identify and select the best alternative to resolve an agreed-upon problem
- To identify and select the best way to exploit an agreed-upon opportunity
- To assess the justification for executing a project
- To gain formal approval to proceed with a proposed project
- To compare options for a project that is already received funding
- To choose between projects competing for limited funds (remember our discussion on capital budgeting?)

It's important to point out that several of these issues could be applied to the *same* initiative, typically in a step-wise fashion.

For example, the process of evaluating the initiative might begin by evaluating whether a given problem is even worth solving. This approach is quite normal, if not prudent. If the problem is worth solving, the next logical step in business case development would be to identify and select the best alternative for solving the problem. Naturally, the overall initiative would have to be formally justified (costs versus benefits) before proceeding any further. Finally, the business case is likely to be molded into a tool for seeking formal management approval to proceed.

The proposed business case structure that we will review a bit later in this chapter is structured in a way that recognizes this kind of *evolutionary development*, which is characteristic of many project initiatives. This configuration incorporates a kind of "phased" approach to business case development, including a number of potential *stop points*. Each of these stop points represents an opportunity to pause and consider whether it's worth proceeding with the initiative—and therefore, whether the business case itself is worthy of further development. Whether or not you choose to adopt the specific structure I suggest, you should try to incorporate the capability to stop for "reality checks" during the course of the business case development cycle. This will undoubtedly save you the time, expense, and agony associated with fully developing a business case, only to find that the proposal should have been squelched considerably earlier in the investigation process.

BENEFITS OF USING A FORMAL BUSINESS CASE APPROACH

To be sure, there are any number of good reasons to use a formalized business case approach. A well-prepared and skillfully delivered business case can reap the following benefits:

- Verify strategic alignment
- Promote consensus among stakeholders
- Support sound risk management
- Promote understanding of the project
- Force decision-makers to follow a format that ensures all relevant factors have been considered as objectively as possible

While all these represent beneficial outcomes, without doubt, my personal favorite is the last one. It is directly tied to my use of the word "formal" in the title of this section. It is in fact the treatment of the business case approach as a *formally adopted corporate procedure* that drives decision-makers to make appropriate, logical, data-driven business decisions. This ensures that business cases are impartial, an issue we will touch on two more times during this chapter.

CONDITIONS THAT TRIGGER A FORMAL BUSINESS CASE APPROACH

While it's true that business cases are valuable decision-making tools, there is no doubt that their preparation may entail a considerable amount of effort. To me, this suggests that the application of a full-blown business case may not be necessary for every single project a company chooses to pursue.

This issue can be partially addressed by developing a separate business case procedure for smaller or less complex projects. Having at least two variations of business case procedure is an approach that I almost always suggest to my clients. But under what conditions would an all-out effort to develop an extensive, formal business case be warranted? Here are a few guidelines to help. I recommend that you consider preparing a formal business case when:

- **The investment size is substantial.** Obviously, the greater the size of the investment, the greater the need to ensure that high-quality, accurate investment decisions are being made. At the risk of looking like I'm hedging, I'm not sure I can crisply define what is meant by the term substantial investment size—it's a relative term. Characterizing a particular project investment as "substantial" depends on the size of your company, the amount of cash available, and its attitude toward investing in projects. The key point here is that thresholds that dictate when the business case approach is to be applied should be formally established and identified as an official procedure. Also, thresholds may be expressed using criteria such as financial expenditure, overall duration, complexity, or risk. Finally, these thresholds should be communicated across the organization and incorporated within your company's project management procedures.
- **The project has a broad stakeholder base.** Seasoned project managers come to recognize that complexity can be a significant challenge in leading projects. They also recognize that the application of technology is not the sole contributor to project complexity. Projects that require the participation or involvement of a wide stakeholder base sometimes can represent an even more challenging form of complexity. Business cases, if developed and delivered using a participative approach, can go a long way in effectively integrating the interests that may exist across a broad range of stakeholder groups. This will, in turn, enable smoother project execution.
- **Widespread understanding of the project is valuable.** Once again, seasoned project managers come to realize that when the people who are connected to a particular project are knowledgeable about that project—what it hopes to accomplish and why it is being pursued—the entire implementation process is positively impacted. A comprehensive business case can be a powerful tool to enhance this kind of cross-functional understanding.
- **Buy-in and commitment are critical success factors.** On some projects, obtaining the buy-in and commitment from various parties across the organization is nice to have. On other projects, it

is an absolute necessity. For example, consider a situation in which the realization of a project's stated benefits requires a particular department to change some of its internal procedures. Although this department was impacted, it is not expected to be heavily involved in the project. This scenario is not all that uncommon.

- **Thrusting these changes upon that department with little or no explanation could result in a considerable amount of resistance—including, perhaps, some level of noncompliance.** This, in turn, may negatively impact the benefits stream. The key point is obvious: When people understand why they are being asked to change, buy-in and commitment is enhanced. A well-prepared business case can be a powerful educational tool, serving to promote the desired cross-functional understanding. The department may not like the change, but it is more likely to comply because it now understands the need.
- **A high level of uncertainty exists in the project.** As we discussed in Chapter 11, the existence of high levels of uncertainty can have a profound impact on project outcomes. Consequently, developing a good understanding of the potential impacts of risk and uncertainty can be a valuable contributor to making high-quality project decisions. In situations in which uncertainty runs high, using a formal business case approach forces all parties involved to confront its existence through a sound, analytical framework of analysis.
- **The project's benefits stream is complex, obscure, or poorly understood.** Until now, we have spoken at considerable length about how companies must do a better job of ensuring that unjustifiable projects do not get approved. It is possible, however, for the opposite situation to exist. From time to time, projects that may represent attractive investment opportunities never see the light of day because the benefits stream isn't properly modeled. Should you encounter a project where you suspect this might be the case, consider employing a formal business case approach. It will allow you to articulate some of the more unusual types of benefits that we discussed in Chapter 9, such as cost protection, cost avoidance, efficiency improvements, and post-project revenue streams.

WHO PREPARES THE BUSINESS CASE?

The answer to this question varies considerably from company to company. However, while the specific players may be different, the basic roles needed to prepare a business case generally remain the same:

- Lead author *(ideally this would be a project manager, but it's more likely to be someone within a business unit or a functional organization)*
- Supporting authors *(typically current or future project team members)*
- Financial expert with organizational knowledge and strong spreadsheet skills *(typically someone from the finance and accounting department)*
- Analysts/researchers *(to perform competitive analyses, marketing studies, tests, etc., as needed)*
- Subject matter experts *(to provide input to analytical processes such as estimating and risk assessment)*
- Stakeholders *(appropriate contributions from those impacted by the project)*

It's critical to pursue a full life cycle approach when determining who should be involved in the preparation of the business case. One of the greatest opportunities for improving the business case preparation process within many companies comes in avoiding the "over the wall" syndrome. This occurs when so-called "front-end" entities, such as marketing and business unit groups, assume the lead in preparing a project's business case. This would be OK, except for the fact that these groups frequently assume the lead *to the exclusion of all other parties*. This approach can lead to a number of serious issues, many of which were discussed throughout our discussion of project portfolio management in Chapters 5 through 7.

THE BUSINESS CASE DEVELOPMENT PROCESS

A view of the fundamental process used in preparing business cases is shown in Figure 12.1. This illustration also points out a number of the key components that comprise this process. As you examine the diagram, you will undoubtedly notice that this process—and many of its key components—is highly correlated to the basic project development process we discussed in Chapter 6 (described in the section entitled "Alternative Identification and Analysis: Step-by-Step" and illustrated in Figure 6.1).

This is a very crucial point. It's important to recognize that a substantial portion of business case preparation is nothing more than *good project management*. Even more important is the recognition that much of the work involved in putting together a business case is really stuff that you would already be doing if you were a top-notch project manager.

Within high-performing project environments, the process of business case preparation is all about organizing and presenting the

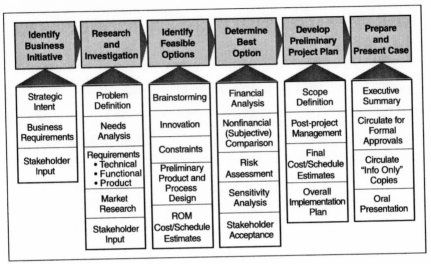

FIGURE 12.1

Key components of the business case preparation process.

information, knowledge, and insights that surface as a result of good, solid project investigation and analysis. It should not be viewed as an externally imposed exercise in generating a bunch of information for the sole purpose of satisfying someone's request to "put a business case together." To be blunt, a project management community that looks at business cases and business case preparation as administrative busy work, an external request for a non–value-added activity, or simply a chore to be endured, may have some serious shortfalls in regard to its basic approach to project management.

CRITICAL SUCCESS FACTORS IN BUSINESS CASE DEVELOPMENT

Few would argue that the most important elements of business case preparation are related to the content—the numerical data and qualitative information, the facts and figures, and the inherent qualities of the project itself. Perhaps equally important, though, are the methods and approaches used in preparing the case, such as the collection of data, the use of assumptions, and the application of analytical tools. These and other methods and approaches are of paramount importance in developing a meaningful understanding of a proposed project and communicating its value to the company, thus securing its support by management decision-makers. However, some of these methods and approaches are not easy to do. And some are more important than others.

In my experience, I have observed several *critical success factors* related to the way business cases are prepared and presented. Most assuredly, certain aspects of business case preparation can have a dramatic effect on the way a given project is perceived. Interestingly, two projects of approximately the same strength may be viewed differently, depending on the methods used in preparing and presenting their respective cases. The following are a few of the more notable critical success factors in business case preparation:

- **Identifying all costs and benefits.** Perhaps one of the easiest traps to fall into when developing a business case preparation is the tendency to restrict your thinking to the obvious costs and obvious benefits associated with an initiative. Project costs and benefits often are subject to a kind of ripple effect. In fact, I have rarely seen situations in which the implementation of a project—particularly a large or complex project—does not precipitate a variety of ancillary effects across the entire company.

  Consider, for example, a relatively straightforward labor savings project, such as the installation of a piece of equipment aimed at eliminating workers in a production department. The obvious cost: *the purchase and installation of the equipment*. The obvious benefit: *a reduction in labor costs*.

  However, it would not be unusual for a project such as this to have an effect on other aspects of the business, such as material expenses, waste levels, supply chain management, product quality issues, supporting tooling or other new process aids, ongoing maintenance considerations, utilities costs, spare parts administration, employee efficiency, product design issues, interface issues with other pieces of equipment, workflow issues with other departments, and more.

  Whoever is responsible for business case preparation must take into consideration the full range of effects that any proposed initiative will have across the entire company. This is not always easy to do.

- **Effectively translating soft (intangible) benefits.** The practice of relying on financial measures such as net present value (NPV) and internal rate of return (IRR) for project evaluation can, at times, be the object of criticism. As we discussed in Chapter 10, this criticism frequently is tied to the inescapable use of so-called *soft* or *intangible benefits*. As you may recall, these terms simply refer to project benefits that are very difficult to convert directly into dollars and cents.

  While I'm more than willing to admit that there are many kinds of benefits whose exact monetary value is difficult to estimate directly, it is nonetheless essential to find an effective way to incorporate them in the business case. We must remind ourselves that the fundamental objective of business case preparation is to help management decision-makers understand exactly what is at stake in any given project decision. Thus, you must include every relevant and meaningful item tied to either costs or benefits—whether or not a given item is difficult to quantify with a high degree of accuracy. Soft benefits (the intangibles, as some call them) are particularly challenging in this regard. Help may be on the way, however.

A technique that I refer to as *benefits translation* can be very helpful in addressing the issue of quantification, because it strives to bridge the gap between soft benefits and hard numbers.

Consider for a moment a classic soft benefit: increased customer satisfaction. I have seen countless examples where this is cited as a project benefit, with little or no additional elaboration. Although few would argue that increased customer satisfaction is a valuable benefit, considering its inclusion in a formal business case instantly (and predictably) triggers a flurry a questions: How valuable is an increase in customer satisfaction? What is it worth to our company financially? Can we estimate its value directly?

The answer is, well...no, not *directly*.

A seemingly intangible benefit like increased customer satisfaction really does not begin to assume a tangible form until we translate it. The translation process is not that difficult, and really requires three things: (1) a little *honest* imagination, (2) an excellent knowledge of the process under consideration, and (3) a proper application of probabilistic estimating techniques.

In many cases, the actual process of benefits translation is little more than an exercise in "if-then" logic. In other words, "If we were to do X, then Y would be the result."

In this case, we could say, "If we were to increase customer satisfaction, then the result would be:
- ...customers will buy bigger, better products from us."
- ...customers will buy some of our other products."
- ...new revenue streams resulting from customer referrals."
- ...a reduction in service and/or warrantee costs."
- ...a reduction in the size of the customer service group."

Using this simple step alone, we have taken a giant leap forward in our ability to quantify a benefit. We can now ask more detailed questions, such as: "What kinds of products?," "How many referrals?," and "How much of a reduction in group size?"

Indeed, we have taken a very large and fuzzy benefit and translated it into five considerably less fuzzy benefits. Although we may need to make assumptions and apply probabilistic estimating techniques to estimate the size of the benefit, the task often is doable. Here's the beauty, though: Even if we were to take the process of quantifying this benefit no further, we still end up with some meaningful attributes that can be plugged into the weighted factor scoring matrix we discussed in Chapter 6. Either way, we have accomplished the mission of incorporating this benefit in the business case.

- **Involving the right people.** There are a few ways of looking at this critical success factor. First, you must be certain to involve all the right people to optimize the accuracy and validity of the data used in your business case. You will need to extract information from many sources, because it will be impossible for you—or even a small core team—to know everything relative to any given project.

    Second, you should consider your logic, analytical methods, and assumptions to be open to scrutiny. This also helps improve the quality of the information used in the case. Finally, there is the issue of buy-in. It is likely that you will require the support and commitment of a variety of people throughout the company. When people are involved, even if only to review the case, they are more likely to support your project.

- **Ensuring impartiality.** This particular critical success factor is really not about whether people understand or support the business case you've written or even whether its well-written in the first place. It's about ensuring that the only business cases that get submitted to management decision-makers are those that are tied to projects that should be approved. We have contended throughout this book that, from a business standpoint, it is imperative that corporate monies should only be applied to the best project opportunities.

    Although this may seem like an obvious point, the reality is that organizational politics can sometimes get in the way of good corporate citizenry. The danger here lies in situations in which individual organization units—whether departments or divisions—have a strong and "personal" incentive for trying to get a project approved. This is one of the many reasons why I advocate some sort of centralized project management group, or project management office (PMO), as the coordinating body for business case preparation. PMOs that are organizationally positioned in a way that allows them to have no particular affiliation to any work group can often be relied on to do what's best for the company. That is an excellent perspective to have when it comes to business case preparation.

- **Using assumptions appropriately.** By design, business case preparation comes early in the life of a project initiative. At the time the business case is being developed, it is impossible to know everything about a project. So, assumptions are used to accommodate the lack of perfect information.

  The inclusion of assumptions in business cases is unavoidable. It is unlikely you will encounter a situation in which you will not need to use assumptions to complete your analysis. And even though assumptions really represent information that you more or less "make up," that does not that suggest that you should take a cavalier attitude toward the role they play. The appropriate use of assumptions in a business case is a critically important issue. Assumptions may be used to serve a variety of purposes, including:

  - *To define a specific basis for analysis (scenario assumption).* Let's say, for example, you are constructing a cash flow chart in preparation for financial analysis. As a way of enabling you to analyze the resource requirements (and costs) on this project, you might define a specific set of conditions—or scenario—by virtue of this assumption: 30% of the execution resources will be supplied by our company and 70% will be outsourced.
  - *To predict future unknowns (forecast assumption).* Once again, let's assume you are further developing the cash flow chart above, which includes cash inflows related to future product sales. Obviously, you cannot see into the future, so you would have to make this kind of forecast assumption: Annual product sales will increase by 10% over the next 5 years.
  - *To simplify data (synthesizing assumption).* This kind of assumption often is used in situations in which a large quantity of individual data points exist. Theoretically, each data point should be individually considered, but doing so would make the analysis excessively complex. Simplifying the entire data set enables you to utilize the data without dragging the analysis down into unnecessary levels of detail. Simplification typically comes in forms such as averaging and aggregating. As an example, let's say that part of your analysis must consider the cycle time of a particular operation that is carried out at a large number of different sites. Unless a good statistical argument existed against doing so, you might very well use this kind of simplifying assumption: Cycle times used in the analysis represent the weighted average of all 14 sites.

Perhaps the most important point about the use of assumptions in business cases comes in recognizing that *the skill with which assumptions are applied can be just as important as the assumptions themselves*. Whenever you use assumptions in business cases, you must make certain that they are:

– *Descriptive*. It is not sufficient to simply inform the reader that you are making an assumption. You should describe the actual data whose place the assumption is taking, the value that the assumption will have in the analytical process, why it is necessary to assume something instead of using actual data (namely, to define a scenario, make a prediction, or simplify a large data set).

– *Reasonable*. It's important to recognize that the quality of your analysis can depend on the accuracy of your assumptions. In fact, this very point forms the basis for the argument that says performing financial calculations are a waste of time. Why? Because they are based on fuzzy, "made-up" numbers (you can refer back to the beginning of Chapter 10 to revisit the discussion on this topic). As the accuracy of assumptions diminishes, so does the credibility of the business case itself. The process begins by ensuring all assumptions are reasonable.

– *Visible*. A considerable amount of judgment often is required to formulate valid assumptions. Assumptions must be a faithful and reasonable substitute for the missing data in order to be valid. To optimize the validity of the overall business case, all assumptions must be visible *and considered to be subject to scrutiny by all*. This approach has two benefits: (1) reviewers may have some specific information or insight that can help you increase the accuracy of an assumption; and (2) people who understand and agree with your assumptions are more likely to support your business case, and therefore, your project.

– *Used only when necessary.* Assumptions should be used as sparingly as possible—only when actual data are either unavailable or prohibitively expensive to obtain. Unfortunately, I have witnessed more cases than I care to admit where assumptions were used in a project analysis, even though data were available. In some cases, the underlying cause was a lack of awareness. But in far too many situations, the issue was one of complacency—or worse—laziness. In one case, for example, I was helping a project team prepare a project plan in which a significant amount of work was to be outsourced. Without doubt, the outsourced work had a major impact on the project's overall cost and duration. Spending an hour or two on the phone, gathering input and insights from the suppliers, would have added significant value to the quality of our cost and schedule estimates. However, instead of doing this, the key players on this project team seemed quite comfortable to simply "wing it." To be honest, I found this approach indefensible.

QUALITIES OF A WELL-PREPARED BUSINESS CASE

Most of our discussion to this point has dealt with the *content* of the business case. In this section, we will be addressing the development of the business case from a *document preparation* standpoint. This aspect of business case development can be a critically important process element, but its importance is sometimes underrated.

You may have noticed that I made several references to the term "well-prepared business case." But what does that really mean? Admittedly, the ordinarily desirable characteristics of documents, such as organization, grammar, and sentence structure certainly contribute to a positive experience for the reader. However, that's not really what I'm referring to. It would be quite possible, for example, for a business case to be a showcase of organization and grammar, yet add little meaningful value to the quality of the decision-making process.

So, in this context, "well-prepared" refers to what I consider to be important *core attributes*. These are characteristics that offer the greatest chance for making the correct decision—or the best possible decision—given the available information. Generally, the highest quality project decisions are made when the business case is:

- **Thorough.** The business case must incorporate all relevant information. It must examine a proposed initiative from all angles—nothing can be left out. It must take into consideration the needs of everyone impacted by the project, not just one or two departments. And to the extent subjective input is used, the business case must strive to represent the interests and opinions of all parties connected to the project. Thoroughness also means that efforts must be made to replace assumptions with actual information whenever available.
- **Unbiased.** The spirit of the business case must be one of total impartiality. Its tone should be that of a fact-finding mission that results in logical conclusions, not a hypothesis to be proved or disproved. The primary function of the business case should be to determine what's best for the company as a whole.
- **Quantitatively focused.** As much as possible, the business case should seek to rally around the best available information, not

emotional arguments or speculation. The use of expert judgment is acceptable, but should not supplant actual data, verifiable information, or thoughtful analysis.

- **Logical.** Simply stated, the business case should make sense. For example, if cause-and-effect relationships are part of the business case, they should be fully explained to the reader. Arguments made during the course of the business case should build on one another. It's quite possible that a business case presented in an illogical fashion could cause management decision-makers to be unsupportive of a project that is an otherwise excellent investment simply because they don't understand the logic behind the analysis.

- **Clear and understandable.** Once again, the issue here is more about the reaction of the reader than the inherent content of the business case. A business case that is difficult to understand runs the risk of being unsupported by management decision-makers. This attribute could relate to a variety of issues, such as excessively complex charts and graphs, a confusing presentation of hard data, the use of undefined acronyms, or a lack of rationale behind the analytical approaches used. While some of these issues may strike you as trivial, they may nonetheless contribute to negative impressions about the initiative itself. Sad, but true.

- **Conclusive.** I specifically recommend that every business case should *finish strong*. One of the most important components of that strong finish should be a set of clearly stated, explicit, and logical *conclusions*. While business cases should strive to be data driven, they should not simply present raw information, facts and figures, and calculations then put the reader in the position of trying to draw the correct conclusions. A well-prepared business case clearly synthesizes and interprets all presented data and converts it into strongly worded conclusions regarding findings as well as the appropriate path forward.

- **Compelling.** A well-prepared business case should assume the form of a carefully crafted set of compelling arguments that incite decision-makers to take the right action. However, it's important to note that "carefully crafted" does not mean that the business case should be fabricated, exaggerated, or even embellished in any way. A strong business case should be able to stand on its own merits. However, I have observed many instances where very strong business cases that are poorly prepared have led decision-makers to react by saying, "So what?" This is particularly sad if the project is strong.

RECOMMENDED BUSINESS CASE STRUCTURE: AN OVERVIEW

By definition, a project business case contains a wide variety of information about a project.

But how should that information be organized? What's the best way to structure the document?

As you might suspect, there are countless variations. Companies that currently use a business case approach will tailor the design of their cases to suit the specific needs of the company. In doing so, they consider generic factors, such as the type of project, the availability of data, and the accessibility of subject matter expertise. They also must consider several factors related to the stakeholder population, such as desired level of detail, preferred communication style, and orientation toward risk.

Appendix A provides detailed guidelines that describe the kind of information that should be included in a project business case. These guidelines follow this general structure:

1. *Front Matter.* Includes administrative information relating to the entire business case document.
2. *Executive Summary.* Summarizes the data and findings incorporated in all subsequent sections of the business case document; it is designed to answer the questions and concerns that are of greatest interest to senior executives.
3. *The Business Case.* Describes what the business case document is about; explains why the business case was developed, how it was developed, and who it was prepared for.
4. *Situational Assessment.* Provides relevant detail about the situation facing the company, including its origin and nature, its importance to the company, and the elements that would characterize a successful outcome.
5. *Alternatives Assessment.* Includes a qualitative and quantitative evaluation, analysis, and comparison of all feasible options for addressing the situation described in the situational assessment.
6. *Risk and Sensitivity Assessment.* Examines the uncertainty associated with all previous data or information. It identifies threats, calculates ranges of possible outcomes, and provides various other insights regarding the effects of uncertainty.
7. *Contingencies and Dependencies.* Describes any specific changes (including any desired actions or behaviors), needed to ensure the long-term success of the initiative; that is, the realization of stated benefits.

8. *Implementation Strategies and Action Planning.* Describes how the preferred alternative would be implemented; forms the basis for preparation of the project plan.
9. *Summary, Conclusions, and Recommendations.* Synthesizes and summarizes the entire business case at a very high level; revisits previous findings, conclusions, and closes with strong recommendations.

PART 5

APPENDIXES

APPENDIX A

Guidelines for Preparing a Project Business Case

In Chapter 12, we addressed a number of general issues related to the preparation of project business cases. We discussed several key foundational topics, including the function, purpose, and timing of business cases. We also reviewed a number of critical aspects of the overall business case preparation process, such as the sequence of steps and the likely participants.

However, we didn't actually get into any specific details describing the *kind of information* that should be included in a business case, and what that information should communicate.

The following information is intended to define exactly *how* to construct a business case. It provides a recommended business case structure and includes specific directions on the nature of the information that should be included in each of the individual fields.

RECOMMENDED BUSINESS CASE STRUCTURE AND PREPARATION GUIDELINES

1.0 Front Matter

Section 1 is the so-called "boilerplate." It includes administrative information relating to the business case document.

1.1 Cover Sheet

As the name suggests, this is the front page of the business case. It should include basic identifying information, such as title, author(s), date, etc.

1.1.1 Title

Summarize the proposed action and the nature of the business case analysis. For example, "Proposed Software Upgrade: Return on Investment Study." If possible, the title should be stated in terms of a problem rather than a solution.

1.1.2 Author and Organization

Identify the person who wrote and/or coordinated the preparation of the business case document.

1.1.3 Contributor(s) and Organization(s)

Identify anyone who had significant input or involvement in the preparation of the business case document. Within reason, identifying the existence of several contributors can often serve to enhance the credibility of the business case.

1.1.4 Current Date

Record the date associated with whatever version of the business case you are now releasing. This will become particularly useful if multiple versions of the business case document are needed.

1.2 Document Control

Serves as an audit trail in cases where multiple versions of the business case document exist.

1.2.1 Version Number

Identify the current version of the business case document being published. Use a traditional version numbering scheme, such as 2.1, 3.0, etc.

1.2.2 Version History

Identify the release date of all previous versions of the business case document.

1.3 Review/Approval Table

Lists who has reviewed the business case and whose formal approval to proceed is being sought. (Before releasing the business case, you should identify two basic groups: those whom you would like to review the document, and those whose formal approval is required before the project can be initiated. I would recommend that you distribute copies to all reviewers in advance of circulating the business case document for formal approval. Offer this group the opportunity to suggest minor revisions, giving them a limited window (perhaps 3 to 5 days) within which they may return comments. It's worth noting that if you had worked with this group during the preparation of the business case, their suggestions are likely to be minimal.) Once you have incorporated all appropriate suggestions from reviewers, circulate the business case for formal management approval. Design the routes in a way that recognizes any hierarchical approval scheme that your organization traditionally recognizes.

1.4 Table of Contents

Self-explanatory. Be sure to list any appropriate appendix items in this table of contents.

2.0 Executive Summary

Section 2 is positioned at the front of the business case document, but should be the last section you prepare. It serves to summarize the data and findings incorporated in all subsequent sections of the business case document, and it may be the only section that some stakeholders read (i.e., senior executives). Accordingly, it is structured to answer the questions and concerns that are of interest to senior executives, and it requires great care in its preparation.

2.1 Description of Business Needs

Provides a brief situational background, including the problem or opportunity, and the proposed solution. Should also identify—in general business terms—how the company will benefit by taking the proposed action.

2.2 Strategic Linkages (Corporate/Organizational/BU)

Identifies how the situation or proposed action ties to existing business strategies. Connections should be made to strategies at all appropriate levels—corporate, organizational, business unit, and even departmental—if appropriate.

2.3 Summary of Options Considered

Briefly identifies and describes all reasonable alternatives that were given full analytical consideration.

2.4 Preferred Option and Justification

Describes the solution and/or course of action that the business case study team views as superior. Briefly justifies the recommendation through a combination of summary-level financial justification (e.g., "This project had a net present value of $350,000"). You may also wish to summarize some of the qualitative attributes that make your recommended course of action more attractive than all other options listed in section 2.3.

2.5 Summary of Financial Analysis

Summarizes the outputs of the study team's detailed financial analysis. You may wish to include a comparison of the net present value

(NPV) results and/or internal rate of return (IRR) results for all options that were considered. You also may wish to incorporate a simplified cash flow chart, showing the major cash inflows in cash outflows.

2.6 Inaction Risks (Do-Nothing Result)

Briefly describes what would happen (or would *not* happen) if your recommended course of action was not approved. One of the most common questions asked by management decision-makers is: "What happens if we do nothing?"

2.7 Key Recommendations

Summarizes the overall situation. You should reiterate the basic problem, your recommended course of action, any kinds of support you may require, any approvals that you may require to keep the initiative moving forward (including timing), and any other relevant points.

3.0 The Business Case

Section 3 is directed at the business case document itself. It should include elements that describe what the business case is about, why the business case was developed, and how it was developed.

3.1 Business Case Subject

Describes what the business case content is intended to cover. Should be very brief, and simply suggest a proposed action ("Implement process change...," "Build new manufacturing line...," "Incorporate product enhancements...," *plus* a business rationale or desired goal ("...to improve data accuracy," "...to meet 3-year growth targets," "...to improve customer satisfaction.") A few qualifying remarks or clarifying points may be included.

3.2 Business Case Purpose

Describes the function that the business case is intended to perform; that is, to support a specific funding request; in support of next year's budget preparation; and to decide between purchasing, building, or leasing a facility.

3.3 Intended Audience

Identifies everyone who is likely to have any appreciable level of interest in the contents of the business case. Included in this group are key decision-makers, key participants in carrying out the proposed action, and those impacted by the proposed action or outcomes described in the business case.

3.4 Analytical Methodology

Describes the limits and limitations of the business case; that is, what is and isn't included in the analysis or the results.

3.4.1 Scope and Boundaries

Describes any relevant limitations related to any number of analytical dimensions, such as time ("Analysis is limited to fiscal years 2000 through 2004"), organizations ("Results apply to marketing and sales only"), or geography ("Study applies to North American subsidiaries only").

3.4.2 Financial Metrics

Identifies any and all specific financial measures, methods, and criteria that are used in the business case for the purpose of analysis, comparison, decision-making, or recommendations. Among the possibilities here are: NPV, IRR, payback period, total cost of ownership, discounted cash flow methodology, etc.). You may also wish to identify how financial metrics will be applied or incorporated, such as: "Alternatives with an NPV of less than $100,000 were not included in the qualitative comparison," or "Alternatives were judged primarily on the basis of total cost of ownership."

3.4.3 Data Sources and Methods

Identifies all relevant and significant sources of input data, for example: workflow analysis, contractor estimates, subject matter expert forecasts, computer simulations, departmental budgets, etc. You may also wish to describe the methods for calculating or establishing certain values; for example: "Labor costs include average base hourly rate plus overhead," or "Used the average of all contractor bids received."

3.5 Disclaimer

Calibrates the target audience's expectations in the case of internal projects (i.e., "Analysis is based upon information supplied by....," or "The validity of results is likely to change over time."). May be done for the purpose of legal protection when the business case is prepared for an audience outside the performing company, such as a contracting or outsourcing situation.

4.0 Situational Assessment

Section 4 provides relevant detail about the situation facing the company, including its origin and nature, its importance and/or value to the company, and the critical elements of a successful outcome.

4.1 Description of the Problem, Need, or Opportunity

Outlines and characterizes the specific issue upon which the business case document is based.

4.1.1 Background and Current Situation

Provides a narrative description of an existing set of circumstances (i.e., a "situation"). The situation could pertain to a *problem* that should be resolved, some kind of *need* that exists within the company, or an *opportunity* that should be exploited. Any relevant situational factors should be quantified, as appropriate.

4.1.2 Gap Statement: Current Situation versus Desired Situation

Provides insight about the possibilities relative to the stated problem, need, or opportunity. Based on a study of current status and a statement of a feasible, desired future state, the gap statement seeks to specifically outline "where the company is positioned today" versus "where the company would like to be positioned."

4.1.3 Stakeholders and Their Interests

Identifies all key stakeholders and characterizes the nature of their stake or the vested interest that each stakeholder has in the initiative.

4.2 Investment Goals

Describes what the company would expect to achieve by resolving the situation.

4.2.1 Business Outcomes and Results

Describes what would be created, altered, or resolved as a result of pursuing the course of action proposed in the business case. Existing business processes should form the foundation for this description. Should be primarily narrative, with limited quantification as needed.

4.2.2 Business Benefits and Key Value Drivers

Describes and quantifies the benefits to be gained by pursuing the proposed course of action and the factors driving the achievement of those benefits. Should be quantified and heavily focused on economic criteria. Answers the question: "What is it worth to the company to solve this problem, satisfy the needs, or exploit this opportunity?"

4.3 Strategic Alignment

Describes the relationship between the proposed initiative and the company's strategic framework, products and processes, and other initiatives currently underway or planned.

4.3.1 Strategic Relationships

Outlines how the situation (or proposed initiative) identified in the business case "ties in" to any existing corporate-level strategies, corporate-level business plans, and business unit and/or functional unit (departmental) strategies.

4.3.2 Integration Considerations

Describes any changes or other actions that would need to take place to ensure that the process of addressing the problem, need, or opportunity will properly integrate with: (1) any existing products and processes; (2) current ongoing operations; (3) other projects or programs currently underway or anticipated in the future; and (4) any companies or other entities outside the performing company.

4.3.3 Position Relative to Other Initiatives

Describes the relative positioning of the initiative proposed in the business case compared to other initiatives currently underway (or planned) within the company, with specific regard to: (1) *urgency* (an expression of need, i.e., how quickly the proposed initiative needs to be done); (2) *priority* (an expression of relative importance, i.e., the perceived value to the company); and (3) *sequence* (an expression of timing, i.e., which initiatives need to be done before others).

4.4 Situational Analysis: Product or Service

The nature of most projects is that they will tend to address either a product or service (e.g., new product introduction), or a process (e.g., process improvement initiative). This section of the business case is intended to provide a detailed analysis of the current situation for proposed initiatives that are primarily *focused on the creation of a new product or service, or the enhancement of an existing product or service.*

4.4.1 Market Analysis

Describes the nature of the current product market. Includes an analysis of current and future issues, such as market demand, supply versus demand, economic trends, etc.

4.4.2 Customer/User Analysis

Defines a number of environmental factors related to the target audience for the products identified in the proposed initiative. These factors may include issues such as the clarification between customers and users (if appropriate), customer/user preferences, the customer/user appeal associated with various features or functionality, etc.

4.4.3 Competitor Analysis

Provides a description of the current competitive environment. Likely to include a listing of viable competitors. Likely to include a detailed comparative study including a variety of factors such as size, comparison of products and product lines, relative market share, and a SWOT Analysis (Strengths, Weaknesses, Opportunities, Threats).

4.4.4 Gap Analysis, Product (Current versus Desired)

Considers a variety of factors in offering an expression of where the product (or product line) is currently positioned compared to where the product could (or should) be positioned. Would typically consider all information uncovered in Sections 4.4.1 through 4.4.3, coupled with the reality of the company's capabilities as well as its long-term goals for the product in question.

4.5 Situational Analysis: Process

The nature of most projects is that they will tend to address *either* a product or service (e.g., new product introduction), *or* a process (e.g., process improvement initiative). This section of the business case is intended to provide a detailed analysis of the current situation for proposed initiatives that are primarily *focused on the development and introduction of a new process, or the enhancement of an existing process.*

4.5.1 Process(es) Affected

Identifies and briefly characterizes the specific process or processes that are the subject of Section 4.5, and those which might be impacted by that process (if appropriate).

4.5.2 Existing Process Model

Provides a detailed description of the current state of the process under consideration with regard to *how* it currently functions, *how effectively* it functions, *how efficiently* it functions, etc.

Specifically identifies the following aspects of the process: (1) process inputs, outputs, and interfaces (a process flow diagram is sometimes used here); (2) processing methods and participants (may include a description of the equipment and/or technology utilized in the process); and (3) process performance metrics (defines the measurement criteria, measurement methods, and current performance levels).

4.5.3 Desired Process Model

Provides exactly the same information identified in section 4.5.1. In this case, however, the detailed description applies to the *future* state process proposed in the business case.

4.5.4 Gap Analysis, Process (Current versus Desired)

Considers a variety of factors in offering an expression of how the process is currently performing compared to where the product could (or should) be performing. Would typically consist of a direct comparison of the information provided in Sections 4.5.1 and 4.5.2, coupled with the reality of the company's capabilities as well as its long-term goals for the process in question.

4.6 Critical Success Factors

Identifies specific, pinpointed metrics by which the success of the proposed initiative will be judged. Would typically focus on the achievement of specific: (1) *project objectives* (e.g., adherence to budget or on-time completion); (2) *functional objectives* (e.g., successful product testing, or an increase in product line flexibility); (3) *operational objectives* (e.g., widespread distribution of the product, or increase in process efficiency); and (4) *business objectives* (increase in product revenues, or reduction in labor expense). The satisfaction of business objectives should be viewed as the most important element of success. In this section, you should also pay close attention to any constraints that may be imposed by the client or your own organization. In other words, *not violating a specific, imposed constraint* may be viewed as a critical success factor.

4.7 Completion Criteria

Identifies specific milestones, achievements, performance metrics, or conditions that will be used to characterize the completion of the proposed initiative. May be closely related (and in some cases, identical) to some of the critical success factors identified in section 4.6.

5.0 Alternatives Assessment

Section 5 is a qualitative and quantitative evaluation, analysis, and comparison of all feasible alternatives.

5.1 Descriptions of Feasible Alternatives

Provides a narrative description of each feasible alternative that is to be evaluated in section 5 of the business case. These descriptions would be similar to the Statement of Work (SOW) found in many projects and/or contractual agreements. The concept of feasibility could apply to resource requirements, specific cost or time limitations, functionality and performance requirements, technology limitations, or any number of other factors that could render a given alternative impractical. In order to provide a valuable basis for comparison, one of the alternatives that should always be included in the alternatives assessment process is the so-called "do-nothing scenario."

5.2 Comparison of Alternatives

Provides a direct, side-by-side comparison of all feasible alternatives. In many cases, the construction of a simple chart or spreadsheet could facilitate this kind of comparison.

5.2.1 Scope and Boundaries

Describes the content, nature, and extent of each alternative, including: (1) what content elements are included; (2) what content elements are not included; (3) what environmental factors may serve to limit its efficacy; and (4) any known limitations, such as constraints or narrow operating conditions, etc.

5.2.2 Results and Effects

Describes which aspects of the originally stated problem, need, or opportunity will be addressed and/or impacted—and how. Are likely to include statements about: (1) what will be delivered; (2) what will be achieved or accomplished; and (3) what will be changed and/or affected, etc.

5.2.3 Advantages and Disadvantages

Describes (in a reasonably unbounded fashion) the various positive and negative aspects related to each alternative. Should be limited to relatively important factors, and to the factors that are greatest interest to the stakeholders identified in section 5.2.4.

5.2.4 Organizational and Stakeholder Impacts

Outlines the effects that each alternative would have on individual stakeholders, stakeholder groups, departments and organizations, as well as the company at large. Should describe both the nature as well as the severity of every impact. The stakeholders identified in this section should correlate with the stakeholders identified in section 4.1.3.

5.2.5 Implementation and Integration Considerations

Outlines any special considerations or circumstances that might relate to the implementation of each specific alternative. Also describes any changes or other actions that would need to take place in order for each alternative to properly integrate with: (1) any existing products and processes; (2) current ongoing operations; (3) other projects or programs currently underway or anticipated in the future; and (4) any companies or other entities outside the performing company. Issues are likely to be similar to the issues discussed in section 4.3.2, but considerably more focused and detailed, because these issues are directly tied to specific alternative solutions.

5.3 Analytical Framework

Identifies all the factors—financial as well as nonfinancial—that will be included in the alternatives analysis process.

5.3.1 Cost Model

Lists all the elements related to the cash outflow—or the "cost side"—of the financial analysis that follows in section 5.4. Identifies all relevant cost and expense types, such as direct labor, indirect labor, materials, operating expenses, maintenance and production costs, overhead expenses, waste, and any number of other relevant cost types.

5.3.2 Benefits Model
Lists all the elements that are included in the cash inflow—or benefits side—of the financial analysis that follows in Section 5.4. Also identifies all the so-called nonfinancial benefits; that is, benefits that are extremely difficult or costly to estimate. The nonfinancial benefits will be considered as part of the comprehensive, qualitative analysis that follows in Section 5.5.

5.4 Financial (Quantitative) Analysis
Provides a detailed cost versus benefit analysis of all alternatives. Typically, the results of this analysis are used for three purposes: to confirm whether a given alternative is financially justified, to calculate the expected financial contribution of each alternative, and as one of the keys in the comprehensive analysis (section 5.5), which is designed to identify the preferred alternative.

5.4.1 Cash Outflows (Items of Cost)
Provides the estimated value (actual dollar amount) of all cost items previously identified in the cost model section 5.3.1. Estimates should be expressed in terms of their *most likely* values.

5.4.2 Cash Inflows (Financial Benefits)
Provides the estimated value (actual dollar amount) of all benefits previously identified in section 5.3.2. Estimates should be expressed in terms of their *most likely* values.

5.4.3 Cash Flow Chart
A simple table (i.e., spreadsheet) that visually displays all the cash inflows and cash outflows identified in sections 5.4.1 and 5.4.2. Cash flows are charted on an annual basis through the useful life of the investment. A separate cash flow chart should be constructed for each alternative under consideration. All appropriate elements of a thorough financial analysis should be included in the chart, such as income tax effects, depreciation, working capital, salvage value, and disposal costs. The cash flow chart should assume a total life cycle perspective, including all post-project, incremental cash flows that are incurred as a direct result of approving a given alternative.

5.4.4 Cash Flow Analysis
Displays the results of a thorough interpretation of the data included in the cash flow chart. May or may not show details of actual compu-

tations. Displays the results of the computations to reveal the value of the desired financial metrics, as indicated in Section 3.4.2.

5.5 Comprehensive (Qualitative) Analysis

Provides a well-rounded, thorough analysis that utilizes both financial and nonfinancial criteria.

5.5.1 Qualitative Benefits/Benefits Rationale

Provides a narrative description of all the significant benefits associated with each alternative. Should be limited to benefits that have very obvious business value to the company, but are difficult to estimate with precision and accuracy. Used in situations in which calculating the actual dollar value of a given benefit is viewed as problematic (ordinarily due to a lack of data), and/or because valid data are prohibitively costly to acquire. Although the dollar value of these qualitative benefits will not actually be calculated, a so-called *benefits rationale* should be provided. A benefits rationale should provide a focused, compelling argument that effectively describes the perceived value of a benefit to the company.

5.5.2 Weighted Factor Scoring Matrix

A method (and graphical tool) that facilitates a direct, but somewhat subjective comparison of alternatives against a broad set of predetermined criteria. Should include a combination of financial and nonfinancial criteria. The financial criteria are obtained from the cash flow analysis of section 5.4.4, and these should be the dominant criteria in determining the relative attractiveness of competing alternatives. The nonfinancial criteria typically include several of the factors identified as *qualitative benefits* in section 5.5.1. If properly constructed, a weighted factor scoring matrix can be an effective tool in driving consensus regarding which alternative is viewed as best.

5.6 Finance and Accounting Effects

Describes any notable impacts on the company's finance and accounting systems. Examples of systems that could be affected include the company's balance sheet, income statement, or statement of cash flows; an organization's expense budget; or the operating budget of a functional department or business unit.

5.7 Summarization of Initial Alternatives Assessment

Provides a synopsis and offers conclusive remarks with respect to all the data and analysis included in Section 5. Involves the process of synthesizing and interpreting the entire alternatives assessment process. Answers a variety of questions regarding: (1) the full range of potential solutions; (2) the impact of taking action versus doing nothing; (3) some of the more noteworthy impacts associated with various alternatives; and (4) which alternative seems to be the best (specifically noting that risk factors have not yet been considered).

6.0 Risk and Sensitivity Assessment

Section 6 examines the extent of uncertainty associated with all previous data or information. It tests limits, identifies threats, calculates ranges of possible outcomes, and provides various other insights regarding the effects of uncertainty. *A risk and sensitivity assessment can be performed on all the alternatives presented in Section 5, or a logical subset thereof.*

6.1 Key Risk Factors

Identifies several specific elements of the overall business case analysis that are suspected of having significant impact on the analytical results. Should focus primarily on how financial results (NPV, IRR, total cost of ownership, etc.) may be affected by changes in the input variables. Will generally include many of the factors that were used as inputs to the financial analysis and were identified as assumptions. Examples include market size, market share, sales volumes, production volumes, manufacturing cycle times, product price points, currency exchange rates, rates of inflation, and countless other factors. You can optimize the value of this information to your management by dividing these factors into two basic groups: (1) factors within their control, and (2) factors beyond their control.

6.2 Risk Quantification and Probability Distributions

Defines and characterizes all the key risk factors identified in section 6.1. Provides estimates on the reasonable limits for each factor (i.e., maximum and minimum values). Should also provide information on *risk profiles*, a graphical and mathematical interpretation of how risk probability is spread throughout the defined range.

6.3 Probabilistic Risk Analysis (Quantitative)

Calculates the specific effect each risk factor can have on the attractiveness and/or viability of a given proposed alternative. The analysis should focus primarily on the economic strength (i.e., financial viability) of an alternative. Outputs can be significantly enhanced through the use of graphical tools, such as a sensitivity graph and/or a tornado diagram. Typically, these kinds of graphical tools will show the correlation between various input values (sales volume, market share, etc.) and their output values (NPV, time to money, etc.).

6.4 Potential Problem Analysis (Qualitative)

Identifies a series of discrete risks (i.e., specific potential problems) that may serve as impediments to achieving a successful outcome of the proposed initiative. The potential problems identified are likely to correlate highly with the critical success factors identified in section 4.6. As with critical success factors, potential problems tend to focus on specific threats to achieving: (1) *project objectives* (e.g., adherence to budget or on-time completion); (2) *functional objectives* (e.g., expected product functionality or desired product line flexibility); (3) *operational objectives* (e.g., timely distribution of the product or assumed increases in process efficiency); and (4) *business objectives* (estimated increase in product revenues or expected reduction in labor expense). The satisfaction of business objectives should be viewed as the most important area of concern regarding potential problems. Following a standard risk management process, "high-threat" potential problems should be identified by evaluating *probability of occurrence* and *estimated impact* of each potential problem.

6.5 Best-Case/Worst-Case Analysis

Provides a scenario-based description of both a highly favorable outcome (best-case scenario) and a highly unfavorable outcome (worst-case scenario). In general terms, both scenarios should describe a set of circumstances and outcomes whereby the likelihood of a more severe outcome would only be about 10% to 15%. Both descriptions should focus heavily on factors related to economic and financial considerations, as well as business impacts.

6.6 Mitigation Strategies

Identifies any recommended actions aimed toward reducing the unfavorable effects that may be caused by the potential problems, uncertainties, unknowns, and unfavorable outcomes identified in section 6.1 through 6.4. May take either of two basic forms: (1) identification of any specific preventive measures and/or contingency plans that should be implemented; and (2) recommended application of other forms of risk accommodation, such as contingency funds or extensions of the project timeline.

6.7 Interpretation of Risk Assessment

Provides a synthesis and summarization of the entire risk analysis process. If possible, should attempt to comprehensively describe the composite effects of all risks, uncertainties, and unknowns that challenge or threaten a successful outcome of the proposed initiative. You should make specific recommendations where management actions are recommended or required. If appropriate, should include a disclaimer, offering reminders that the nature of the outcome may be highly variable and somewhat unpredictable.

6.8 Preferred Alternative

Provide a specific, definitive recommendation regarding which alternative under consideration is viewed as the most attractive, using all previous data. As appropriate, this recommendation should summarize and reinforce any necessary *conditions for success*. Typically, conditions for success will tend to map back to any critical assumptions that were utilized as part of the overall business case analysis. If the alternative being recommended in this section is different from the preferred alternative identified in section 5.7, an explanation should be provided. The alternative recommended in this section is the only alternative to be further developed in upcoming Sections 7 and 8 (the reader should be reminded of this).

7.0 Contingencies and Dependencies

Section 7 identifies any specific contributions that may be needed, or changes that may be required, in order to: (1) ensure that the proposed initiative is feasible; (2) enable the proposed initiative to be a success; and (3) enable the realization of any benefits claims.

7.1 Organizational Contingencies and Dependencies (Value Chain Analysis)

Provides a broad perspective of any changes or contributions required across the entire company. A thorough and comprehensive evaluation can often be facilitated through an examination of a company's organization structure and/or through value chain analysis. The value chain refers to the sequence of business functions within which usefulness is added to the products and services of a company. Typical value chain components include research and development functions, engineering and design functions, manufacturing and production functions, marketing functions, distribution functions, and customer service functions.

7.2 Product and Process Contingencies and Dependencies

Defines what specific products, product lines, business processes, and operating processes should be modified or adapted to properly integrate or accommodate the proposed initiative.

7.3 Functional and Operational Contingencies and Dependencies

Defines the relationship between existing functions and operations and the proposed initiative. May involve relatively significant changes in approach, such as revisions to functional group structures or relationships. May involve a broad range of issues, such as the way operations are currently managed, the methods used to allocate resources, the configuration of existing product lines, materials management methods, approaches to sales and marketing, distribution methods, and any number of modifications required to accommodate the proposed initiative.

7.4 Procedural Contingencies and Dependencies

Describes what specific procedures or policies should be modified or adapted to properly integrate or accommodate the proposed initiative.

7.5 Summary and Key Responsibilities

Clearly identifies what actions and behaviors are needed by specific individuals or specific workgroups to enable a successful outcome of the proposed initiative. The term "actions and behaviors" might refer to specific requirements for on-time decision-making or the provision of the required resources, or explicit agreement to abide by the changes outlined in Sections 7.1 through 7.4. (*Note:* It is critical that the owners of the responsibilities described in this section formally acknowledge and agree to their responsibilities *before* any project implementation begins).

8.0 Implementation Strategies and Action Planning

Section 8 describes how the preferred alternative identified in section 6.7 would be carried out. This section forms the basis for preparation of the project plan.

8.1 Preferred Alternative: Description of Scope

Provides a narrative description of the preferred alternative. Descriptions would be similar to an SOW that can be found in many projects and/or contractual agreements. This section specifically answers the question: "What will be done?"

8.2 Enabling Implementation Activities

Breaks down the overall implementation plan into specific types of execution approaches and enabling methodologies.

8.2.1 Product Development Activities

Defines the research and development work (if any) that would be required for successful implementation of the proposed initiative.

Relates exclusively to any *products* that are created or modified as a result of implementing the proposed initiative. If any product development effort is required, this section would be highly correlated with the information included in Section 4.4.

8.2.2 Process Development Activities

Defines the research and development work (if any) that would be required for successful implementation of the proposed initiative. Relates exclusively to any *processes* that are created or modified as a result of implementing the proposed initiative. If any process development effort is required, this section would be highly correlated with the information included in section 4.5.

8.2.3 Capital Improvements

Defines what specific assets (equipment, facilities, intellectual property, etc.) will be created and placed into service as a result of implementing the proposed initiative. Could also include enhancements to existing company assets.

8.2.4 Product and Process Certifications

Describes any testing and evaluation processes and methods that will be used in gaining assurance that any prescribed performance and quality targets will be upheld. May also refer to any number of certification standards mandated by regulatory agencies, such as the Environmental Protection Agency (EPA) or the Occupational Safety and Health Administration (OSHA).

8.3 Funding Strategy

Provides a formal estimate of all expenditures required to implement the proposed initiative. May identify the source of funding for the initiative. May define timing; that is, when various amounts of funds will need to be released.

8.4 Project Management Strategies

Provides details regarding how the implementation of the proposed initiative will be managed.

Functionally equivalent to the process of *project planning*.

8.4.1 Project Governance Model

Identifies the key decision-makers involved in the project implementation process, including: (1) the business owner (or "client"); (2) the management sponsor (typically exists within the performing organization); and (3) the project owner (ordinarily the group which actually executes the project).

8.4.2 Resource Requirements
Describes who will be required to work on the project. In many cases, this section will probably identify only departments, not specific individuals.

8.4.3 Execution Methods
Describes the methods, procedures, and approaches that will be used in accomplishing the work described in sections 8.1 and 8.2.

8.4.4 Procurement and Acquisition Methods
Describes how contracted or purchased resources, services, or goods will be acquired from outside the performing organization. Should include estimated amounts of labor and materials required to carry out the proposed initiative.

8.4.5 Implementation Timeline
Provides the schedule for project implementation. Level of detail could vary according to how much investigation is performed prior to preparation of the business case.

8.5 *Key Deliverables and Results*

Identifies what will be produced, created, accomplished, altered, etc. as a result of implementing the proposed initiative. All stated outcomes and predicted results should be directly tied to the attainment of key business objectives identified in Section 4.2.

8.6 *Verification of Deliverables and Results*

Describes the methods for measuring and verifying that the key deliverables and results identified in Section 8.5 have been successfully achieved. Methods could include: (1) performing analyses or conducting formal tests; (2) performing actual product or process demonstrations; (3) inspecting or observing; and (4) conducting simulations.

8.7 *Transition Considerations*

Describes any critical issues that may need to be addressed and/or resolved as the proposed initiative transitions from the *project execution phase* to the *post-project implementation phase*. In the case of product-oriented initiatives, this might refer to the transition from the development of manufacturing capability (the project) to ongoing product sales and distribution. In the case of process-oriented initiatives, this transition might refer to the transition from the act of building and installing a new process (the project) to the downstream utilization of that process. A total life cycle mentality is a necessary component of good business case preparation.

8.8 Management Model, Post-Project

Defines how the proposed initiative will be managed once the project has been successfully completed. Post-project management considerations are intended to address a variety of post-project issues, such as how the initiative will be managed on a day-to-day, ongoing basis, to who will be responsible for ensuring the ongoing realization of the benefit stated in the business case, and to provide detail on any post-implementation reviews, if appropriate.

9.0 Summary, Conclusions, and Recommendations

Section 9 should restate and summarize the entire business case at a very high level. Findings and conclusions should be anchored to the business objectives stated in the business case subject (Section 3.1). Conclusions should be explicit. *Do not* assume that everyone reading the business case will be able to draw the same conclusion as you did—or worse, be able to draw any conclusion at all. Finish strong: Close with a specific recommendation, especially if the case involves a funding request. Make it very clear that the ball is now in the decision-makers court.

APPENDIX B

Interest Tables

TABLE B.1

Future Value of $1 at the End of n Periods: $\text{FVIF}_{r,n} = (1 + r)^n$

Period	1%	2%	3%	4%	5%	6%	7%	8%	9%	10%
1	1.0100	1.0200	1.0300	1.0400	1.0500	1.0600	1.0700	1.0800	1.0900	1.1000
2	1.0201	1.0404	1.0609	1.0816	1.1025	1.1236	1.1449	1.1664	1.1881	1.2100
3	1.0303	1.0612	1.0927	1.1249	1.1576	1.1910	1.2250	1.2597	1.2950	1.3310
4	1.0406	1.0824	1.1255	1.1699	1.2155	1.2625	1.3108	1.3605	1.4116	1.4641
5	1.0510	1.1041	1.1593	1.2167	1.2763	1.3382	1.4026	1.4693	1.5386	1.6105
6	1.0615	1.1262	1.1941	1.2653	1.3401	1.4185	1.5007	1.5869	1.6771	1.7716
7	1.0721	1.1487	1.2299	1.3159	1.4071	1.5036	1.6058	1.7138	1.8280	1.9487
8	1.0829	1.1717	1.2668	1.3686	1.4775	1.5938	1.7182	1.8509	1.9926	2.1436
9	1.0937	1.1951	1.3048	1.4233	1.5513	1.6895	1.8385	1.9990	2.1719	2.3579
10	1.1046	1.2190	1.3439	1.4802	1.6289	1.7908	1.9672	2.1589	2.3674	2.5937
11	1.1157	1.2434	1.3842	1.5395	1.7103	1.8983	2.1049	2.3316	2.5804	2.8531
12	1.1268	1.2682	1.4258	1.6010	1.7959	2.0122	2.2522	2.2182	2.8127	3.1384
13	1.1381	1.2936	1.4685	1.6651	1.8856	2.1329	2.4098	2.7196	3.0658	3.4523
14	1.1495	1.3195	1.5126	1.7317	1.9799	2.2609	2.5785	2.9372	3.3417	3.7975
15	1.1610	1.3459	1.5580	1.8009	2.0789	2.3966	2.7590	3.1722	3.6425	4.1772
16	1.1726	1.3728	1.6047	1.8730	2.1829	2.5404	2.9522	3.4259	3.9703	4.5950
17	1.1843	1.4002	1.6528	1.9479	2.2920	2.6928	3.1588	3.7000	4.3276	5.0545
18	1.1961	1.4282	1.7024	2.0258	2.4066	2.8543	3.3799	3.9960	4.7171	5.5599
19	1.2081	1.4568	1.7535	2.1068	2.5270	3.0256	3.6165	4.3157	5.1417	6.1159
20	1.2202	1.4859	1.8061	2.1911	2.6533	3.2071	3.8697	4.6610	5.6044	6.7275
21	1.2324	1.5157	1.8603	2.2788	2.7860	3.3996	4.1406	5.0338	6.1088	7.4002
22	1.2447	1.5460	1.9161	2.3699	2.9253	3.6035	4.4304	5.4365	6.6586	8.1403
23	1.2572	1.5769	1.9736	2.4647	3.0715	3.8197	4.7405	5.8715	7.2579	8.9543
24	1.2697	1.6084	2.0328	2.5633	3.2251	4.0489	5.0724	6.3412	7.9111	9.8497
25	1.2824	1.6406	2.0938	2.6658	3.3864	4.2919	5.4274	6.8485	8.6231	10.835
26	1.2953	1.6734	2.1566	2.7725	3.5557	4.5494	5.8074	7.3964	9.3992	11.918
27	1.3082	1.7069	2.2213	2.8834	3.7335	4.8223	6.2139	7.9881	10.245	13.110
28	1.3213	1.7410	2.2879	2.9987	3.9201	5.1117	6.6488	8.6271	11.167	14.421
29	1.3345	1.7758	2.3566	3.1187	4.1161	5.4184	7.1143	9.3173	12.172	15.863
30	1.3748	1.8114	2.4273	3.2434	4.3219	5.7435	7.6123	10.063	13.268	17.449
40	1.4889	2.2080	3.2620	4.8010	7.0400	10.286	14.974	21.725	31.409	45.259
50	1.6446	2.6916	4.3839	7.1067	11.467	18.420	29.457	46.902	74.358	117.39
60	1.8167	3.2810	5.8916	10.520	18.679	32.988	57.946	101.26	176.03	304.48

*FVIF > 99,999.

TABLE B.1

continued

Period	12%	14%	15%	16%	18%	20%	24%	28%	32%	36%
1	1.1200	1.1400	1.1500	1.1600	1.1800	1.2000	1.2400	1.2800	1.3200	1.3600
2	1.2544	1.2996	1.3225	1.3456	1.3924	1.4400	1.5376	1.6384	1.7424	1.8496
3	1.4049	1.4815	1.5209	1.5609	1.6430	1.7280	1.9066	2.0972	2.3000	2.5155
4	1.5735	1.6890	1.7490	1.8106	1.9388	2.0736	2.3642	2.6844	3.0360	3.4210
5	1.7623	1.9254	2.0114	2.1003	2.2878	2.4883	2.9316	3.4360	4.0075	4.6526
6	1.9738	2.1950	2.3131	2.4364	2.6996	2.9860	3.6352	4.3980	5.2899	6.3275
7	2.2107	2.5023	2.6600	2.8262	3.1855	3.5832	4.5077	5.6295	6.9826	8.6054
8	2.4760	2.8526	3.0590	3.2784	3.7589	4.2998	5.5895	7.2058	9.2170	11.703
9	2.7731	3.2519	3.5179	3.8030	4.4355	5.1598	6.9310	9.2234	12.166	15.917
10	3.1058	3.7072	4.0456	4.4114	5.2338	6.1917	8.5944	11.806	16.060	21.647
11	3.4785	4.2262	4.6524	5.1173	6.1759	7.4301	10.657	15.112	21.199	29.439
12	3.8960	4.8179	5.3503	5.9360	7.2876	8.9161	13.215	19.343	27.983	40.037
13	4.3635	5.4924	6.1528	6.8858	8.5994	10.699	16.386	24.759	36.937	54.451
14	4.8871	6.2613	7.0757	7.9875	10.147	12.839	20.319	31.691	48.757	74.053
15	5.4736	7.1379	8.1371	9.2655	11.974	15.407	25.196	40.565	64.359	100.71
16	6.1304	8.1372	9.3576	10.748	14.129	18.488	31.243	51.923	84.954	136.97
17	6.8660	9.2765	10.761	12.468	16.672	22.186	38.741	66.461	112.14	186.28
18	7.6900	10.575	12.375	14.463	19.673	26.623	48.039	85.071	148.02	253.34
19	8.6128	12.056	14.232	16.777	23.214	31.948	59.568	108.89	195.39	344.54
20	9.6463	13.743	16.367	19.461	27.393	38.338	73.864	139.38	257.92	468.57
21	10.804	15.668	18.822	22.574	32.324	46.005	91.592	178.41	340.45	637.26
22	12.100	17.861	21.645	26.186	38.142	55.206	113.57	228.36	449.39	866.67
23	13.552	20.362	24.891	30.376	45.008	66.247	140.83	292.30	593.20	1178.7
24	15.179	23.212	28.625	35.236	53.109	79.497	174.63	374.14	783.02	1603.0
25	17.000	26.462	32.919	40.874	62.669	95.396	216.54	478.90	1033.6	2180.1
26	19.040	30.167	37.857	47.414	73.949	114.48	268.51	613.00	1364.3	2964.9
27	21.325	34.390	43.535	55.000	87.260	137.37	332.95	784.64	1800.9	4032.3
28	23.884	39.204	50.066	63.800	102.97	164.84	412.86	1004.3	2377.2	5483.9
29	26.750	44.693	57.575	74.009	121.50	197.81	511.95	1285.6	3137.9	7458.1
30	29.960	50.950	66.212	85.850	143.37	237.38	634.82	1645.5	4142.1	10143
40	93.051	188.88	267.86	378.72	750.38	1469.8	5455.9	19427	66521	*
50	289.00	700.23	1083.7	1670.7	3927.4	9100.4	46890	*	*	*
60	897.60	2595.9	4384.0	7370.2	20555	56348	*	*	*	*

*FVIF > 99,999.

TABLE B.2

Present Value of $1 Received at the End of n Periods:

$$PVIF_{r,n} = 1/(1 + r)^n = (1 + r)^{-n}$$

Period	1%	2%	3%	4%	5%	6%	7%	8%	9%	10%
1	.9901	.9804	.9709	.9615	.9524	.9434	.9346	.9259	.9174	.9091
2	.9803	.9612	.9426	.9246	.9070	.8900	.8734	.8573	.8417	.8264
3	.9706	.9423	.9151	.8890	.8638	.8396	.8163	.7938	.7722	.7513
4	.9610	.9238	.8885	.8548	.8227	.7921	.7629	.7350	.7084	.6830
5	.9515	.9057	.8626	.8219	.7835	.7473	.7130	.6806	.6499	.6209
6	.9420	.8880	.8375	.7903	.7462	.7050	.6663	.6302	.5963	.5645
7	.9327	.8706	.8131	.7599	.7107	.6651	.6227	.5835	.5470	.5132
8	.9235	.8535	.7894	.7307	.6768	.6274	.5820	.5403	.5019	.4665
9	.9143	.8368	.7664	.7026	.6446	.5919	.5439	.5002	.4604	.4241
10	.9053	.8203	.7441	.6756	.6139	.5584	.5083	.4632	.4224	.3855
11	.8963	.8043	.7224	.6496	.5847	.5268	.4751	.4289	.3875	.3505
12	.8874	.7885	.7014	.6246	.5568	.4970	.4440	.3971	.3555	.3186
13	.8787	.7730	.6810	.6006	.5303	.4688	.4150	.3677	.3262	.2897
14	.8700	.7579	.6611	.5775	.5051	.4423	.3878	.3405	.2992	.2633
15	.8613	.7430	.6419	.5553	.4810	.4173	.3624	.3152	.2745	.2394
16	.8528	.7284	.6232	.5339	.4581	.3936	.3387	.2919	.2519	.2176
17	.8444	.7142	.6050	.5134	.4363	.3714	.3166	.2703	.2311	.1978
18	.8360	.7002	.5874	.4936	.4155	.3503	.2959	.2502	.2120	.1799
19	.8277	.6864	.5703	.4746	.3957	.3305	.2765	.2317	.1945	.1635
20	.8195	.6730	.5537	.4564	.3769	.3118	.2584	.2145	.1784	.1486
21	.8114	.6598	.5375	.4388	.3589	.2942	.2415	.1987	.1637	.1351
22	.8034	.6468	.5219	.4220	.3418	.2775	.2257	.1839	.1502	.1228
23	.7954	.6342	.5067	.4057	.3256	.2618	.2109	.1703	.1378	.1117
24	.7876	.6217	.4919	.3901	.3101	.2470	.1971	.1577	.1264	.1015
25	.7798	.6095	.4776	.3751	.2953	.2330	.1842	.1460	.1160	.0923
26	.7720	.5976	.4637	.3607	.2812	.2198	.1722	.1352	.1064	.0839
27	.7644	.5859	.4502	.3468	.2678	.2074	.1609	.1252	.0976	.0763
28	.7568	.5744	.4371	.3335	.2551	.1956	.1504	.1159	.0895	.0693
29	.7493	.5631	.4243	.3207	.2429	.1846	.1406	.1073	.0822	.0630
30	.7419	.5521	.4120	.3083	.2314	.1741	.1314	.0994	.0754	.0573
35	.7059	.5000	.3554	.2534	.1813	.1301	.0937	.0676	.0490	.0356
40	.6717	.4529	.3066	.2083	.1420	.0972	.0668	.0460	.0318	.0221
45	.6391	.4102	.2644	.1712	.1113	.0727	.0476	.0313	.0207	.0137
50	.6080	.3715	.2281	.1407	.0872	.0543	.0339	.0213	.0134	.0085
55	.5785	.3365	.1968	.1157	.0683	.0406	.0242	.0145	.0087	.0053

*The factor is zero to four decimal places.

TABLE B.2

continued

Period	12%	14%	15%	16%	18%	20%	24%	28%	32%	36%
1	.8929	.8772	.8696	.8621	.8475	.8333	.8065	.7813	.7576	.7353
2	.7972	.7695	.7561	.7432	.7182	.6944	.6504	.6104	.5739	.5407
3	.7118	.6750	.6575	.6407	.6086	.5787	.5245	.4768	.4348	.3975
4	.6355	.5921	.5718	.5523	.5158	.4823	.4230	.3725	.3294	.2923
5	.5674	.5194	.4972	.4761	.4371	.4019	.3411	.2910	.2495	.2149
6	.5066	.4556	.4323	.4104	.3704	.3349	.2751	.2274	.1890	.1580
7	.4523	.3996	.3759	.3538	.3139	.2791	.2218	.1776	.1432	.1162
8	.4039	.3506	.3269	.3050	.2660	.2326	.1789	.1388	.1085	.0854
9	.3606	.3075	.2843	.2630	.2255	.1938	.1443	.1084	.0822	.0628
10	.3220	.2697	.2472	.2267	.1911	.1615	.1164	.0847	.0623	.0462
11	.2875	.2366	.2149	.1954	.1619	.1346	.0938	.0662	.0472	.0340
12	.2567	.2076	.1869	.1685	.1372	.1122	.0757	.0517	.0357	.0250
13	.2292	.1821	.1625	.1452	.1163	.0935	.0610	.0404	.0271	.0184
14	.2046	.1597	.1413	.1252	.0985	.0779	.0492	.0316	.0205	.0135
15	.1827	.1401	.1229	.1079	.0835	.0649	.0397	.0247	.0155	.0099
16	.1631	.1229	.1069	.0930	.0708	.0541	.0320	.0193	.0118	.0073
17	.1456	.1078	.0929	.0802	.0600	.0451	.0258	.0150	.0089	.0054
18	.1300	.0946	.0808	.0691	.0508	.0376	.0208	.0118	.0068	.0039
19	.1161	.0829	.0703	.0596	.0431	.0313	.0168	.0092	.0051	.0029
20	.1037	.0728	.0611	.0514	.0365	.0261	.0135	.0072	.0039	.0021
21	.0926	.0638	.0531	.0443	.0309	.0217	.0109	.0056	.0029	.0016
22	.0826	.0560	.0462	.0382	.0262	.0181	.0088	.0044	.0022	.0012
23	.0738	.0491	.0402	.0329	.0222	.0151	.0071	.0034	.0017	.0008
24	.0659	.0431	.0349	.0284	.0188	.0126	.0057	.0027	.0013	.0006
25	.0588	.0378	.0304	.0245	.0160	.0105	.0046	.0021	.0010	.0005
26	.0525	.0331	.0264	.0211	.0135	.0087	.0037	.0016	.0007	.0003
27	.0469	.0291	.0230	.0182	.0115	.0073	.0030	.0013	.0006	.0002
28	.0419	.0255	.0200	.0157	.0097	.0061	.0024	.0010	.0004	.0002
29	.0374	.0224	.0174	.0135	.0082	.0051	.0020	.0008	.0003	.0001
30	.0334	.0196	.0151	.0116	.0070	.0042	.0016	.0006	.0002	.0001
35	.0189	.0102	.0075	.0055	.0030	.0017	.0005	.0002	.0001	*
40	.0107	.0053	.0037	.0026	.0013	.0007	.0002	.0001	*	*
45	.0061	.0027	.0019	.0013	.0006	.0003	.0001	*	*	*
50	.0035	.0014	.0009	.0006	.0003	.0001	*	*	*	*
55	.0020	.0007	.0005	.0003	.0001	*	*	*	*	*

*The factor is zero to four decimal places.

TABLE B.3

Sum on an Annuity of $1 per Period for n Periods:

$$\text{FVIFA}_{r,t} = \sum_{t=1}^{n} (1+r)^{t-1} = \frac{(1+r)^n - 1}{r}$$

Number of Periods	1%	2%	3%	4%	5%	6%	7%	8%	9%	10%
1	1.0000	1.0000	1.0000	1.0000	1.0000	1.0000	1.0000	1.0000	1.0000	1.0000
2	2.0100	2.0200	2.0300	2.0400	2.0500	2.0600	2.0700	2.0800	2.0900	2.1000
3	3.0301	3.0604	3.0909	3.1216	3.1525	3.1836	3.2149	3.2464	3.2781	3.3100
4	4.0604	4.1216	4.1836	4.2465	4.3101	4.3746	4.4399	4.5061	4.5731	4.6410
5	5.1010	5.2040	5.3091	5.4163	5.5256	5.6371	5.7507	5.8666	5.9847	6.1051
6	6.1520	6.3081	6.4684	6.6330	6.8019	6.9753	7.1533	7.3359	7.5233	7.7156
7	7.2135	7.4343	7.6625	7.8983	8.1420	8.3938	8.6540	8.9228	9.2004	9.4872
8	8.2857	8.5830	8.8923	9.2142	9.5491	9.8975	10.260	10.637	11.028	11.436
9	9.3685	9.7546	10.159	10.583	11.027	11.491	11.978	12.488	13.021	13.579
10	10.462	10.950	11.464	12.006	12.578	13.181	13.816	14.487	15.193	15.937
11	11.567	12.169	12.808	13.486	14.207	14.972	15.784	16.645	17.560	18.531
12	12.683	13.412	14.192	15.026	15.917	16.870	17.888	18.977	20.141	21.384
13	13.809	14.680	15.618	16.627	17.713	18.882	20.141	21.495	22.953	24.523
14	14.947	15.974	17.086	18.292	19.599	21.015	22.550	24.215	26.019	27.975
15	16.097	17.293	18.599	20.024	21.579	23.276	25.129	27.152	29.361	31.772
16	17.258	18.639	20.157	21.825	23.657	25.673	27.888	30.324	33.003	35.950
17	18.430	20.012	21.762	23.698	25.840	28.213	30.840	33.750	36.974	40.545
18	19.615	21.412	23.414	25.645	28.132	30.906	33.999	37.450	41.301	45.599
19	20.811	22.841	25.117	27.671	30.539	33.760	37.379	41.446	46.018	51.159
20	22.019	24.297	26.870	29.778	33.006	36.786	40.995	45.762	51.160	57.275
21	23.239	25.783	28.676	31.969	35.719	39.993	44.865	50.423	56.765	64.002
22	24.472	27.299	30.537	34.248	38.505	43.392	49.006	55.457	62.873	71.403
23	25.716	28.845	32.453	36.618	41.430	46.996	53.436	60.893	69.532	79.543
24	26.973	30.422	34.426	39.083	44.502	50.816	58.177	66.765	76.790	88.497
25	28.243	32.030	36.459	41.646	47.727	54.865	63.249	73.106	84.701	98.347
26	29.526	33.671	38.553	44.312	51.113	59.156	68.676	79.954	93.324	109.18
27	30.821	35.344	40.710	47.084	54.669	63.706	74.484	87.351	102.72	121.10
28	32.129	37.051	42.931	49.968	58.403	68.528	80.698	95.339	112.97	134.21
29	33.450	38.792	45.219	52.966	62.323	73.640	87.347	103.97	124.14	148.63
30	34.785	40.568	47.575	56.085	66.439	79.058	94.461	113.28	136.31	164.49
40	48.886	60.402	75.401	95.026	120.80	154.76	199.64	259.06	337.88	442.59
50	64.463	84.579	112.80	152.67	209.35	290.34	406.53	573.77	815.08	1163.9
60	81.670	114.05	163.05	237.99	353.58	533.13	813.52	1253.2	1944.8	3034.8

*FVIFA > 99,999.

TABLE B.3

continued

Number of Periods	12%	14%	15%	16%	18%	20%	24%	28%	32%	36%
1	1.0000	1.0000	1.0000	1.0000	1.0000	1.0000	1.0000	1.0000	1.0000	1.0000
2	2.1200	2.1400	2.1500	2.1600	2.1800	2.2000	2.2400	2.2800	2.3200	2.3600
3	3.3744	3.4396	3.4725	3.5056	3.5724	3.6400	3.7776	3.9184	4.0624	4.2096
4	4.7793	4.9211	4.9934	5.0665	5.2154	5.3680	5.6842	6.0156	6.3624	6.7251
5	6.3528	6.6101	6.7424	6.8771	7.1542	7.4416	8.0484	8.6999	9.3983	10.146
6	8.1152	8.5355	8.7537	8.9775	9.4420	9.9299	10.980	12.136	13.406	14.799
7	10.089	10.730	11.067	11.414	12.142	12.916	14.615	16.534	18.696	21.126
8	12.300	13.233	13.727	14.240	15.327	16.499	19.123	22.163	25.678	29.732
9	14.776	16.085	16.786	17.519	19.086	20.799	24.712	29.369	34.895	41.435
10	17.549	19.337	20.304	21.321	23.521	25.959	31.643	38.593	47.062	57.352
11	20.655	23.045	24.349	25.733	28.755	32.150	40.238	50.398	63.122	78.998
12	24.133	27.271	29.002	30.850	34.931	39.581	50.895	65.510	84.320	108.44
13	28.029	32.089	34.352	36.786	42.219	48.497	64.110	84.853	112.30	148.47
14	32.393	37.581	40.505	43.672	50.818	59.196	80.496	109.61	149.24	202.93
15	37.280	43.842	47.580	51.660	60.965	72.035	100.82	141.30	198.00	276.98
16	42.753	50.980	55.717	60.925	72.939	87.442	126.01	181.87	262.36	377.69
17	48.884	59.118	65.075	71.673	87.068	105.93	157.25	233.79	347.31	514.66
18	55.750	68.394	75.836	84.141	103.74	128.12	195.99	300.25	459.45	700.94
19	63.440	78.969	88.212	98.603	123.41	154.74	244.03	385.32	607.47	954.28
20	72.052	91.025	102.44	115.38	146.63	186.69	303.60	494.21	802.86	1298.8
21	81.699	104.77	118.81	134.84	174.02	225.03	377.46	633.59	1060.8	1767.4
22	92.503	120.44	137.63	157.41	206.34	271.03	469.06	812.00	1401.2	2404.7
23	104.60	138.30	159.28	183.60	244.49	326.24	582.63	1040.4	1850.6	3271.3
24	118.16	158.66	184.17	213.98	289.49	392.48	723.46	1332.7	2443.8	4450.0
25	133.33	181.87	212.79	249.21	342.60	471.98	898.09	1706.8	3226.8	6053.0
26	150.33	208.33	245.71	290.09	405.27	567.38	1114.6	2185.7	4260.4	8233.1
27	169.37	238.50	283.57	337.50	479.22	681.85	1383.1	2798.7	5624.8	11198.0
28	190.70	272.89	327.10	392.50	566.48	819.22	1716.1	3583.3	7425.7	15230.3
29	214.58	312.09	377.17	456.30	669.45	984.07	2129.0	4587.7	9802.9	20714.2
30	241.33	356.79	434.75	530.31	790.95	1181.9	2640.9	5873.2	12941	28172.3
40	767.09	1342.0	1779.1	2360.8	4163.2	7343.9	22729	69377	*	*
50	2400.0	4994.5	7217.7	10436	21813	45497	*	*	*	*
60	7471.6	18535	29220	46058	*	*	*	*	*	*

*FVIFA > 99,999.

TABLE B.4

Present Value of an Annuity of $1 per Period for n Periods:

$$\text{PVIFA}_{r,t} = \sum_{t=1}^{n} \frac{1}{(1 + r)^t} = \frac{1 - 1/(1 + r)^n}{r}$$

Number of Periods	1%	2%	3%	4%	5%	6%	7%	8%	9%	10%
1	0.9901	0.9804	0.9709	0.9615	0.9524	0.9434	0.9346	0.9259	0.9174	0.9091
2	1.9704	1.9416	1.9135	1.8861	1.8594	1.8334	1.8080	1.7833	1.7591	1.7355
3	2.9410	2.8839	2.8286	2.7751	2.7232	2.6730	2.6243	2.5771	2.5313	2.4869
4	3.9020	3.8077	3.7171	3.6299	3.5460	3.4651	3.3872	3.3121	3.2397	3.1699
5	4.8534	4.7135	4.5797	4.4518	4.3295	4.2124	4.1002	3.9927	3.8897	3.7908
6	5.7955	5.6014	5.4172	5.2421	5.0757	4.9173	4.7665	4.6229	4.4859	4.3553
7	6.7282	6.4720	6.2303	6.0021	5.7864	5.5824	5.3893	5.2064	5.0330	4.8684
8	7.6517	7.3255	7.0197	6.7327	6.4632	6.2098	5.9713	5.7466	5.5348	5.3349
9	8.5660	8.1622	7.7861	7.4353	7.1078	6.8017	6.5152	6.2469	5.9952	5.7590
10	9.4713	8.9826	8.5302	8.1109	7.7217	7.3601	7.0236	6.7101	6.4177	6.1446
11	10.3676	9.7868	9.2526	8.7605	8.3064	7.8869	7.4987	7.1390	6.8052	6.4951
12	11.2551	10.5753	9.9540	9.3851	8.8633	8.3838	7.9427	7.5361	7.1607	6.8137
13	12.1337	11.3484	10.6350	9.9856	9.3936	8.8527	8.3577	7.9038	7.4869	7.1034
14	13.0037	12.1062	11.2961	10.5631	9.8986	9.2950	8.7455	8.2442	7.7862	7.3667
15	13.8651	12.8493	11.9379	11.1184	10.3797	9.7122	9.1079	8.5595	8.0607	7.6061
16	14.7179	13.5777	12.5611	11.6523	10.8378	10.1059	9.4466	8.8514	8.3126	7.8237
17	15.5623	14.2919	13.1661	12.1657	11.2741	10.4773	9.7632	9.1216	8.5436	8.0216
18	16.3983	14.9920	13.7535	12.6593	11.6896	10.8276	10.0591	9.3719	8.7556	8.2014
19	17.2260	15.6785	14.3238	13.1339	12.0853	11.1581	10.3356	9.6036	8.9501	8.3649
20	18.0456	16.3514	14.8775	13.5903	12.4622	11.4699	10.5940	9.8181	9.1285	8.5136
21	18.8570	17.0112	15.4150	14.0292	12.8212	11.7641	10.8355	10.0168	9.2922	8.6487
22	19.6604	17.6580	15.9369	14.4511	13.1630	12.0416	11.0612	10.2007	9.4424	8.7715
23	20.4558	18.2922	16.4436	14.8568	13.4886	12.3034	11.2722	10.3711	9.5802	8.8832
24	21.2434	18.9139	16.9355	15.2470	13.7986	12.5504	11.4693	10.5288	9.7066	8.9847
25	22.0232	19.5235	17.4131	15.6221	14.0939	12.7834	11.6536	10.6748	9.8226	9.0770
26	22.7952	20.1210	17.8768	15.9828	14.3752	13.0032	11.8258	10.8100	9.9290	9.1609
27	23.5596	20.7069	18.3270	16.3296	14.6430	13.2105	11.9867	10.9352	10.0266	9.2372
28	24.3164	21.2813	18.7641	16.6631	14.8981	13.4062	12.1371	11.0511	10.1161	9.3066
29	25.0658	21.8444	19.1885	16.9837	15.1411	13.5907	12.2777	11.1584	10.1983	9.3696
30	25.8077	22.3965	19.6004	17.2920	15.3725	13.7648	12.4090	11.2578	10.2737	9.4269
35	29.4086	24.9986	21.4872	18.6646	16.3742	14.4982	12.9477	11.6546	10.5668	9.6442
40	32.8347	27.3555	23.1148	19.7928	17.1591	15.0463	13.3317	11.9246	10.7574	9.7791
45	36.0945	29.4902	24.5187	20.7200	17.7741	15.4558	13.6055	12.1084	10.8812	9.8628
50	39.1961	31.4236	25.7298	21.4822	18.2559	15.7619	13.8007	12.2335	10.9617	9.9148
55	42.1472	33.1748	26.7744	22.1086	18.6335	15.9905	13.9399	12.3186	11.0140	9.9471

TABLE B.4

continued

Number of Periods	12%	14%	15%	16%	18%	20%	24%	28%	32%
1	0.8929	0.8772	0.8696	0.8621	0.8475	0.8333	0.8065	0.7813	0.7576
2	1.6901	1.6467	1.6257	1.6052	1.5656	1.5278	1.4568	1.3916	1.3315
3	2.4018	2.3216	2.2832	2.2459	2.1743	2.1065	1.9813	1.8684	1.7663
4	3.0373	2.9137	2.8550	2.7982	2.6901	2.5887	2.4043	2.2410	2.0957
5	3.6048	3.4331	3.3522	3.2743	3.1272	2.9906	2.7454	2.5320	2.3452
6	4.1114	3.8887	3.7845	3.6847	3.4976	3.3255	3.0205	2.7594	2.5342
7	4.5638	4.2883	4.1604	4.0386	3.8115	3.6046	3.2423	2.9370	2.6775
8	4.9676	4.6389	4.4873	4.3436	4.0776	3.8372	3.4212	3.0758	2.7860
9	5.3282	4.9464	4.7716	4.6065	4.3030	4.0310	3.5655	3.1842	2.8681
10	5.6502	5.2161	5.0188	4.8332	4.4941	4.1925	3.6819	3.2689	2.9304
11	5.9377	5.4527	5.2337	5.0286	4.6560	4.3271	3.7757	3.3351	2.9776
12	6.1944	5.6603	5.4206	5.1971	4.7932	4.4392	3.8514	3.3868	3.0133
13	6.4235	5.8424	5.5831	5.3423	4.9095	4.5327	3.9124	3.4272	3.0404
14	6.6282	6.0021	5.7245	5.4675	5.0081	4.6106	3.9616	3.4587	3.0609
15	6.8109	6.1422	5.8474	5.5755	5.0916	4.6755	4.0013	3.4834	3.0764
16	6.9740	6.2651	5.9542	5.6685	5.1624	4.7296	4.0333	3.5026	3.0882
17	7.1196	6.3729	6.0472	5.7487	5.2223	4.7746	4.0591	3.5177	3.0971
18	7.2497	6.4674	6.1280	5.8178	5.2732	4.8122	4.0799	3.5294	3.1039
19	7.3658	6.5504	6.1982	5.8775	5.3162	4.8435	4.0967	3.5386	3.1090
20	7.4694	6.6231	6.2593	5.9288	5.3527	4.8696	4.1103	3.5458	3.1129
21	7.5620	6.6870	6.3125	5.9731	5.3837	4.8913	4.1212	3.5514	3.1158
22	7.6446	6.7429	6.3587	6.0113	5.4099	4.9094	4.1300	3.5558	3.1180
23	7.7184	6.7921	6.3988	6.0442	5.4321	4.9245	4.1371	3.5592	3.1197
24	7.7843	6.8351	6.4338	6.0726	5.4509	4.9371	4.1428	3.5619	3.1210
25	7.8431	6.8729	6.4641	6.0971	5.4669	4.9476	4.1474	3.5640	3.1220
26	7.8957	6.9061	6.4906	6.1182	5.4804	4.9563	4.1511	3.5656	3.1227
27	7.9426	6.9352	6.5135	6.1364	5.4919	4.9636	4.1542	3.5669	3.1233
28	7.9844	6.9607	6.5335	6.1520	5.5016	4.9697	4.1566	3.5679	3.1237
29	8.0218	6.9830	6.5509	6.1656	5.5098	4.9747	4.1585	3.5687	3.1240
30	8.0552	7.0027	6.5660	6.1772	5.5168	4.9789	4.1601	3.5693	3.1242
35	8.1755	7.0700	6.6166	6.2153	5.5386	4.9915	4.1644	3.5708	3.1248
40	8.2438	7.1050	6.6418	6.2335	5.5482	4.9966	4.1659	3.5712	3.1250
45	8.2825	7.1232	6.6543	6.2421	5.5523	4.9986	4.1664	3.5714	3.1250
50	8.3045	7.1327	6.6605	6.2463	5.5541	4.9995	4.1666	3.5714	3.1250
55	8.3170	7.1376	6.6636	6.2482	5.5549	4.9998	4.1666	3.5714	3.1250

Glossary

The following are brief definitions of some key business-related items. As a business-savvy project manager, you should have some level of familiarity with each of them. Most are described and/or discussed somewhere within this book. For those that are not, you should consider learning more about them through other reference materials.

Activity-based costing—a control system that identifies the resources employed to produce a product and allocates product costs accordingly.

Accelerated depreciation method—a depreciation methodology that provides for a high depreciation expense in the first year of use of an asset, and gradually declining expense thereafter.

Accrual basis—a basis of accounting in which revenues are recognized in the period earned, and expenses are recognized in the period incurred in the process of generating revenues.

Activity-based costing—an accounting framework based on determining the cost of activities and allocating these costs to products, using activity rates. Uses the cost of these activities as the basis for assigning costs to other cost objects such as products, services, or customers. Provides more accurate allocation of indirect costs and traditional methods.

Assets (also real assets)—any number of items that have value and are owned by the business entity; includes physical items, such as facilities, equipment, and offices (referred to as *tangible assets*), and nonphysical items, such as technical expertise, trademarks, and patents (referred to as *intangible assets*).

Balance sheet—a financial statement that shows the firm's financial position with respect to assets and liabilities at a specific point in time; it displays three basic pieces of information:
(1) how the company's assets are deployed (cash versus inventory versus property); (2) the extent of the company's liabilities (how much is owed to whom); and (3) the breakdown of owner's equity (shareholder contributions plus any retained earnings)

Balanced scorecard—a comprehensive management control system that balances traditional financial measures with measures of customer service, internal business processes, and the organization's capacity for learning and growth.

Business process improvement—refers to the concept of continuous improvement, applied to all processes within a company; one of the more notable forms of ongoing business process improvement is *kaizen*, a Japanese term that means "gradual and orderly continuous improvement."

Business process redesign—changes in business processes that are often precipitated when a problem or opportunity is identified; customers or users (internal or external) are frequently the driving force behind the redesign process.

Business process reengineering—a somewhat more radical approach to business process management than continuous improvement; it is the fundamental rethinking of business processes, aimed at achieving dramatic improvements in critical measures of performance, such as cost, quality, efficiency, and service.

Cannibalization—a phenomenon that occurs in situations in which the introduction of a new product into the marketplace precipitates a decline in the sales of that company's existing product(s).

Capacity planning—the determination and adjustment of the organization's ability to produce products and services to match customer demand.

Capital budget (also capital expenditures budget)—the budget that summarizes future plans for acquiring fixed assets.

Capital budgeting—the process of identifying, evaluating, and planning long-term asset investment decisions.

Capital rationing—the process by which management allocates available investment funds among competing capital investment proposals.

Cash flow diagram—a graphical tool used to illustrate and visualize any combination of cash inflows and cash outflows. As a graphical tool, the cash flow diagram is very simple, yet eloquent and powerful.

Cash flow statement—describes all the changes with respect to cash over a specified period of time; has strong ties to project work; includes *cash flows from financing activities* (such as the funding of projects), *cash flows from investing activities* (which includes investing in projects and the assets they create), and *cash flows from* *operating activities* (closely aligned with the fundamental objective of most projects).

Cash inflow—an influx of cash or a financial benefit associated with a particular capital investment decision (i.e., project).

Cash outflow—a loss of cash or an additional expenditure associated with a particular capital investment decision (i.e., project).

Competitive advantage—an element of tactical planning that addresses how a company can go about achieving an advantage with respect to their competitors.

Controllable costs—costs that can be influenced (increased, decreased, or eliminated) by someone such as a manager or factory worker.

Control system design—an element of tactical planning that establishes and imposes boundaries by which a company's day-to-day business processes are conducted; the mechanism by which managers may be assured that processes are being applied in an appropriate manner in accomplishing the company's strategic objectives. A secondary, more detailed, function of control system design is to ensure that specific tasks are being carried out and resources are being applied effectively and efficiently.

Core competence—a business activity that an organization does particularly well in comparison to competitors.

Cost—a resource sacrificed or foregone to achieve a specific objective; usually measured by the monetary amount (i.e., dollars) that must be paid to acquire goods and services.

Cost allocation—the process of assigning indirect cost to a cost object, such as a job, product, or project.

Cost avoidance—a category of project cash flows; relates to situations in which a financial threat comes from outside the company. One classic example of cost avoidance arises when the government mandates some kind of corporate reform—for example, a new set of safety requirements. By taking action now (i.e., pursuing a project), companies avoid the imposition of unfavorable, externally driven costs. These avoided costs should be listed as cash inflows in the financial analysis.

Cost center—a responsibility center in which a manager is accountable for costs only. A decentralized unit in which the department or division manager has responsibility for the control costs incurred and the authority to make decisions that affect these costs.

Cost driver—any factor that causes a change in the cost of an activity.

Cost leadership—a type of competitive strategy with which the organization aggressively seeks efficient facilities, cuts costs, and employs tight cost controls to be more efficient than competitors.

Cost object—any customer, product, service, project, or other work unit for which a separate cost measurement is desired.

Cost protection—a category of project cash flow; by approving certain projects, a company is able to protect itself against the potential future costs that would be associated with the catastrophic failure of equipment, including loss of sales and equipment damage. The value of these items is recorded as a cash inflow under a line item called *cost protection*.

Cost of quality—costs incurred in assuring quality of a product or service. Includes four categories of quality costs: internal failure costs (costs associated with defects found before delivery of product or service); external failure costs (costs associated with defects found during or after product or service delivery); appraisal costs (costs incurred to determine the degree of conformance to quality requirements); and prevention costs (costs incurred to keep failure and appraisal costs to a minimum).

Current assets—cash or other assets that are expected to be converted to cash, sold, or used up, usually within a year or less.

Current liabilities—liabilities that are due within a short time (usually 1 year or less) and that are to be paid out of current assets.

Customer relationship management—the process of identifying, attracting, differentiating, and retaining customers; relies on processes that profile key segments, so that marketing and retention strategies can be customized for these customers.

Debt financing (also debt capital)—how much money a company has borrowed from financial institutions to finance its operations and invest in asset creation; the act of borrowing money that has to be repaid at a later date in order to conduct business.

Declining balance depreciation method—the methodology of depreciation that provides declining periodic depreciation expense over the estimated life of an asset.

Depreciation—the decrease in utility of plant assets other than land; in accounting terms, refers to the systematic allocation of a fixed asset's cost to expense.

Depreciation expense—the portion of the cost of a fixed asset that is recorded as an expense every year throughout its useful life.

Differentiation—a type of competitive strategy in which an organization seeks to distinguish its products or services from competitors.

Direct costs—any costs that are an integral part of the finished product; costs that can be reasonably measured and attributed to a work activity or a specific output.

Discounting—the process of devaluing some future amount of money so that it may be expressed in terms of equivalent worth today; relies on the time value of money concept.

Discount rate (also hurdle rate)—the rate at which future cash flows are devalued, to express them in terms of current-day dollars; ordinarily expressed as an annual percentage rate.

Economic value added (EVA)—the amount of wealth returned to the company in any given year; a measure of management's ability to create value using the existing assets of the company; it is actually a truer estimate of a company's economic profit for the year, because it considers the carrying costs of the assets needed to generate a given amount of wealth.

Equity capital (also equity financing)—the money a company has received from the owners of stock (shareholders' amount of money that the company has kept for the purpose of reinvesting in the company), plus that kept on the shareholder's behalf (called *retained earnings*); generally acquired through the sale of stock, which, in turn, is interpreted as part ownership in that company.

Financial accounting—a component of an organization's internal accounting system that provides information primarily for users outside the organization; concerned with the recording of transactions using generally accepted accounting principles (GAAP) for a business or any other economic unit; includes the periodic preparation of various statements from these transaction records.

Fixed assets—physical resources that are owned and used by a business; generally, they are permanent or viewed as having a long life.

Fixed cost—the portion of the total cost that does not depend on the volume; this cost remains the same no matter how much is produced.

Functional design—the process of configuring and organizing a company's individual operating units (i.e., departments) so that the functions (1) support the company's strategic goals and (2) are properly coordinated with the functions performed by other departments within the company.

Future value—the estimated worth in the future of an amount of cash on hand today invested at a fixed rate of interest.

Generally accepted accounting principles (GAAP)—a set of accounting procedures and practices used in the United States that are handed down by the Financial Standard Standards Board, a recognized standard-setting body; applied in the preparation of financial statements and accounting reports.

Global strategy—the high-level approach a company uses to conduct business within and across national borders; approaches include globalization, multidomestic, and transnational.

Grand strategy—the highest level of a company's strategic positioning. While the choice of a grand strategy may be a purposeful decision made by upper management, it can also be forced upon a company as a result of the company's financial strength, competitive position, future growth potential, or even the general economy. Grand strategies tended to fall into three general categories: growth, stability, and retrenchment.

Income statement—a summary of the revenues and expenses of a business entity for a specific period; shows how profitable a company was during that period.

Incremental cost—a change in a company's cash flows that occurs as a direct result of accepting a certain decision; frequently, this "decision" refers to the approval of a proposed project. Every item of costs included in a project financial analysis is expressed in terms of incremental costs.

Indirect costs—costs that cannot be reasonably attributed to a specific output, but are still considered part of "doing business" at a company; examples of indirect costs include utilities costs or insurance premiums; other terms include *overhead costs* and *burden costs*.

Internal process design—the foundation of operational planning; consists of the development of approaches, methods, and guidelines for guiding virtually every activity performed within the company, and may include detailed prescriptions for issues such as behavior, methods, and documentation around a wide variety of business functions.

Internal rate of return method—a method of analyzing proposed capital investments that focuses on using present value concepts to compute the rate of return from the net cash flows expected from that investment.

Investment center—a responsibility center in which the manager is responsible for costs, revenues, profits, and investment in the assets. A decentralized unit in which the manager has responsibility and authority to make decisions that affect not only the cost and revenues, but also the plant assets available to the center.

Justification (or financial justification)—describes a condition in which it makes sense to approve a project from a purely financial standpoint; any project whose net present value is greater than zero, or whose internal rate of return is greater than the weighted average cost of capital, or whose profitability index is greater than 1 is considered to be a prudent investment, because that project will make more money than it costs to implement it. Also represents the formal meaning of the term "justified project," or as many say, "financially justified project."

Managerial accounting—a component of an organization's internal accounting system that provides information primarily for users inside the organization; includes a combination of financial and non-financial information; used by managers and others within the organization for purposes of conducting daily operations, planning future operations, and developing overall business and operating strategies.

Market value added (MVA)—the difference between what investors have put into the company and what they could now get out of it; the goal of corporate managers should be to maximize that difference.

Master budget—the comprehensive budget plan encompassing all the individual budgets related to sales, cost of goods sold, operating expenses, capital expenditures, and cash.

Maximum exposure—the largest amount of money that will be tied up in a given project at any given time; a method for expressing the riskiness of a project.

Mission statement—a broadly stated definition of an organization's basic business scope and operations that distinguishes it from similar types of organizations.

Net present value (NPV)—the amount of wealth that any single project is expected to return to the company; the difference between the initial investment and the present value of all expected future cash inflows and outflows that are incurred as a result of that investment; a positive NPV (greater then zero) means that a project is generating more than enough cash to service the debt incurred to finance that project.

Noncontrollable costs—costs that cannot be influenced (increased, decreased, or eliminated) by someone such as a manager or factory worker.

Opportunity cost—the amount of income that is given up as a result of choosing a particular alternative or making a particular decision.

Overhead costs—all the costs required to run an operation, except for direct materials and direct labor.

Owner's equity—the shareholders' right to the assets of a company after the total liabilities are deducted.

Payback period (also time-to-money)—a capital budgeting method that measures the time it will take to recoup, in the form of net cash flows, the net dollars invested in a project.

Present value—an estimated worth today of an amount of cash to be received (or paid) in the future.

Primary competitive strategy—a high-level strategy that describes the *basic orientation* a company will assume with respect to the way it competes.

Profit center—a responsibility center in which the manager is responsible for both revenues and costs. A decentralized unit in which the manager has responsibility and the authority to make decisions that affect both cost and revenues (and therefore profits).

Profitability index—also referred to as the *benefit/cost ratio*, because it is a simple comparison of all the benefits and costs associated with executing a project. Specifically, it is defined as ratio of the equivalent worth of benefits to the equivalent worth of costs.

Project capital costs—costs that are clearly and directly assignable to the creation of an asset; the sum of all capital costs is recorded as the value of that asset.

Project expense costs—costs that are associated with the supporting environment of the project, but not directly attributable to the creation of an asset.

Ratio analysis—a process to facilitate understanding of a company's business position, general health, or growth prospects; in ratio analysis, bits and pieces of information are extracted from the three basic financial statements (balance sheet, income statement, and statement of cash flows), and combined to create financial ratios; typically used by three groups: company managers, credit analysts, and stock analysts or investment analysts; there are five general categories of ratios: liquidity, leverage, profitability, asset management, and market value.

Responsibility center—an organizational unit under the supervision of a single individual who is responsible for its activity.

Return on investment (ROI)—an umbrella term for a variety of ratios measuring an organization's business performance. ROI calculations are made by dividing some measure of return by a measure of investment and multiplied by 100 to provide a percentage.

Revenue center—a responsibility center in which a manager is accountable for revenues only. A decentralized unit in which the department or division manager has responsibility for the generation of revenues, and the authority to make decisions that affect their acquisition.

Situation analysis—an evaluative technique that includes an examination of the strengths, weaknesses, opportunities, and threats that can affect a company's ability to achieve its strategic goals; often referred to as a SWOT analysis.

Straight-line depreciation method—a method of depreciation that provides for equal periodic depreciation expense over the estimated life of an asset.

Strategic planning—the process of deciding on the goals of the organization and the strategies for attaining these goals.

Structural design—the way that a company chooses to organize itself; the structural design process naturally leads to the design and development of a formalized organizational structure whose purpose is to define job duties and effectively deploy human resources.

Sunk cost—monies that have already been spent; any cost that is not affected by subsequent decisions.

Supply chain management—managing the sequence of suppliers and purchasers, covering all stages of processing from obtaining raw materials to distributing finished goods to final customers.

Tactical plans—short-term plans, usually of 1- to 2-year duration, that describe actions the organization intends to take to meet its strategic business plan.

Time value of money—a concept that deals with the issue of how the dollar's worth can change over time.

Total cost of ownership—a cluster estimating methodology that considers not only the purchase price of an item, but also a wide array of other factors such as maintenance, operating cost, etc.; evaluates the cost of an item throughout its entire life cycle.

Total life cycle perspective—the recognition that activities such as project investigation, research and development, operations, product utilization, and asset retirement (among others) are all part of the life of a project; management appropriately considers these factors when making key decisions.

Useful life—the time period within which a project financial analysis is performed; typically determined by the company's accounting department.

Variable cost—portion of the total cost that depends on and varies with the volume.

Voice of the customer—an expression of the preferences, opinions, and motivations of customers and end-users; used to guide functions such as product design, design engineering, marketing, and sales.

Weighted average cost of capital (WACC)—the mathematical blending of the cost of debt financing with the cost of equity financing; typically viewed as the borrowing rate applied to monies used to finance projects.

Index

Note: Boldface numbers indicate illustrations; *t* indicates a table.